New Perspectives in Service-Learning

Research to Advance the Field

A Volume in
Advances in Service-Learning Research

New Perspectives in Service-Learning

Research to Advance the Field

Edited by

Marshall Welch
Lowell Bennion Community Service Center
University of Utah

Shelley H. Billig
RMC Research Corporation

80 Mason Street • Greenwich, Connecticut 06830 • www.infoagepub.com

Library of Congress Cataloging-in-Publication Data

New perspectives in service-learning : research to advance the field /
[edited by] Shelley H. Billig, Marshall Welch.
    p. cm. – (Advances in service-learning research)
  Includes bibliographical references and index.
  ISBN 1-59311-157-6 (paperback) – ISBN 1-59311-158-4 (hardcover)
  1. Student service–Congresses. 2. Student
service–Research–Congresses. I. Billig, Shelley. II. Welch, Marshall.
III. Advances in service-learning.
  LC220.5.N49 2004
  361.3'7–dc22

                                 2004020286

Printed in the United States of America

ACKNOWLEDGMENTS

We gratefully acknowledge the fastidious work of our editor, Mary Ann Strassner, and all of the scholars who wrote for this book and presented at the Third Annual K–H Service-Learning Research Conference. This book could not have been finished without the generous funding of the W.K. Kellogg Foundation. Special thanks to the continuing support of Bob Long, Anne Petersen, and Chris Kwak.

CONTENTS

Part III
Institutionalization of Service-Learning

Part IV
Reflections on Today and Tomorrow

INTRODUCTION

The Third Annual International K–H Service-Learning Research Conference that took place in November 2003, in Salt Lake City, Utah, played an important role in continuing the interest and stimulating dialogue about service-learning. Service-learning, a teaching and learning approach wherein the provision of community service is used as a vehicle for learning and civic engagement, continues to be of interest to teachers, students, parents, administrators, and policymakers in K–12 and higher education. This interest and growth is evident by the number of articles, books, Web sites, and organizations devoted to the topic. Increasing numbers of professional organizations and disciplines in public and higher education are allocating portions or entire conferences to service-learning. As interest in service-learning becomes more widespread, the need for high-quality research to understand issues of effective practice, capacity building, and institutionalization come to the fore. The annual conference and accompanying book series serve as a catalyst for dissemination of theory and research, and as a venue for presentation and publication.

The first book in the *Advances of Service-Learning Research* series was published in conjunction with the initial conference in Berkeley, California, in 2001. The introduction to that book acknowledged the limited research base in the field. In a mere 2 years, considerable progress has been made. Since the first conference, service-learning researchers and practitioners have made strides in moving from embracing the intuitive appeal of service-learning to taking a critical examination of its impact on students, faculty, educational institutions, and the community. Momentum was sustained during the second conference in Nashville, Tennessee, in 2002 by

New Perspectives in Service-Learning: Research to Advance the Field, pages ix–xii
Copyright © 2004 by Information Age Publishing

expanding the discussion of theoretical frameworks and methodologies. This book continues the process by sharing exciting new approaches and outcomes as well as presenting new questions and avenues for further research. The chapters found in this collection were selected through a refereed, blind review process from papers presented at the third annual conference held in November 2003 in Salt Lake City, Utah.

This book is organized into four parts. The first part provides a foundation for our understanding of service-learning as a form of civically engaged scholarship. The first chapter is an expansion of the keynote speech from the conference by Ira Harkavy who inspired and challenged the audience to use service-learning as a means of creating democratic schools and society. The chapter provides a historical frame of reference and documents the democratic mission of higher education and K–12 schools. Harkavy identifies obstacles for realizing that mission and concludes by proposing ways in which service-learning can be a key implementation strategy for revitalizing the democratic spirit and activities of young people and their teachers. Ziegert and McGoldrick present a unique perspective on the challenges of rigor of research in the second chapter. They compare the current state of service-learning research to similar challenges associated with the methodological progression that took place during the early history of research in the field of economics. Their analysis illuminates many pitfalls that can be avoided with foresight and strategic decisions.

Part II is devoted to assessing the impact of service-learning. In chapter 3, Roldan, Strage, and David present two examples using a framework for assessing the effects of service-learning. They describe how their university used the framework to infuse service-learning into courses across disciplines. Their chapter includes the results of two assessment studies to illustrate the use of their framework in assessing outcomes of service-learning. Meyer, Billig, and Hofschire present a conceptual model in chapter 4 that suggests service-learning's effect on K–12 students' academic outcomes as mediated through its impact on student cognitive, affective, and behavioral engagement. Their research presents an examination of both academic growth using state-mandated standardized tests and changes in civic engagement as a result of participating in service-learning. In chapter 5, Warchal and Ruiz respond to the ongoing call for longitudinal research on the long-term impact of service-learning. Their research examines postgraduate employment choices, evidence of community engagement, and examples of civic leadership of college graduates. Krumboltz's (1994) Social Learning Theory of Career Decision Making serves as the theoretical framework of their study. The results of their quantitative analysis suggest that service-learning experiences play a significant factor in graduates' choices for employment and levels of volunteerism.

Using Perry's (1968/1999) scheme of intellectual and ethic development and Bennett's (1993) Developmental Model of Intercultural Sensitivity as theoretical models, Fitch in chapter 6 describes how a small, coeducational, faith-based liberal arts college utilized service-learning to promote students' intellectual development and intercultural sensitivity. The work presented in this chapter reflects an important response to previous calls for theoretically based investigations of the impact of service-learning on students' awareness and openness to race and diversity. Community-based research is often touted in much of the current literature as a viable means of promoting civic engagement as it provides an interface of students, faculty, and community partners for addressing critical social needs. In chapter 7, Marsteller-Kowaleski writes of an innovative approach of incorporating community-based research as a pedagogy within an introductory research methods service-learning class. She uses the tenets of community-based research as the rubric to assess the impact of the class on students, the instructor, and the community partners.

Part III addresses the critical issue of institutionalizing service-learning. Each of the three chapters in this section presents a unique perspective and context of making service-learning an integral part of educational settings. Mintz and Abramovitz describe teacher perceptions on implementing service-learning in public school settings in chapter 8. Using guiding principles from theories of intrinsic motivation and self-determination, they examined the effect of five influential forces that motivate teachers to implement service-learning. Their work presents an interesting examination of school culture and personal attributes. Chapter 9 continues this examination within higher education. Based on initial work that began as a round-table discussion at the first service-learning research conference in Berkeley, Mundy reports findings from a comprehensive national survey examining faculty engagement in service-learning at various types of institutions of higher education. She examined characteristics of faculty, disciplines, and institutions of 15 colleges and universities. This portion of the book concludes with chapter 10 in which Gelmon, Sherman, Gaudet, Mitchell, and Trotter make international comparisons of the process of institutionalizing service-learning in higher education in the United States, Canada, and South Africa. The authors provide a useful illustration of how Furco's (2003) rubric can be used to assess levels of institutional implementation of service-learning, and conduct a compelling analysis of the history of service-learning adoption and diffusion at their sites.

Part IV provides a reflective chapter written by Billig and Welch on the challenges of service-learning as civically engaged scholarship. They look at common characteristics and issues from two views: one from the K–12 perspective and another from that of higher education, and discuss the challenges presented by both systems.

All of these chapters provide useful new information that addresses critical needs and questions in various contexts. Each chapter is firmly grounded in theoretical constructs. Much of the work presented in this collection represents applied research that can be used as tools or a foundation for hypothesis testing by colleagues in the field. The research prompts new questions, and each chapter presents suggestions for additional work needed to increase understanding and effectiveness of practice. Most exciting is the growing realization and application of service-learning as a form of civically engaged scholarship. The work of the scholars presented here demonstrates how this form of experiential pedagogy fosters the civic responsibility of students, faculty, and educational institutions as citizens while contributing to the theories and research base in this exciting and growing field.

REFERENCES

Bennett, M. J. (1993). Towards ethnorelativism: A developmental model of intercultural sensitivity. In R. M. Paige (Ed.), *Education for the intercultural experience* (2nd ed., pp. 21–71). Yarmouth, ME: Intercultural Press.

Furco, A. (2003) *Self-assessment rubric for the institutionalization of service-learning in higher education*. Providence, RI: Campus Compact.

Krumboltz, J. D. (1994). Improving career development theory from a social learning perspective. In M. L. Savickas & R. W. Lent (Eds.), *Convergence in career development theories: Implications for science and practice* (pp. 9–31). Palo Alto, CA: Consulting Psychologist Press.

Perry, W. G. (1999). *Forms of intellectual and ethical development in the college years: A scheme*. New York: Holt, Rinehart and Winston. (Original work published 1968)

PART I

FOUNDATIONS

CHAPTER 1

SERVICE-LEARNING AND THE DEVELOPMENT OF DEMOCRATIC UNIVERSITIES, DEMOCRATIC SCHOOLS, AND DEMOCRATIC GOOD SOCIETIES IN THE 21ST CENTURY

Ira Harkavy

It is not possible to run a course aright when the goal itself is not rightly placed.

—Bacon, *Novum Organum* (1620)

In conception, at least, democracy approaches most nearly the ideal of all social organization; that in which the individual and the society are organic to each other.

—Dewey, *The Ethics of Democracy* (1888)

Democracy has been given a mission to the world, and it is of no uncertain character. I wish to show that the university is the prophet of this democracy, as well as its priest and its philosopher; that in other words, the university is the Messiah of the democracy, its to-be-expected deliverer.

—Harper, *The University and Democracy* (1899)

New Perspectives in Service-Learning: Research to Advance the Field, pages 3–22
Copyright © 2004 by Information Age Publishing
All rights of reproduction in any form reserved.

Democracy must begin at home, and its home is the neighborly community.

—Dewey, *The Public and Its Problems* (1927)

To be a great university we must be a great local *university.*

—Kenny, President, State University of New York, Stony Brook,
New York Times (August 18, 1999)

I had the good fortune to participate in the Wingspread meeting that drafted a research agenda entitled *Research Agenda for Combining Service and Learning in the 1990s* (Giles, Porter Honnet, & Migliore, 1998), which is often cited as one of the foundational documents for the field. In retrospect I have found the two broad thematic questions generated by the Wingspread conference to be particularly compelling: (1) What is the effect of service-learning on intellectual, moral, and citizenship development of participants? and (2) What is the effect of service-learning on the advancement of social institutions and democracy?

In my judgment, these questions remain among the most central questions for a service-learning research agenda. But as impressed as I was with the research agenda developed in 1991, as well as other research agendas developed over the past dozen years, upon reflection I have grown concerned with the actual progress we have made. The very state of our universities, schools, indeed society itself, may well indicate that service-learning has not nearly fulfilled the promise of service-learning.

Is that a fair conclusion? Am I claiming too much for service-learning? After all, service-learning is merely a technique, a method, one way of teaching and studying society. Or is service-learning much more than that? More precisely, can service-learning have a higher, much more significant purpose?

In the *Encyclopedia of Community*, Benson and I (2003b) defined service-learning as:

an active, creative...[pedagogy] that integrates community service with academic study in order to enhance a student's capacity to think critically, solve problems practically, and function as a life-long moral, democratic citizen in a democratic society.

In most cases, service-learning takes place within an academic course.... Service-learning also involves student reflection on the service experience, an emphasis on providing genuine service to the community, and the development of democratic, mutually beneficial, and respectful relationships between the students and the community members with whom they work. (p. 1223)

For Benson and me, service-learning best accomplishes its goals by engaging students in collaborative, action-oriented, reflective, real-world problem solving designed to develop the knowledge and related practice necessary for an optimally democratic society.

Given our definition of service-learning, it follows that a service-learning research agenda should work to develop strategies and actions to help fulfill the democratic promise of America's colleges and universities in particular and the democratic promise of American society in general. We should, therefore, evaluate service-learning by the extent to which it actually advances democracy in our classrooms, communities, and society. To be more specific, the evaluation of the impact of service-learning on student learning should be one component, not the primary focus, of a research agenda. Similarly, increased acceptance of service-learning in the disciplines, while important, is not an indication that anything like serious, substantial, significant change in higher education is occurring. To be even more direct, if research on service-learning conceptualizes learning outcomes and acceptance by disciplines as ends, rather than as means to larger educational and societal ends, the service-learning movement will lose its way and result in the inevitable reduction of service-learning to just another technique, method, or field.

The reduction of service-learning would be even more devastating than the reduction of disciplines (e.g., history, political science, economics, sociology) that occurred in the early decades of the 20th century. Founded for the purpose of advancing "scientific…study" and "practical reform (DuBois, 1899/1967, p. 4), the disciplines, largely in reaction to the horrors of World War I, turned inward, focusing on themselves rather than contributions they could make, to use Francis Bacon's phrase, to "the relief of man's estate" (Benson, 1972, p. x). Why will the reduction of service-learning have even more negative consequences than the post–World War I taming of the disciplines? Simply put, because service-learning should not be conceived of as a discipline, but as a systematic, democratic, collaborative, experimental approach to learning, personal and civic development, knowledge production, and societal change. Even more important, service-learning can and has served as the driving force and center of an intellectual movement to create democratic schooling from pre-K education through higher education. It has been the leading edge of an academic glasnost to create democratic, engaged, civic universities after nearly a century (to mix metaphors) of the narrowing and hardening of academic arteries. In short, the reduction of service-learning would be particularly devastating because it would result in dashing hope that significant schooling and societal change can occur, creating a perception and feeling that no matter how promising the strategy, in the end it will be "the same old same old."

In effect, I am calling for a Baconian-inspired strategy for the development and advancement of a comprehensive service-learning research agenda. To Bacon, the first principle for progress is "know thy goals." As Bacon wrote in 1620, "It is not possible to run a course aright when the goal itself is not rightly placed" (Benson, 1972, p. xi). The goal and research agenda for service-learning should be to contribute *significantly* to developing and sustaining democratic schools, colleges, universities, communities, and societies. By working to realize that goal, service-learning will powerfully help American higher education in particular, and American schooling in general, return to their core mission of educating students for a democratic society.

Given the position outlined above, I must do three things to give credence to my argument:

1. Demonstrate that a democratic mission is the core mission of American higher education.
2. Identify the obstacles that have helped prevent higher education from realizing its democratic mission.
3. Propose a practical strategy by which service-learning can help reduce those obstacles and help higher education realize its democratic mission.

DEMOCRATIC MISSION AS CORE MISSION

If we are to fulfill the democratic promise of America for *all* Americans, we need to be a nation comprised of individuals with an "inclination joined with an ability to serve." I take this phrase from Benjamin Franklin, the extraordinary patriot, statesman, scientist, educator, scholar, and activist. In 1749, Franklin published a pamphlet entitled, *Relating to the Education of Youth in Pennsilvinia* [*sic*] to describe the purposes and curriculum of the "Academy of Philadelphia," later named the University of Pennsylvania. To quote Franklin's *Proposals* more fully:

> The idea of what is true merit, should also be often presented to youth, explain'd and impress'd on their minds, as consisting in an inclination join'd with an ability to serve Mankind, one's Country, friends and family…which ability should be the great aim and end of all learning. (Best, 1962, pp. 150–151)

An inclination joined with an ability to serve was the original rationale for public schools, which were to educate youth for citizenship. Moreover, colonial colleges were founded with service as a central aim. While Franklin founded the University of Pennsylvania (Penn) as a secular institution to educate students in a variety of fields, the other colonial colleges were largely created to educate ministers and religiously orthodox men capable of creating good communities built on religious denominational principles.

These institutions were created specifically with religiously based service as a central purpose.

- Harvard (Congregationalist)
- William and Mary (Anglican)
- Yale (Congregationalist)
- Princeton (Presbyterian)
- Columbia (Anglican)
- Brown (Baptist)
- Rutgers (Dutch Reformed)
- Dartmouth (Congregationalist)

Service to society, fulfilling America's democratic mission, was the founding purpose of the land-grant universities. Established by the Morrill Act of 1862, land grant colleges and universities were designed to spread education, advance democracy, and improve the mechanical, agricultural, and military sciences. The spirit of the Morrill Act was perhaps best expressed at the University of Wisconsin, which at the turn of the century designed programs around the educational needs of adult citizens across the state. In 1912, Charles McCarthy, a graduate of the University of Wisconsin and the first legislative reference librarian in the United States, coined the phrase "The Wisconsin Idea" to describe a concept that had been in practice for a number of years (McCarthy, 1912). The Wisconsin Idea began its "take-off phase" in 1903 when Charles Van Hise became president of the University of Wisconsin and joined forces with his former classmate, Governor Robert La Follette, to make "the boundaries of the university...the boundaries of the state" (Stark, 1995/1996, pp. 2–3). When asked what accounted for the great progressive reforms that spread across the Midwest in the first two decades of the 20th century, McCarthy replied, "a combination of soil and seminar." McCarthy's answer captured the essence of the Wisconsin Idea—focusing academic resources on improving the life of the farmer and the lives of citizens across the entire state (Stark, pp. 2–3).[1]

The urban research universities founded in the late 19th century also made service their central goal. In 1876, Daniel C. Gilman, in his inaugural address as the first president of Johns Hopkins University, expressed the hope that universities should "make for less misery among the poor, less ignorance in the schools, less bigotry in the temple, less suffering in the hospitals, less fraud in business, less folly in politics" (Long, 1992, p. 184). Following Gilman's lead, the abiding belief in the democratic purposes of the American research university echoed throughout higher education at the turn of the 20th century. In 1899, for example, William Rainey Harper, the University of Chicago's first president, identified the university as the "prophet of democracy, as well as its priest and its philosopher; that in other words, the university is the Messiah of the democracy, its to-be-expected deliverer" (1905, p. 12). And in 1908, Charles W. Eliot, the president of Harvard, proclaimed:

> At bottom most of the American institutions of higher education are filled with the democratic spirit of serviceableness. Teachers and students alike are profoundly moved by the desire to serve the democratic community. (cited in Long, 1992, p. 112)

Simply put, the democratic mission served as *the* central mission for the development of the American research university, including both land-grant institutions *and* urban universities such as Hopkins, Chicago, Columbia, and Penn. As political scientist Charles Anderson (1993) observed in *Prescribing the Life of the Mind:*

> With deliberate defiance, those who created the American university (particularly the public university, though the commitment soon spread throughout the system) simply stood this [essentially aristocratic] idea of reason on its head. Now it was assumed that the widespread exercise of self-conscious, critical reason was essential to *democracy* [italics added]. *The truly remarkable belief arose that this system of government would flourish best if citizens would generally adopt the habits of thought hitherto supposed appropriate mainly for scholars and scientist* [italics added]. We vastly expanded access to higher education. We presumed it a general good, like transport, or power, part of the infrastructure of the civilization. (pp. 7–8)

History is not the only useful guide to help us determine whether the democratic mission should be the primary mission of American higher education. Astin's (1997) contemporary research on the "public pronouncements that U.S. colleges and universities make in their catalogues and mission statements" is also helpful (p. 210). He found:

> In many ways, these sometimes lofty statements come as close as anything to Dewey's conception of the proper role of education in society. If we were to study the mission statements of a randomly selected group of U.S. higher education institutions, we would seldom, if ever, find any mention of private economic benefits, international competitiveness, or filling slots in the labor market. On the contrary, when it comes to describing its educational mission, the typical college or university will use language such as "preparing students for responsible citizenship" "developing character," "developing future leaders," "preparing students to serve society," and so forth. In other words, if we are to believe our own rhetoric, those of us who work in the academy see ourselves as *serving the society and promoting and strengthening our particular form of democratic self-government.* (italics added, pp. 210–211)

American higher education in general, however, has, in my judgment, very far to go before it actually fulfills its historic public purposes. In her study for the Grantmaker Forum on National and Community Service, Gibson (2001) noted that when it comes to civic engagement, higher education's rhetoric far exceeds its performance. Weaving together her own words with those of Checkoway and Mattson, Gibson observed:

> Other higher education leaders have echoed Derek Bok's concern that universities are disassociated with the civic missions on which they were founded—missions that assumed responsibility for preparing students for active participation in a democratic society and developing students' knowledge for the improvement of communities. Currently, it is "hard to find top administrators with consistent commitment to this mission; few faculty members consider it central to their role, and community groups that approach the university for assistance often find it difficult to get what they need." In short, the university has primarily become "a place for professors to get tenured and students to get credentialed." (p. 11)

How far higher education *is* from where it *should* be is also evident in the parlous state of democracy on campus, which is exemplified by the hierarchical, elitist, competitive culture that pervades the academy, the state of the communities in which our institutions are located, and the state of American democracy itself.

OBSTACLES TO THE REALIZATION OF HIGHER EDUCATION'S DEMOCRATIC MISSION

Why has American higher education failed to realize its democratic mission? Summarily stated, the forces of Platonization, commodification, and disciplinary ethnocentrism, tribalism, and guildism continue to prevent American higher education, indeed American society, from translating its democratic mission into democratic practice.

Platonization

Plato's elitist, idealist theory of schooling has incalculable day-to-day impacts on education and society. In part, the extraordinary impact of Plato's antidemocratic, idealist theory on American democracy can be explained by Dewey's failure to translate his own ideas into practical action.

The philosopher Dewey most liked to read was Plato. Though he admired Plato, their worldviews differed radically. Plato's worldview was aristocratic and contemplative while Dewey's was democratic and activist. Despite their many differences, in certain crucial respects Dewey shared Plato's views about the relationships between education and society. Like the ancient Greek philosopher, Dewey theorized that education and society were dynamically interactive and interdependent. Plato's philosophy of education aimed to achieve aristocratic order while Dewey's aimed to achieve democratic community. For Dewey it followed, then, that if human beings hope to develop and maintain a participatory democratic society, they must develop and maintain a participatory democratic schooling system.

Ironically, in direct contrast to Plato who pragmatically created a remarkably influential Academy to implement his aristocratic philosophy of education and society, the philosophical activist Dewey failed to work to institutionalize his democratic philosophy of education and society, except by "lay preaching"; that is, despite the powerful example of Plato's Academy—an Academy whose elitist, idealist philosophy continues to dominate Western schooling systems to this day—Dewey flagrantly violated his own general theory of thinking and action. Oversimply stated, Plato's idealist theory of education, his corollary theory of knowledge (i.e., the great superiority of elegant *pure theory* and *pure science* compared to *inferior* real-world practice, as well as his elitist theory of governance) are deeply embedded in the culture and structure of American colleges and universities (Benson & Harkavy, 2000).

The dead hand of Plato continues to shape American higher education and through American higher education it shapes the entire schooling system. Broadly viewed, service- learning can be conceptualized as a strategy to release the vise-like grip of Plato's dead hand (Harkavy & Benson, 1998). Overthrowing Plato, however, would only achieve a partial victory. A clear and present danger to the democratic mission of higher education and to American democracy in general also comes from the forces of commodification (i.e., education for profit, students as customers, syllabi as content, academics as superstars). It is worth emphasizing that these forces, although particularly pernicious at this time, were alive and well at the very birth of the colonial college (Benson & Harkavy, 2002).

Commodification

More than an ethic of religious-inspired service inspired the colonial colleges. They were also a significant form of community competition. Colleges, it was anticipated, would bring more than religious and educational benefits to a local community. They would bring economic (and a wide variety of other) benefits. The Brown brothers of Providence, Rhode Island, provided a particularly clear statement of anticipated economic benefits. Appealing for support to "businessmen of Providence and...surrounding towns," they promised:

> Building the college here will be the means of bringing great quantities of money into the place, and thereby greatly increasing the markets for all kinds of the country's produce, and consequently increasing the value of estates to which this town is a market. (p. 2)[2]

Succinctly stated, "contradictory capitalist market motives," not simply traditional medieval, Christian motives, inspired and shaped the contradictory origins and increasingly contradictory development of the American higher education system.

To systematically discuss the history of commodification in American higher education would require a series of books. I merely note, therefore, that it was the Cold War and its extraordinarily complex consequences, direct and indirect, short term and long term, that redefined American science and accelerated and deepened the commodification of American universities in powerful and, in my judgment, deeply disturbing ways.

To place that highly complex development in historical perspective, consider Leslie's (1993) analysis that, during World War II, to a far greater extent than during World War I, universities had

> won a substantial share of the funds [going into wartime mobilization], with research and development contracts that actually dwarfed those of the largest industrial contractors.... Vannevar Bush, the chief architect of wartime science policy and a strong advocate of university research, was the man behind the change. (p. 6)

Bush engineered that change as director of the powerful wartime Office of Scientific Research and Development. Late in 1944, President Roosevelt, highly impressed by its accomplishments, asked Bush to draft a long-term plan for postwar science. Bush delivered his famous report, *Science, the Endless Frontier,* in 1945. General agreement exists that, since 1945, the report has profoundly influenced America's science policy. For my purposes, the chief importance of Bush's *Basic Science Manifesto* is that it rapidly produced what Benson and I (2002) have previously characterized as the Big Science, Cold War, Entrepreneurial, Commodified, American Research University System (p. 192). Bok (2003) brilliantly stigmatized this development in his recent book, *Universities in the Marketplace,* as the commercialization of higher education.

Perhaps the most important consequence of the commercialization of higher education is the devastating impact that it has on the values and ambitions of college students. When universities openly and increasingly pursue commercialization, the pursuit of economic self-interest by students tends to be legitimized and reinforced and contributes to the widespread sense among them that they are in college solely to gain career skills and credentials. It would only belabor the argument to comment further on how student idealism is even more sharply diminished, and student disengagement is even more sharply increased, when students see their universities abandon academic values and scholarly pursuits to openly, enthusiastically function as entrepreneurial, ferociously competitive, profit-making corporations.

Disciplinary Ethnocentrism, Tribalism, and Guildism

Disciplinary ethnocentrism, tribalism, and guildism strongly dominate American universities today and strongly work against their actually doing what they rhetorically promise to do (Benson & Harkavy, 2003a). The famous postmodern literary theorist Stanley Fish, a dean at the University of Illinois at Chicago, pontifically provides us with a marvelous case in point. In his monthly column in the *Chronicle of Higher Education* (May 16, 2003), he caustically attacked

the authors of a recent book [Colby, Ehrlich, Beaumont, & Stephens, 2003], *Educating Citizens: Preparing America's Undergraduates for Lives of Moral and Civic Responsibility*. A product of the Carnegie Foundation for the Advancement of Teaching, the volume reports on *a failure that I find heartening*. (italics added, p. C5)

What precisely is the failure? Why does Fish find it heartening? The failure is that, according to Colby and colleagues (2003), undergraduate education now does not prepare students to become involved and responsible citizens. Why is that failure "heartening" to the Dean of Liberal Arts and Sciences at the University of Illinois at Chicago? Because, he insists unequivocally, professors cannot possibly provide that kind of learning and should never try to provide it. Their job is simply to teach what their discipline calls for them to teach and to try to make their students into good disciplinary researchers. Professors cannot make their students "into good people and...shouldn't try" (p. C5). Indeed, for Fish, "emphasis on broader goals and especially on the therapeutic goal of 'personal development' can make it difficult to interest students in the disciplinary training it is our job to provide" (p. C5).

In effect, Fish not only calls on American academics to repudiate Dewey and his democratic adherents, he calls on them to repudiate Plato and his antidemocratic elitist adherents. Since Plato's philosophy of education, like Dewey's, gives its highest priority to making good citizens, according to the Fish doctrine of professorial responsibility, they were both completely wrong. As teachers, the only duty of professors is to teach their discipline; it emphatically does not require or permit them to try to make their students "into good people."

In a perverse way, Fish's caustic attack on the authors of *Educating Citizens* actually performs a valuable function. It splendidly illuminates what might be called the disciplinary fallacy afflicting American universities; namely, the fallacy that professors are duty-bound only to serve the scholastic interests and preoccupations of their disciplines and have neither the responsibility nor the capacity to help their universities keep their long-standing promises to prepare *America's Undergraduates for Lives of Moral and Civic Responsibility* (Colby et al., 2003). In effect, Fish boldly asserted what most professors now believe and practice but strongly tend not to admit openly. This belief and practice also strongly tends to produce disciplinary isolation and "silo-ization," which strongly inhibits the interdisciplinary cooperation and integrated specialization necessary to solve significant, highly complex, real-world problems. (See Center for Educational Research and Innovation, 1982, p. 127.)

TOWARD A STRATEGY TO HELP HIGHER EDUCATION PRACTICALLY REALIZE ITS DEMOCRATIC MISSION

Having briefly—and oversimply—identified the obstacles that prevent higher education from realizing its democratic mission, I turn now to the really hard, really significant question: What is to be done to release higher education from the dead hand of Plato and the live hands of commodification and the disciplinary fallacy? More specifically, what is a practical strategy that would enable service-learning to help American higher education overthrow Plato and institute Dewey, reject commodification and disciplinary guildism, and practically realize its democratic mission?

Focus on Undergraduate Education

In the Foreword to *Educating Citizens*, Shulman, President of the Carnegie Foundation, emphasized the critically important role colleges play in the development of the virtues and understanding vital for democratic citizenship. Observing that a democratic society required an "educated citizenry blessed with virtue as well as wisdom," Shulman (p. viii) hailed the book's demonstration that achieving the requisite

> ...combination of moral and civic virtue accompanied by the development
> of understanding occurs best when fostered by our institutions of higher
> education. It does not occur by accident, or strictly through early experience.
> Indeed, I argue that there may well be a critical period for the development

of these virtues, and that period could be the college years. During this developmental period, defined as much by educational opportunity as by age, students of all ages *develop the resources needed for their continuing journeys through adult life.* [italics added, p. viii]

Shulman's astute observation helps us see the critically important role that, in a wide variety of ways, colleges play in the lifelong, all-encompassing development of all the different types of personnel who, directly and indirectly, control and operate the American schooling system. If their critically formative years at college neither contribute to their own development as democratic citizens nor concretely demonstrate to them how schools can function to produce democratic citizens, they will necessarily reproduce what they have learned—more precisely, failed to learn—in college. As a result of that disastrously flawed reproductive process, the schooling system will be incapable of developing an effective program for democratic citizenship. Put another way, I contend that American colleges constitute the strategically important component of American universities when the goal is to help develop an American schooling system capable of producing students who possess the set of attributes they must possess to function as democratic citizens.

Shame and Cognitive Dissonance

For many years my colleagues and I have argued that the immoral state of America's cities and the enlightened self-interest of colleges and universities would lead higher education to embrace significant service-learning partnerships with their communities. More significantly, my colleagues and I argued that the increasingly obvious, increasingly immoral contradiction between the increasing status, wealth, and power of American universities—particularly elite research universities—and the increasingly pathological state of a great many American cities would *shame* them into taking action to reduce the contradiction. In addition, we argued that universities would not only be pressured by external agencies (e.g., federal and state governments) to work hard to improve the quality of their local schools and communities but would increasingly recognize that it was in their own enlightened self-interest to do that.[3]

It has recently become clear to me, however, that my colleagues and I seriously underestimated the ability of universities to effectively resist making substantive changes of the kind many academics have been advocating since the 1980s. Probably the main form of resistance has been for universities to make eloquent rhetorical pledges of support for community engagement and service-learning and then fail to put "their money (and other necessary resources) where their mouth is."

Aside from deploring it, what can practically be done to overcome or reduce that hypocritical form of university resistance to change? That is the problem. What is the solution? Part of the solution, I believe, is to follow Bok's (2003) lead in *Universities in the Marketplace* and apply the powerful social psychological theory of cognitive dissonance. Bok did not explicitly cite that theory, but he used it with devastating effect in his book-length demonstration that "the commercialization of higher education" not only fundamentally contradicts traditional "academic standards and institutional integrity" but, in a "process [which] may be irreversible," threatens to sacrifice "essential values that are all but impossible to restore" (p. 208).

In *A Theory of Cognitive Dissonance* (1957), Festinger published in book form the theory that became one of the most influential theories in social psychology. Summarized in oversimplified form, the theory focuses on "the feeling of psychological discomfort produced by the combined presence of two thoughts that do not follow from one another [e.g., smokers who agree that smoking is very unhealthy but continue to smoke].[4] Festinger proposed that the greater the discomfort, the greater the desire to reduce the dissonance of the two cognitive elements."

In *Universities in the Marketplace*, Bok (2003) clearly wanted to produce such great discomfort among university administrators and faculty members who either engaged in commercial activities or tolerated them that they would feel compelled to change their behavior. In similar fashion, the egalitarian values proclaimed in the Declaration of Independence have long been invoked in American history to produce the cognitive dissonance and great discomfort indispensable to "agitators" who wanted to abolish slavery, win equal rights for women, overcome segregation, and achieve similar egalitarian goals.

Learning from history and following Bok's lead, I hope to help stimulate a sustained, massive campaign designed to shame universities into translating their democratic rhetoric into practical action. Taking a leaf from Steffens's (1957) famous muckraking work on *The Shame of the Cities*, that campaign would try to overcome "The Shame of the Universities." A highly effective way to conduct the campaign is to quote freely from Astin's (1997) powerful essay, *Liberal Education and Democracy: The Case for Pragmatism*. In effect, Astin skillfully used the theory of cognitive dissonance to develop a devastating critique of the hypocrisy of universities, which rhetorically proclaim that their mission is to help their students become responsible democratic citizens and then do almost nothing *positive* to realize that mission. In fact, as Astin observed, by their antidemocratic organization and functioning, "by their obvious preoccupation with enhancing [their] resources and reputations," and in a variety of other ways, universities strongly contribute to their students accepting the "values of materialism, competitiveness, and individualism" (p. 221). Guided by cognitive dissonance theory and American history (and the history of other countries' reforms and revolutions), I am convinced that a sustained, massive, many-sided campaign to expose and denounce university hypocrisy can produce sufficient great discomfort to *help* change American university behavior for the better. But in itself such a campaign will not bring about the radical changes I call for. We need additional prongs in our strategy, two of which are briefly described here.

Act Locally

In her edited volume, *Building Partnerships for Service-Learning,* Jacoby and colleagues (2003) emphasized that creating effective, democratic, mutually beneficial, mutually respectful partnerships should be a primary, if not *the* primary, goal for service-learning in the first decade of the 21st century. Jacoby called on colleges and universities to focus their attention on improving democracy and the quality of life in their local communities. Here Jacoby is echoing one of Dewey's (1927/1954) most significant propositions: "Democracy must begin at home, and its home is the neighborly community" (p. 213). Democracy, Dewey emphasized, has to be built on face-to-face interactions in which human beings work together cooperatively to solve the ongoing problems of life. In effect, Jacoby and colleagues have updated Dewey and advocated this proposition: *Democracy must begin at home, and its home is the engaged, neighborly college or university and its local community partner.*

The benefits of a local community focus for college and university service-learning courses and programs are manifold. Ongoing, continuous interaction is facilitated through work in an easily accessible local setting. Relationships of trust, so essential for effective partnerships and effective learning, are also built through day-to-day work on problems and issues of mutual concern. In addition, the local community also provides a convenient setting in which a number of service-learning courses based in different disciplines can work together on a complex problem to produce substantive results. Work in a college or university's local community, since it facilitates interaction across schools and disciplines, can create interdisciplinary learning opportunities. And finally, the local community is a real-world site in which community members and academics can pragmatically determine whether the work is making a real difference and whether *both* the neighborhood and the institution are better as a result of common efforts.

Focus on Significant Community-Based, Real-World Problems

To Dewey (1910) knowledge and learning were most effective when human beings worked collaboratively to solve specific, strategic real-world problems. "Thinking," he wrote, "begins in . . . a *forked road* situation, a situation which is ambiguous, which presents a dilemma, which poses alternatives" (p. 11). A focus on global problems, such as poverty, substandard housing, hunger, and inadequate, unequal education, that manifest themselves locally are, in my judgment, the best way to apply Dewey's brilliant proposition in practice. To support the argument, I turn to the example I know best, the University of Pennsylvania's work with its local ecological community, West Philadelphia.

The lack of accessible, affordable, effective health care has been increasingly recognized as one of the most serious problems afflicting poor urban communities. In fact, since my colleagues and I began our work in 1985, community leaders have identified improving health care as a critical need. As a result, beginning in the late 1980s, we have been trying, largely unsuccessfully, to develop a sustainable, comprehensive, effective health care program at local public schools. In the spring and summer of 2002, however, a group of undergraduates in an academically based community service seminar focused their research and service on helping to solve the health care crisis in West Philadelphia. Their research and work with the community led them to propose establishment of a health promotion and disease prevention center at a public school in West Philadelphia, the Sayre Middle School.

From their research, they were well aware that community-oriented primary-care projects frequently flounder because of an inability to sustain adequate external funding. The students concluded that, for a school-based community health care project to be sustained and successful, it had to be built into the curriculum at both the university and the public school levels. Only then would it gain a degree of permanence and stability over time. They proposed, therefore, creation of a health promotion/disease prevention center at a local school that would serve as a teaching and learning focus for medical, dental, nursing, arts and sciences, social work, education, design, and business students. The proposal proved to be so compelling that it led to the development of a school-based Community Health Promotion and Disease Prevention Center at Sayre Middle School. It is worth noting that Mei Elansary, one of the undergraduates who developed the Sayre project, received the 2003 Howard R. Swearer Humanitarian Award given by Campus Compact to students for outstanding public service.

The School-Based Community Health Promotion and Disease Prevention Center at Sayre Middle School was formally launched in January 2003. It functions as the central component of a university-assisted community school designed both to advance student learning and democratic development and to help strengthen families and institutions within the community. A community school is an ideal location for health care programs since it is not only where children learn, but also where community members gather and participate in a variety of activities. Moreover, the multidisciplinary character of the Sayre Health Promotion and Disease Prevention Center enables it to be integrated into the curriculum and co-curriculum of both the public school and the university, ensuring an educational focus as well as sustainability for the Sayre Center. In fact, the core of the program is to integrate the activities of the Sayre Center with the educational programs and curricula at both Sayre Middle School and Penn. To that end, Penn faculty, and students in medicine, nursing, dentistry, social work, arts and sciences, and design as well as other schools to a lesser extent, now work at Sayre through new and existing courses, internships, and research projects. Health promotion and service activities are also integrated into the Sayre students' curriculum. In effect, Sayre students serve as agents of health care change in the Sayre neighborhood.

The Health Promotion and Disease Prevention Center at Sayre is connected to a small learning community (SLC) that involves 350 students from Grades 6 through 8. In that SLC, health promotion activities are integrated with core subject learning in science, social studies, math, and language arts, among other areas. Ultimately, every curriculum unit will have a community education and/or community problem-solving component (usually this will function as the organizing theme of the unit). Given this approach, Sayre students are not passive recipients of health information. Instead, they are active deliverers of information and coordination and creative providers of service.

A considerable number and variety of Penn academically based community service courses provide the resources and support that make it possible to operate, sustain, and develop the Sayre Health Promotion and Disease Prevention Center. Literally hundreds of Penn students (professional, graduate, and undergraduate) and over a dozen faculty members (from a wide range of Penn schools and departments) work at Sayre. Because they are performing community service while engaged in academic research and teaching and learning, they are simultaneously practicing their specialized skills and developing, to some extent at least, their moral and civic consciousness and democratic character. Because they are engaged in a highly integrated common project, they are also learning how to communicate, interact, and collaborate with each other in wholly unprecedented ways that have measurably broadened their academic horizons.

CONCLUSION

In conclusion, I must point out that Penn is perhaps the only major university where all of its schools and colleges are located on a contiguous urban campus. In the early 1970s, Penn's President Meyerson emphasized the extraordinary intellectual and societal benefits that would result if the university took optimum advantage of the ease of interaction that a single campus location provides. To realize those benefits he called for the implementation of a "One University" organizational realignment—a realignment in which Penn would be characterized by an intellectual collaboration and synergy across departments, divisions, colleges, and schools that would result in powerful advances in knowledge and human welfare.

This was easier said than done. In practice, overcoming Penn's long-standing disciplinary fragmentation and conflict, narrow specialization, and bureaucratic barriers (and what Benjamin Franklin once stigmatized as ancient customs and habitudes) proved enormously difficult to achieve, and the One University idea remained an idea, not an action program. The Sayre Project, however, is beginning to create One University in practice through its focus on solving the global problem of community health as it is manifested in a given community in West Philadelphia. The complex, real-world problem of improving the health of an actual community simply requires multischool, multidisciplinary, interdepartmental collaboration, as well as deep, sustained collaboration with the community itself.

It is still the early days for the Sayre Project. But the project appears to hold promise for West Philadelphia, Penn, and maybe for other communities and universities. My key point, however, is more general. Working to solve significant, serious, strategic, community-identified, real-world problems in a university's local community may well be among the most promising ways for service-learning to advance its research agenda, fulfill its promise, and significantly, substantially contribute to the development of democratic universities, democratic schools, and democratic good societies in the 21st century.

ACKNOWLEDGMENT

This chapter is a summary of the keynote speech provided during the Third Annual K–H International Service-Learning Research Conference, Salt Lake City, Utah.

NOTES

1. For additional information on the Wisconsin Idea, see Fitzpatrick, E. J. (1944). *McCarthy of Wisconsin.* New York: Columbia University Press; McCarthy, C. in the References; Rudolph, F. (1962). *The American college and university.* New York: Alfred A. Knopf, pp. 355–372; Veysey, L. R. (1965). *The emergence of the American university.* Chicago: University of Chicago Press; First Phoenix Edition, 1970, pp. 104–109.

2. The Brown brothers' quotation can be found in Cochran, T. C. (1972). *Business in American life: A history.* New York: McGraw Hill, p. 35; see also Brubacher, J. S., & Rudy, W. (1976). *Higher education in transition: A history of American colleges and universities, 1636–1976.* New York: Harper & Row, 3rd ed., pp. 3–9.

3. These arguments have been made in a variety of articles and chapters dating from 1991, including: Benson, L., & Harkavy, I. (1991). Progressing beyond the welfare state: A neo-Deweyan strategy. *Universities and Community Schools, 2*(1–2), 2–28; Harkavy, I., & Benson, L. (1992, April 29). Universities, schools, and the welfare state. *Education Week,* 27; Harkavy, I., & Puckett, J. L. (1994). Lessons from Hull House for the contemporary urban university. *Social Service Review, 68*(3), 299–321; Harkavy, I. (1996). Back to the future: From service-learning to strategic academically-based community service as an approach for advancing knowledge and solving the problem of the American city. *Metropolitan Universities, 7*(1), 57–70; Harkavy, I. (1997). The demands of the times and the American research university. *Journal of Planning Literature, 11*(3), 33–36; Harkavy, I. (1999). School-community-university partnerships: Effectively integrating community building and education reform. *Universities and Community Schools,* 6(1–2), 7–24; Benson, L., & Harkavy, I. (1997). Integrating the American systems of higher, secondary, and primary education. In R. Orrill (Ed.), *Education and democracy: Re-imagining liberal learning in America* (pp. 174–196). New York: College Entrance Examination Board.

4. Harmon-Jones, E., & Mills, J. (1999). (Eds.), *Cognitive dissonance: Progress on a pivotal theory in social psychology.* Washington, DC: American Psychological Association.

REFERENCES

Anderson, C. W. (1993). *Prescribing the life of the mind.* Madison: University of Wisconsin Press.

Astin, A. W. (1997). Liberal education and democracy: The case for pragmatism. In R. Orrill (Ed.), *Education and democracy: Re-imagining liberal learning in America* (pp. 210–211). New York: College Entrance Examination Board.

Benson, L. (1972). *Toward the scientific study of history.* Philadelphia: Lippincott.

Benson, L., & Harkavy, I. (2000). Integrating the American systems of higher, secondary, and primary education to develop civic responsibility. In T. Ehrlich (Ed.), *Civic responsibility and higher education* (pp. 174–196). Phoenix, AZ: Oryx Press.

Benson, L., & Harkavy, I. (2002). Saving the soul of the university: What is to be done? In K. Robins & F. Webster (Eds.), *The virtual university? Information, markets, and management* (pp. 169–209). Oxford, UK: Oxford University Press.

Benson, L., & Harkavy, I. (2003a). *Informal citizenship education: A neo-Platonic, neo-Deweyan, radical program to develop democratic students, K–16.* Discussion paper, University of Pennsylvania.

Benson, L., & Harkavy, I. (2003b). Service-learning. In K. Christian & D. Levinson (Eds.), *Encyclopedia of community: From the village to the virtual world* (p. 1223). Thousand Oaks, CA: Sage.

Best, J. H. (1962). *Benjamin Franklin on education.* New York: Teachers College Press.

Bok, D. (2003). *Universities in the marketplace: The commercialization of higher education.* Princeton, NJ: Princeton University Press.

Center for Educational Research and Innovation. (1982). *The university and the community: The problems of changing relationships.* Paris: Organization for Economic Development.

Colby, A., Ehrlich, T., Beaumont, E., & Stephens, J. (2003). *Educating citizens: Preparing America's undergraduates for lives of moral and civic responsibility.* San Francisco: Jossey-Bass.

Dewey, J. (1910). *How we think.* Lexington, MA: D.C. Heath.

Dewey, J. (1954). *The public and its problems.* Denver, CO: Alan Swallow. (Original work published 1927)

DuBois, W. E. B. (1967). *The Philadelphia negro: A social study.* Philadelphia: University of Pennsylvania Press. (Original work published 1899)

Festinger, L. (1957). *A theory of cognitive dissonance.* Evanston, IL: Row, Peterson & Company.

Fish, S. (2003, May). Aim low. *Chronicle of Higher Education.* Retrieved June 15, 2004, from http://chronicle.com/jobs/2003/05/2003051601c.htm

Gibson, C. (2001). *From inspiration to participation: A review of perspectives on youth civic engagement.* Berkeley, CA: The Grantmaker Forum on Community and National Service.

Giles, D., Porter Honnet, E., & Migliore, S. (1998). Research agenda for combining service and learning in the 1990s. *Advances in Educational Research, 3,* 119–128.

Harkavy, I., & Benson, L. (1998). De-Platonizing and democratizing education as the bases of service-learning. In R. A. Rhoads & J. P. F. Howard (Eds.), *Academic service learning: A pedagogy of action and reflection: New Directions for Teaching and Learning, 73* (pp. 11–19). San Francisco: Jossey-Bass.

Harper, W. R. (1905). *The trend in higher education.* Chicago: University of Chicago Press.

Jacoby, B., & Associates. (2003). *Building partnerships for service-learning.* San Francisco: Jossey-Bass.

Leslie, S. (1993). *The Cold War and American science: The military–industrial–academic complex at MIT and Stanford.* New York: Columbia University Press.

Long, E. L. (1992). *Higher education as a moral enterprise.* Washington, DC: Georgetown University Press.

McCarthy, C. (1912). *The Wisconsin idea.* New York: MacMillan.

Shulman, L. S. (2003). Foreword. In A. Colby, T. Ehrlich, E. Beaumont, & J. Stephens (Eds.), *Educating citizens: Preparing America's undergraduates for lives of moral and civic responsibility* (pp. vii–x). San Francisco: Jossey-Bass.

Stark, J. (1995/1996). *The Wisconsin Idea: The university's service to the state.* Retrieved
    December 26, 2003, from www.legis.state.wi.us/lrb/pubs/feature/wisidea.pdf
Steffens, L. (1957). *The shame of the cities.* New York: Hill & Wang.

CHAPTER 2

ADDING RIGOR TO SERVICE-LEARNING RESEARCH

An Armchair Economists' Approach

Andrea L. Ziegert and KimMarie McGoldrick

ABSTRACT

Service-learning research has come under recent criticism for not being grounded sufficiently in theory and for lacking precision in specification and measurement. A review of recent research in light of these criticisms reveals that these efforts are at a methodological crossroads. This chapter describes an analogous period in the economics discipline in order to describe potential pitfalls that need to be avoided in the process of moving the research agenda forward. Specifically, knowledge of service-learning can only be as exact and as precise as the most imprecise component of the research process. The precision of a component of the research process says nothing about the precision of the conclusions if researchers do not also address how the parts make a whole. Service-learning research should be built on a strong foundation of theory, values discussion, and concern for context. Each of these elements demands different skills, and researchers should specialize in that area of research in which they are most skilled. Failure to consider any one of these components, theories, values, or context will result in an imprecise and incomplete understanding of service-learning.

New Perspectives in Service-Learning: Research to Advance the Field, pages 23–36
Copyright © 2004 by Information Age Publishing

INTRODUCTION

Advocates of service-learning as an effective pedagogy are increasingly challenged to provide more than antidotal evidence to support their claims. This challenge is consistent with ongoing educational research more generally. For example, the U.S. Department of Education's What Works Clearinghouse (www.w-w-c.org) recently adopted a set of standards for scientific evidence on the effectiveness of particular educational methodologies and pedagogical interventions. These standards provide decision makers with the scientific evidence necessary to differentiate high-quality, credible research claims from less reliable research and promotional claims. For service-learning researchers, this translates into a call for increased rigor in service-learning research.

Much of the initial research in service-learning is descriptive of service-learning interventions in various academic disciplines and has documented the pedagogical techniques' long and rich history. Much of this history is better known with Stanton, Giles, and Cruz's 1999 publication, and many service-learning practitioners benefiting from insights of American Association of Higher Education (AAHE) *Series on Service-Learning in the Disciplines* (Zlotkowski, 1997–2000). McGoldrick and Ziegert (2002) developed a similar volume for the discipline of economics. Their work detailed the theory of service-learning as a method of teaching economic theory, motivations for faculty use of service-learning, assessment issues, resources for interested economists, and nine course-specific applications. While these volumes serve an important descriptive role, they do not address the recent call for rigor in service-learning research and instead are limited to descriptions of programs, classes, and the reflection process. In order to validate the effectiveness of service-learning as a pedagogical technique and to move the practice forward, more rigorous research is needed. The difficulty of this can seem enormous at times. The mere fact that service-learning is not discipline specific makes this a daunting task.

This purpose of this chapter is to raise important questions about the *process* by which service-learning research responds to the challenges of a call for more rigorous research. This chapter addresses how researchers can meet the call for more rigorous research and is not meant to be a criticism of the current status of service-learning research. Our analysis is based on a comparison of the current state of service-learning research to that of economics when research in that discipline was at a similar historical junction. The choices made by those leading the field of economics over 100 years ago had profound ramifications for the way research is conducted today. Some critiques of current economic methodology suggest that these past choices have severely limited progress in the field and have adversely affected the quality of economic research today. It is the authors' hope that similar limitations can be avoided by analyzing both the current state of service-learning research and the concurrent call for more rigorous work as the research agenda progresses, in context with the methodological progression that occurred in economics.

This chapter begins with a review of the current call for a more rigorous service-learning research agenda, followed by a description of the methodological crossroads in economics and a discussion of how a return to earlier methodological categorizations and practices would enrich economics research. A discussion of the current state of service-learning research reveals a similar methodological crossroads that the authors then use to discuss their vision of the future of service-learning research.

THE CALL FOR RIGOR IN SERVICE-LEARNING LITERATURE

The push for a more rigorous research process has been persuasively argued by a number of service-learning practitioners, most recently Eyler (2002) and Furco and Billig (2002). In her work, Eyler made a case for a more precise and robust research process and cited selectivity biases as one example of the problems inherent in current research. Such biases arise when research does not control for the possibility that those who are more likely to be benefited through service-learning practices are indeed the individuals who choose such experiences. The lack of control groups in such research brings into question the true magnitude of the impact of service-learning on measured outcomes. In addition, Eyler argued that long-term learning evaluations need to be undertaken in order to show post-semester impacts and the contribution of service-learning to life-long learning. Specification of actual measurements remains a major issue in this body of research, and Eyler reiterated the need for more careful specification of both independent and dependent variables in empirical work that will generate "research [that] is systematic and contains procedural rules for analysis that mitigate building arguments from selecting anecdotes to fit one's point of view" (p. 7).

Furco and Billig (2002) suggested that the inconsistent and often ungeneralizable results found in previous research is a direct result of the huge variation in research questions addressed, theories that ground such work, and methodological practices. They called for a validation of research through the use of norms and reviewed the National Research Council's six core principles for research and applied them to service-learning research (p. 17). It is argued that the use of these principles would provide a uniform process through which research on service-learning outcomes would be consistently performed despite its inherent multidisciplinary nature.

The call for a more rigorous research agenda and process was also identified in "Strategic Directions for Service-Learning Research," a special issue of the *Michigan Journal of Community Service Learning*. Articles in this issue included:

- A summary of the history of the research movement (Howard, Gelmon, & Giles, 2000);
- An argument for the development of a task force of experts instead of the more individualistic approach followed to date (Eyler, 2000);
- The recognition that a simple call for more systematic research is not sufficient and a process for doing so, such as that based on research validity, must be provided (Bringle & Hatcher, 2000);
- The recognition that any single technique will not likely be satisfactory, but that a key is the matching of research questions, methods, and the paradigm design (Shumer, 2000); and
- The call for multiple levels of assessment via students, faculty, institutions, and community (Gelmon, 2000).

More recently, two papers focused on elements of the research process as crucial to improving the quality of service-learning research. Bringle (2003) argued that theory can provide important conceptual grounding, which will, in turn, provide structure and coherence to service-learning research. He suggested ways in which service-learning researchers can develop and test their own theories or those developed by other researchers, such as social and cognitive psychologists. Work by Hecht (2003) focused on the important role of context in understanding service-learning outcomes. She argued that since students construct meaning from the service-learning experience, it is important to understand the site, student and teacher backgrounds, and reflective and planning contexts of that experience. In sum, as the service-learning research agenda continues to develop, issues such as theoretical constructs and context are being woven into the mix.

Multiple definitions of service-learning interventions and outcomes and a wide variety of research agendas and methods is evidence of the need for further discussion of methodology. The call for rigor in service-learning research is also evidence of a methodological crossroads. At such junctures, researchers must respond by making methodological choices. Choices made today can have profound impact on the future of service-learning research. Insights from the economics discipline at a similar juncture provide an initial starting point for the discussion of how these choices should be made.

ECONOMICS AT A METHODOLOGICAL CROSSROADS

Although every discipline reaches a crossroads, which is generally later determined to have profound effects on the direction in which the field progresses, this is often only viewed from a historical perspective.[1] In economics, this major methodological shift began in the late 1800s. John Neville Keynes (father of John Maynard Keynes, one of the founders of modern economics) first described three related but different methodological practices in his 1891 book, *The Scope and Method of Political Economy.* Colander (2001) noted:

> According to Keynes, positive economics is the study of what is and the way the economy works; it is pure science, not applied economics. Normative economics is the study of what should be; it is not applied economics. The art of economics is applied economics. It relates the lessons learned in positive economics to the normative goals determined in normative economics. (p. 20)

As described, there were actually three different methodological choices in economics research, each contributing to the development of the field and, when combined, addressed all areas of research. As initially developed by Keynes (1891/1955), this threefold approach would incorporate quantitative and qualitative research methods familiar to researchers today. In addition, this threefold vision of research makes explicit the importance of context. As Keynes noted, because countries have different social, political, and economic contexts, they also are likely to differ along theoretical lines.

This approach to a methodological division of labor is not unlike that which happens in other fields, such as medicine. Positive research in medicine would be analogous to the investigation of how organisms or diseases function. Researchers are often driven to this work by the sheer interest in discovery simply for the sake of discovery. They might, for example, discover how neurotransmitters function or how the poison from a blowfish affects living tissue. Much of this work would be considered positivist research as it is building the theoretical foundations of how things work with no clear intent to apply these discoveries to a specific real-world problem. These discoveries are then linked to current medical problems through what might be termed applied research. A drug derived from the blowfish poison may be used "to help cancer patients suppress pain or to wean heroine addicts off their habit" (Younglai, 2003). Finally, normative work in this field is analogous to the ethical review board that oversees clinical trials and more generally sets the guidelines within which medical practices and theoretical research are bound.

But this threefold version of research is not what economics research looks like today. Mainstream neoclassical economics relies on a positivist, almost exclusively quantitative methodology. The movement away from Keynes' vision of economic research is aptly displayed by both the content and title of an essay by one of the most famous economics researchers, Milton Friedman. In his essay, "Methodology of Positive Economics," Friedman (1952) succeeded in persuading the profession that the dominant methodology in economics should be positivist, a view that is inconsistent with Keynes's tripartite vision of economic research. In his argument, he indicated that positive theoretical and applied policy research could be accomplished concurrently. Friedman's essay was the beginning of the current methodological division along positive and normative lines through which the art of economics was lost. His argument was also consistent with the drive to move the discipline of economics from the philosophical roots in which it was viewed previous to the 1950s to a more scientifically based discipline.[2] This push called for a more mathematically based analysis to provide the level of rigor worthy of a science.[3] Colander (2001) argued that this process created a distinct methodological conflict because the processes and rules that govern theoretical research are dramatically different from those that govern applied policy research (p. 31). As a result, positivist economics of today is described as analysis that is based on fact divorced from political, social, and emotional context.[4] Normative economics, shunned by most economists, is viewed as opinion-based, subjective research. Consequently, good economic methodology is positivist and "value free." Clearly this is decidedly divergent from Keynes's vision.

The question that naturally arises is, What has been lost because of this alternative progression? In an attempt to add rigor to economic analysis through a positivist, scientific approach, mainstream economic research methods are limited to quantitative methods. This narrowing of methodological approaches has limited the types of economic phenomena studied, the way in which economic issues are studied, and the possible insights available. For example, insights from qualitative methods are almost nonexistent in economics, and when present, are dismissed or given second-class status. Besides limiting methodological approaches undertaken, the positivist progression in economics has blurred the lines between theory, values, and the art of economic research.

The push for rigor restricted the development of theory to that which could be expressed mathematically. So even though economics as a social science should be multidisciplinary, theoreticians in economics have largely ignored insights from other disciplines. For example, consumer theory in economics borrows little from psychology, and the economics of gender borrows little from women's studies or other related fields. In addition, because positivist economics, as currently defined, encompasses all fact-based research, theorists are forced to both advance theory and be relevant to the world, typically by providing some last-minute policy recommendations. Thus, they are constrained from taking full advantage of their theoretical talents and making substantial advances in theory. As a result, a loss in economic theory occurs because it is far less imaginative than it might otherwise be.

On the other hand, empiricists are also constrained by a positivist methodology. Colander (2001) observed that they apply the theoretical advances handed down by the theorists (p. 21). But given that this theory is an obvious simplification of the real world and void of political, social, and emotional context, the best that can be achieved is an abstract precise and inapplicable result.[5] Given these constraints, applied economics has come to be characterized by increasingly sophisticated empirical techniques in which better methods and data are assumed to be the key to advancement in and for the science. As a result, the discipline lost because economists tend to focus on exceedingly narrow questions and apply statistical techniques that are (absurdly) precise as opposed to increasing their understanding of how the economy works.[6] This extreme precision is just one pitfall that is inherent in a push for better, more precise measurement as aptly summarized by the words of Einstein, "Not everything that can be counted counts and not everything that counts can be counted."

The normative component of economic research was originally described by Keynes (1891/1955) as an objective consideration of the goals and values of our economic system. Yet economics research today is often claimed by mainstream economists as being scientific in the purest sense and thus is typically viewed as void of value judgments and independent of the researcher. Nelson (1996) suggested:

> Objectivity is assumed to be assured by adherence to positive (i.e., value-free) analysis, an arm's length detachment from practical or political concerns, the use of formal and mathematical methods, and the search for ever more general theories. (p. 22)

Many non-mainstream (heterodox) economic researchers suggest that such a claim is not realistic. Nelson continued, "Complete detachment is impossible. This should be obvious in the social sciences, where the researcher may be a member of the society he or she wishes to examine" (p. 42). In fact, researchers in economics make value-laden choices such as what can be defined as economics and thus what is even relevant to study let alone how data is collected and which techniques are chosen to study a particular topic. Even the discussion of the definition of economics as the study of choice (mainstream) compared to the study of provisioning (heterodox) depends on the value assumptions on which economics rests. The failure to openly discuss values as relevant to economic research has resulted in a discipline blind to the values implicit in its analysis and incapable or unwilling to discuss the human consequences of those values.

Colander (2001) built the case that reintroducing the threefold vision of economics would allow for greater advancement of the field. Theorists would be charged with making purely theoretical advancements in the study of how the economy works independent of their relevance (p. 28). They would engage in what Keynes would define as positivist economics. Advances would come as researchers were no longer constrained in their creativity by the need for policy implications. Empirical work would simply be used to test such theories. Normative economics, on the other hand, would include objective discussion of what goals economics should achieve (p. 29). It would focus directly on values and differences across individuals. It is the art of economics that would, in a sense, reconcile the two. This is where truly applied work would be completed. Real-world relevancy becomes paramount in achieving the goals set out by normative economics via the insights achieved through the theoretical research into how the economy works (positive economics) (p. 23). Empirical work under the art of economics is a matter of testing "whether or not the theory fits the real world" (p. 30). It is in doing the art of economics that the institutions become relevant. Political, social, and emotional contexts become part of the analysis. As a result, many different contexts could and should be studied.

Our analysis of the historical development of methodology in economics suggests that meaningful research requires a discipline to be cognizant of theory (positivist analysis), values (normative analysis), and have the ability to combine the two in a particular context (the art). So what does this have to do with today's research in service-learning?

IMPLICATIONS FOR SERVICE-LEARNING RESEARCH

The call for more rigor in service-learning research is evidence of a methodological crossroads, not unlike that of economics as described above. In a recent summary of service-learning research efforts, Eyler, Giles, Stenson, and Gray (2001) reviewed nearly 150 separate service-learning research projects undertaken between 1993 and 2000 and found that much of this research is primarily descriptive of service-learning interventions and outcomes rather than being theoretically driven. These studies also differed by the underlying samples studied (student, faculty, etc). Similarly, Billig and Eyler (2003) identified a number of similar emergent themes, such as the impact on students

in the areas of personal/social development, academic achievement, civic responsibility and citizenship, and career exploration. There is less research on the impacts on participating community members, participating faculty, and institutions in which service-learning occurs. (p. 257)

This diversity of focus and descriptive nature is not surprising since, as a field, service-learning is in its infancy. Consequently, the purposes of service-learning research are many and the methods and study designs used to investigate these goals are even more numerous.

It is also evident from a review of service-learning research that these efforts vary substantially from Keynes' threefold approach of positive (theoretical), normative (values), and the art (empirical contextual application) of research. The lack of theoretical development and the lack of theoretically based empirical research adversely impact the field of service-learning research. Without a theoretical foundation, research remains primarily descriptive rather than predictive, interventions and outcome measures are ill-defined and inconsistent, and the research base remains incoherent and disorganized. In addition, without theoretical grounding, much of the empirical research undertaken merely involves testing the correlation of service-learning to some outcome measure or determining the statistical significance of the presence of service-learning, rather than a discussion of how or why service-learning is effective. Such empirical results may incorrectly be overstated and given predictive power beyond the confines of the original study.

In addition, values underlying service-learning research remain unspoken despite the fact that they drive much of this research. As Billig and Eyler (2003) noted, while faculty may value service-learning for the opportunities for academic learning that it offers, the experience itself is valuable to students for a variety of personal reasons and social outcomes (p. 259). This lack of an explicit discussion of values, together with the lack of theoretical grounding, sets the stage for confusing the differing roles of theory, values, and empiricism and results in a diverse literature that lacks clarity and cohesion and an art of service-learning research that falls well short of its potential.

The call for more rigor in service-learning research is an attempt to focus the efforts of researchers. Responding to this call and moving beyond the current methodological crossroads requires researchers to be more explicit about the processes and procedures of research. It involves defining the parameters under which research will subsequently be undertaken, and this will have a profound influence on the state of service-learning research, as evidenced in the case of economics. The call for a more rigorous research agenda without a well-defined process of achieving this goal, such as the threefold vision of positive, normative, and art, has the potential for further hampering the advancement of the field. Indeed, a review of the literature suggests two potential problems already arising.

Some researchers have responded to the call by attempting to do too much, as evidenced by the multiple methods and outcomes in many of the articles summarized in Eyler and colleagues (2001). Researchers may have unintentionally adopted too broad a role by assuming all of the roles in the research process as described by Keynes: theoretician, normative researcher, and practitioner of the art of applied service-learning research. As a result, the call might encourage some researchers to do work outside their own area of expertise as theoreticians; for example, when their skills are as empirical researchers.

An additional problem arises as service-learning researchers respond to the call for more rigor in research by providing more precision in the measurement of outcomes through the adoption of improved metrics of cognitive development or civic engagement. While there are certainly benefits associated with these more precise measures, enhanced precision without the underlying theory to explain these outcomes may be an example of misplaced rigor, akin to the problems economists face when applying incredibly powerful statistical methods to increasingly narrow questions. This greater precision in outcome measures leads to no gains in the field if they are applied in an attempt to generalize a process that is, in fact, not generalizable because of context specificity. Thus, the call for more rigorous research runs the risk of being misguided as it ends up focusing precision at a level that is impossible in the context of the real world.

RECOMMENDATIONS

In order to address some of these problems and to most effectively advance the current state of service-learning research, researchers should think seriously about the process and procedures of doing service-learning research. This chapter has offered the threefold process of Keynes as an initial starting point. Service-learning research should be built on a strong foundation of theory, values discussion, and concern for context. Each of these elements demands different skills, and researchers should specialize in that area of research in which they are most skilled. This is consistent with and a natural extension of Eyler's (2000) call for a task force of experts.

We agree with Bringle (2003) that a stronger theoretical foundation is necessary to advance service-learning research. Without this foundation, any empirical work is by its nature ad hoc and incoherent. For example, without a theory of student learning, how can we investigate the role of service-learning in that process? Furthermore, the theory that explains service-learning's contribution to student understanding of course content will not be the theory necessary to explain what motivates student civic engagement, or the theory necessary to explain enhanced student appreciation of multiculturalism or ethnic diversity. Service-learning research can best move forward if a cadre of theoreticians devote themselves to developing this theoretical foundation. Theoreticians will need to specialize, and those best at discovering the underpinnings of civic engagement will be different from those developing the self-efficacy models, but all will ultimately contribute. Individuals best suited to these roles will not be the average faculty member who uses service-learning in their classes. Instead educational or cognitive psychologists or others trained in learning theories or other relevant theory should undertake this work. These theories will provide insights into why service-learning works and not just whether the presence of service-learning is statistically significant. Besides providing insights into modus operandi of service-learning, the growing literature on service-learning could be organized along theoretical constructs that would add much-needed coherence and clarity to the literature.

Insights from the economics profession would suggest that theories should be developed, without concern for the practical issues of political, social, and economic context; to do otherwise runs the risk of unnecessarily limiting the development of theory. But this is not to say that context does not matter—it does a great deal. For example, sending students out into the community can be messy: A service site undergoing an unexpected change in key personnel provides students with a different set of experiences than does an agency whose personnel is more stable. And since student experiences form the basis for additional learning, it is likely that these different contexts matter a great deal to the outcome of the service-learning experience. Yet few researchers know how these differences affect student learning or why else they might matter. Such details are not currently included in empirical analyses of service-learning outcomes. That's the art of service-learning research. Besides testing the hypotheses provided by the theoreticians, researchers should look at the role that context plays in our understanding of the process and outcomes of service-learning. Lessons from the economics profession suggest that the failure to consider context can result in abstract analysis detached from the situation it was meant to explain, and thus is of limited value. On the other hand, one of the downsides of context, if it is shown to matter, is that it will add an additional layer of complexity to the literature. But researchers who neglect context make the mistake of attributing more power to theories than is actually the case. Hecht's work (2003) provided a starting point for incorporating context in service-learning research.

Values matter too. Most agree that service-learning is valuable, but researchers may value this pedagogy for different reasons. Some value it for its ability to teach course content in a concrete, hands-on environment; others value it for its ability to promote community and civic engagement. These goals may not be compatible and may even be at odds with one another. The goals and values professors bring to the table will affect how service-learning is incorporated into a classroom setting, which community partners are chosen, and a host of other issues that will directly impact the outcomes of the service-learning experience. While service-learning researchers have not adopted the economists' professed "value-free" analysis, researchers seldom state up front what their values and goals are for using service-learning in the first place, and are even less likely to evaluate the process and outcomes of service-learning in light of these stated values. Better to be up front about goals and values in the first place, and then ask what difference it makes rather than to omit a discussion of values. This, too, is the art of service-learning research.

Advocating a role for values in analysis is not suggesting that research is subjective. Instead we are arguing that as researchers we should discuss our goals and our reasons for selecting particular goals. Indeed, Keynes noted (as cited in Colander) "a normative or regulative science [is]...a body of systematized knowledge discussing criteria of what ought to be" (p. 19). The art of service-learning research would then concern itself with the most effective methods of obtaining these goals.

Failure to consider any one of these components, theories, values, or contexts will result in an imprecise and incomplete understanding of service-learning. Knowledge of service-learning can only be as exact and as precise as the most imprecise component of the research process. The precision of a component of the research process says nothing about the precision of the conclusions, if researchers are unsure of how the parts make a whole. Therefore, adding rigor and advancing service-learning research requires researchers to carefully consider the role of theory, values, and context in service-learning research. That is the art of service-learning research.

CONCLUSION

So where does this leave service-learning research? The arguments provided above are not meant to suggest that current research in service-learning is unimportant or lacking in sophistication. This chapter has described a framework for providing *increased* cohesion and rigor to service-learning research. It argues that service-learning research is at a methodological crossroads similar to one faced by the discipline of economics nearly 100 years ago. In order to move beyond this crossroads and to effectively respond to the call in the service-learning literature for a more rigorous research base, researchers should consider three areas— theory, values, and the art of applied empirical research—and should concentrate their efforts in areas in which they are most skilled. The context of a particular service-learning experience matters and should also inform the analysis. By following this advice, service-learning research will avoid some of the problems that have plagued the economics profession.

NOTES

1. This section relies heavily on the work of Colander, 2001.

2. The work completed at the RAND institution typifies this movement. The organization "attracted a younger generation of mathematically sophisticated economists who embraced the new methods and tools, including the computer, and attempted to turn economics from a branch of political philosophy into a precise, predictive science" (Nassar, p. 107).

3. Whether this was a gain for the profession is somewhat debatable. Consider the words attributed to Kenneth Boulding (economist): "Mathematics brought rigor to economics. Unfortunately, it also brought mortis." Retrieved June 14, 2004, from http://netec.mcc.ac.uk/JokEc.html

4. A common joke about economists reflects this divorce from context: To economists, real life is a special case.

5. Reflective of this imprecision is another common joke about economists: "Recession is when your neighbor loses his job. Depression is when you lose your job." These economic downturns are very difficult to predict, but sophisticated econometric modeling houses like Data Resources and Chase Econometrics have successfully predicted 14 of the last three recessions. Retrieved June 15, 2004, from http://www.csuchico.edu/econ/old/links/econhumor.html

6. Some economists are beginning to question this progression. At a 1986 National Science Foundation–supported symposium on the state of economics, participants argued that training in economics focuses too much on statistical tools and theories and not enough on creativity and real-world problem solving (Krueger, 1991, p. 1039).

REFERENCES

Billig, S. H., & Eyler, J. (2003). The state of service-learning and service-learning research. In S. H. Billig & J. Eyler (Eds.), *Advances in service-learning research: Vol. 3. Deconstructing service-learning: Research exploring context, participation, and impacts* (pp. 253–264). Greenwich, CT: Information Age.

Bringle, R. G. (2003). Enhancing theory-based research on service-learning. In S. H. Billig & J. Eyler (Eds.), *Advances in service-learning research: Vol. 3. Deconstructing service-learning: Research exploring context, participation, and impacts* (pp. 3–24). Greenwich, CT: Information Age.

Bringle, R. G., & Hatcher, J. A. (2000). Meaningful measurement of theory-based service-learning outcomes: Making the case with quantitative research. *Michigan Journal of Community Service Learning* [Special Issue], 68–75.

Colander, D. (2001). *The lost art of economics.* Aldershot, UK: Edward Elgar.

Eyler, J. (2000). What do we most need to know about the impact of service-learning on student learning? *Michigan Journal of Community Service Learning* [Special Issue], 11–17.

Eyler, J. (2002). Stretching to meet the challenge: Improving the quality of research to improve the quality of service-learning. In S. H. Billig & A. Furco (Eds.). *Advances in service-learning research: Vol. 2. Service-learning through a multidisciplinary lens* (pp. 3–14). Greenwich, CT: Information Age.

Eyler, J., Giles, D. E., Stenson, C., & Gray, C. (2001). *At a glance: What we know about the effect of service-learning on college students, faculty, institutions, and communities, 1993–2000* (3rd ed.). Washington, DC: Corporation for National Service, Learn and Serve America National Service-Learning Clearinghouse.

Friedman, M. (1953). Methodology of positive economics. In M. Friedman, *Essays in positive economics* (pp. 3–43). Chicago: University of Chicago Press.

Furco, A., & Billig, S. H. (2002). Establishing norms for scientific inquiry in service-learning. In S. H. Billig & A. Furco (Eds.), *Advances in service-learning research: Vol. 2. Service-learning through a multidisciplinary lens* (pp. 15–32). Greenwich, CT: Information Age.

Gelmon, S. B. (2000). Challenges in assessing service-learning. *Michigan Journal of Community Service Learning* [Special Issue], 76–83.

Hecht, D. (2003). The missing link: Exploring the context of learning in service-learning. In S. H. Billig & J. Eyler (Eds.), *Advances in service-learning research: Vol. 3. Deconstructing service-learning: Research exploring context, participation, and impacts* (pp. 25–50). Greenwich, CT: Information Age.

Howard, J. P. F., Gelmon, S. B., & Giles, D. E., Jr. (2000). From yesterday to tomorrow: Strategic directions for service-learning research. *Michigan Journal of Community Service Learning* [Special Issue], 5–10.

Keynes, J. N. (1955). *The scope and method of political economy* (4th ed.). New York: Kelley & Millman, Inc. (Original work published 1891)

Krueger, A. O. (1991). Report of the Commission on Graduate Education in Economics. *Journal of Economic Literature, 29*(3), 1035–1053.

McGoldrick, K., & Ziegert, A. (Eds.). (2002). *Putting the invisible hand to work: Concepts and models of service-learning in economics.* Ann Arbor: University of Michigan Press.

Nassar, S. (2001). *A beautiful mind: The life of mathematical genius and Nobel Laureate John Nash.* New York: Touchstone Books.

Nelson, J. A. (1996). *Feminism, objectivity and economics.* London: Routledge.

Shumer, R. (2000). Science or storytelling: How should we conduct and report service-learning research? *Michigan Journal of Community Service Learning* [Special Issue], 76–83.

Stanton, T. K., Giles, D. E., Jr. & Cruz, N. I. (1999). *Service-learning: A movement's pioneers reflect on its origins, practice, and future.* San Francisco: Jossey-Bass.

Younglai, R. (2003, November). *Poison from lethal fish could be a painkiller.* Retrieved December 1, 2003, from http://www.boston.com/news/world/canada/articles/2003/11/28/poison_from_lethal_fish_could_be_a_painkiller/

Zlotkowski, E. (Ed.). (1997–2000). American Association of Higher Education's *Series on Service-Learning in the Disciplines.* Washington, DC: American Association for Higher Education.

PART II

IMPACT OF SERVICE-LEARNING

CHAPTER 3

A FRAMEWORK FOR ASSESSING ACADEMIC SERVICE-LEARNING ACROSS DISCIPLINES

Malu Roldan, Amy Strage, and Debra David

ABSTRACT

This chapter proposes a framework for the systematic study of service-learning across disciplines with the explicit intention of guiding practice. Two studies, one from management information systems and another from child development, are presented, to illustrate the utility of the framework for facilitating integration across studies and influencing future course design. Results suggest that, in contrast to findings in other fields, management information systems students showed greatest gains in civic engagement when conducting indirect service. In child development, students who were in service-learning courses in the early part of their studies performed better on courses requiring real-world experience, compared to their counterparts who were not in service-learning classes early in their studies.

Evidence substantiating the benefits of service-learning continues to grow. It has been shown to:

New Perspectives in Service-Learning: Research to Advance the Field, pages 39–59
Copyright © 2004 by Information Age Publishing

- Enhance student engagement with and commitment to school (Sax & Astin, 1997);
- Prepare students to be contributing citizens in their broader communities (Eyler & Giles, 1996; Giles & Eyler, 1998; Kendrick, 1996; Markus, Howard, & King, 1993);
- Have a significant impact on students' social and emotional development (Eyler & Giles, 1996, 1999; Kendrick, 1996; Ostrow, 1995; Rhoads, 1997); and
- Enhance the achievement of the curricular goals of the courses in which it is embedded (Astin & Sax, 1998; Cohen & Kinsey, 1994; Eyler & Giles, 1996; Gray et al., 1996; Kendrick, 1996; Markus et al., 1993; Strage, 2000).

This progress notwithstanding, there is consensus in the field that studies of this pedagogy and its effectiveness must become more sophisticated (Astin, Vogelgesang, Ikeda, & Yee, 2000; Billig & Furco, 2002; Eyler, 2002; Eyler & Giles, 1999; Furco & Billig, 2002; Hecht, 2003; Howard, 2001). As Eyler (2002) has noted, the evidence "is neither precise nor robust enough to guide decision making about practice" (p. 4).

As the popularity of service-learning increases, a more systematic and complete knowledge base about the effectiveness of this particular instructional strategy becomes all the more important, to both guide and improve practice (Howard, 2003). For example, until recently, at San José State University only a core group of well-versed faculty members employed service-learning in their courses. Currently, between 40 and 50 faculty include service-learning requirements in their courses in any given semester. While most of these faculty are dedicated and effective instructors, few immersed themselves in the literature on service-learning as part of their preparation, and even fewer conduct any sort of systematic investigation of the impact of "their" service-learning versus others'. It comes as little surprise, then, that anecdotal and informal reports from the field suggest uneven success and contradictory opinions on the effectiveness of service-learning pedagogy.

This chapter addresses the gap in the field. The purpose of this chapter is twofold:

1. To present a framework to systematically assess the effects of the infusion of different kinds of academic service-learning into courses across disciplines. The intent is to use this framework to guide programmatic efforts to support and improve service-learning implementation locally, and eventually to facilitate cross-university collaborations (cf. Strage, Knutson Miller, Gomez, & Garcia, 2004).

2. To illustrate the use of the framework to contextualize the results of two studies of service-learning.

THEORETICAL MOORINGS

The constructs that anchor the perspective taken in this chapter attempt to identify causal connections among variables in multivariate domains of inquiry, and favor context-specific and interactive effects over broad, one-size-fits-all generalizations. Specifically, from human development, the work draws upon Bronfenbrenner's (1979) ecological systems theory, the Piagetian and Vygotskian principles of constructivism (Piaget, 1954; Vygotsky, 1930/1978), and experiential learning (Kolb, 1984; Perry, 1970/1999); from business and management theory, the work draws upon contingency theory (Galbraith, 1973; Lawrence & Lorsch, 1967). Each of these theoretical perspectives can readily account for the varied results across broad-strokes, univariate studies of the effects of service-learning (e.g., studies contrasting service-learning vs. non-service-learning groups), and also set the stage for developing a theory of context-specific effects of different configurations of service-learning experiences. As Eyler (2002) pointed out, there is some evidence that the small size of differences found in studies of service-learning outcomes could be attributable to differences that exist independently of the service-learning experience and that introduce additional variance in the data.

As depicted in Figure 3.1, the framework distinguishes four categories of *independent variables* associated with the *context:*

1. Community characteristics;
2. Student characteristics;
3. Institutional characteristics; and
4. Faculty characteristics.

There are two categories associated with the *service-learning experience:* course variables and service-learning activity variables. In terms of *dependent variables*, the framework distinguishes outcomes for the community, the student participants, the participating institutions, and participating faculty. With respect to effects on students, the framework focuses on short- and long-term *academic outcomes, civic engagement, and personal growth.*

The presence of shaded boxes in Figure 3.1 suggests that the framework is still something of a work in progress. Ultimately, it will further specify context and outcome variables pertaining to the *broader community,* to the *service-learning sites,* to the *institution* (college or university) *where the course is housed,* and to the *faculty member(s)* teaching the course (Cruz & Giles, 2000; Hecht, 2003; Howard, 2003).

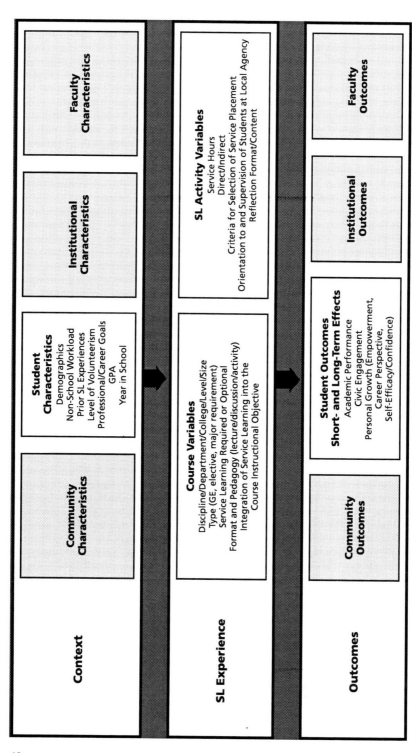

Context

Community Characteristics

Student Characteristics
Demographics
Non-School Workload
Prior SL Experiences
Level of Volunteerism
Professional/Career Goals
GPA
Year in School

Institutional Characteristics

Faculty Characteristics

SL Experience

Course Variables
Discipline/Department/College/Level/Size
Type (GE, elective, major requirement)
Service Learning Required or Optional
Format and Pedagogy (lecture/discussion/activity)
Integration of Service Learning into the Course Instructional Objective

SL Activity Variables
Service Hours
Direct/Indirect
Criteria for Selection of Service Placement
Orientation to and Supervision of Students at Local Agency
Reflection Format/Content

Outcomes

Community Outcomes

Student Outcomes
Short- and Long-Term Effects
Academic Performance
Civic Engagement
Personal Growth (Empowerment, Career Perspective, Self-Efficacy/Confidence)

Institutional Outcomes

Faculty Outcomes

Figure 3.1. Service-Learning Research Framework.

Student Outcome Variables

Most of the literature on the effects of service-learning on students has focused on three general areas of impact: academic achievement, civic engagement, and personal growth. The most widely measured outcomes of service-learning experiences, particularly among studies conducted in higher education settings, is students' *academic achievement* (Eyler & Giles, 1999; Knutson Miller, Yen, & Merino, 2002; Mabry, 1998; Markus et al., 1993; Steinke & Buresh, 2002). Studies typically examined fairly broad-strokes indices of academic outcomes, such as grade point average (GPA) and course grades, or more subjective measures such as student self-reports of learning or academic attainment (Eyler & Giles, 1999). They employed both quantitative (e.g., exam scores) and qualitative (e.g., content analyses of students' written products) measures. Occasionally, they looked more closely at student performance indices reflecting different kinds of cognitive challenge or levels of mastery of course content (e.g., Strage, 2000). Evidence that any pedagogy significantly enhances what students learn in a particular course will be of significant interest to faculty who teach that course, and to others more generally concerned with maximizing teaching effectiveness and student outcomes. Systematic and reliable evidence of circumstances under which service-learning is especially effective will strengthen the case and provide useful guidelines for its adoption.

A second, extensively studied outcome variable is participants' levels of *civic engagement* (Covitt, 2002; Eyler & Giles, 1999; Guarasci, Cornwell, & Erlandson, 1997; Vernon & Foster, 2002; Vogelgesang & Astin, 2000). Campus Compact (n.d.) suggests that evidence that service-learning enhances participants' commitment to social issues served as a powerful incentive for its widespread adoption. Instruments and tools used to measure students' civic engagement range from self-report questionnaires (Diaz-Gallegos, Furco, & Yamada, 1999), to interviews with members of community agencies (Vernon & Foster, 2002), to open-ended questions in surveys (Steinke, Fitch, Johnson, & Waldstein, 2002). Most university mission statements speak to an institutional commitment to supporting and guiding students as they engage in the social issues of their day. As is the case for academic benefits, evidence of circumstances under which service-learning is especially effective will strengthen the case and provide useful guidelines for its adoption.

A third category of student outcome that has been the subject of much research is *personal growth* (Boss, 1994; Delve, Mintz, & Steward, 1990; Eyler & Giles, 1999; Gorman, 1994; Steinke et al., 2002). Studies have examined effects of participating in service-learning experiences on qualities of moral character (i.e., altruism, compassion, honesty), self knowledge, leadership, personal efficacy, the ability to work well with others, and career orientation. One of the tensions on metropolitan university campuses, such as San Jose State, is whether faculty and students view college more as an opportunity for a broad, liberal education, or as an opportunity for vocational preparation (Votruba, 2003). Evidence of when and how service-learning experiences enable students to feed two birds with one piece of bread, by supporting their personal as well as academic growth, can make a valuable contribution to this discussion.

Most research examining effects of service-learning has concentrated on the relatively immediate gains associated with the pedagogy, and indeed, there have been calls for studies to focus on possible lasting or sleeper effects (Billig & Furco, 2002). From an institutional point of view, individual courses are typically considered in the context of a broader curriculum. Thus, it is important for research studies to take the longer view, and identify evidence of effects of service-learning experiences that (continue to) manifest themselves beyond the course in which they are embedded.

Context: Student Characteristic Variables. Applying the framework to the task of assessing the effects of service-learning in courses on a campus involves the examination of the effects associated with variation in student demographics, number of hours spent in non-school-related work, extent of prior service-learning experience, level of volunteerism that a student normally engages in, professional and career goals, GPA, and year in school. Ideally, the aim is to randomly assign students to service-learning and non-service-learning groups, as suggested by Eyler (2002). However, for the most part efforts may be limited to quasi-experimental studies. Measures of these context variables will be used to statistically control for their effects and identify effects of service-learning experiences independent of such student characteristics.

Service-Learning Experience Variables. The framework differentiates between variables that characterize *courses in their entirety* and variables that characterize the *course-embedded service-learning activities* themselves. Course variables include:

- The discipline/department, college, or level of the course;
- Whether the course is part of the general education curriculum, a major requirement, or an elective;
- Whether service-learning is a required component of the course;
- The format and pedagogy of the course (lecture/seminar/lab/practicum/capstone); and
- The degree of integration of the service-learning experiences into the instructional objectives for the course.

The first course variable, *discipline/department*, will be useful for the interpretation of outcomes across the curriculum. Service-learning is most frequently a component of courses in the humanities and the arts, in the social sciences, in education, and in social and health services. Faculty in these disciplines can readily find a natural fit between core curricular objectives and opportunities for service-learning activities. Faculty from the physical sciences and from engineering are more skeptical about the possibility that this pedagogy can seriously enhance student learning, and fear that time dedicated to activities in the field will detract from time students can spend on the more central and important course material. The design characteristics of effective service-learning opportunities may differ from one course context to another because of the unique requirements of each *discipline*. A growing literature documents the growing infusion of service-learning across disciplines, most notably in the 19 disciplines covered by the American Association for Higher Education (AAHE) Monograph Series on Service-Learning in the Disciplines (Zlotkowski, 2001), and in edited collections listed by the National Service-Learning Clearinghouse (Seifer, 2002). The current framework forms the basis for "a more multifaceted, comprehensive approach to service-learning" called for by Zlotkowski, editor of the aforementioned AAHE Monograph Series on Service-Learning in the Disciplines (p. 33).

Where the course in which the service-learning is embedded fits in the student's agenda; that is, whether it is required or not, and whether it is a core, major course or a breadth/general education course may well have an impact on students' enthusiasm for the subject matter as well as on their intrinsic motivation to undertake a service-learning activity. For example, students are far more mastery oriented in their approach to major coursework than they are to general education requirements (Strage et al., 2002). Similarly, service-learning may well work differently in large lecture classes than it does in smaller courses, where opportunities for discussion and individual attention are more frequent, and where students are encouraged to play a more vocal and active role in the classroom (Howard, 2001).

Whether the service-learning is a required element of the course is a significant variable, both in terms of the pedagogical decision about how the course instructional objectives are to be met, and also in terms of research methodology. Where service-learning is an option, research designs must consider possible confounding student characteristic variables that influence positive (or negative) outcomes that might otherwise be attributed to the pedagogy itself. Such concerns are now frequently voiced in calls for future research (e.g., Billig & Furco, 2002).

Lastly, measuring *the degree of integration of service-learning into the course objectives* will enable better understanding of the minimal requirements for effective service-learning, and serve as the basis for recommendations about practice (Howard, 2001).

Service-learning activity variables include:

- The *number of hours* of service students must provide;
- Whether the *service brings students into direct contact with clients*;
- The *criteria used to select service placements*;
- The *orientation to and supervision of students at the service-learning site*; and
- The quality, format, and content of *activities designed to help students reflect* on their experiences at the service-learning site.

There is strong evidence to suggest that a higher number of required service hours enhances student outcomes. Furthermore, several studies suggest that service-learning may be significantly more effective when the service activities bring students into *direct contact* with clients. Knutson Miller and her colleagues (2002, 2003) reported beneficial academic and civic engagement effects for students who worked directly with young children as part of their service-learning, and null or even negative effects for students who merely provided indirect service, such as developing age-appropriate curriculum for them.

Research also highlights the importance of *careful planning, preparation, and partnership* in ensuring successful outcomes of service-learning. Site characteristics, mutual understanding by site, and campus constituents of the nature of the course and the nature of the services provided, as well as the ways in which students will be expected to contribute, have significant impacts (Hecht, 2003; Howard, 2001). The *orientation to and supervision of students* at the service-learning site have both been found to influence the quality of students' service-learning experiences (Eyler & Giles, 1999; Howard, 2001).

Finally, there are strong claims that reflection activities are key to the success of a service-learning effort, and some progress has been made in identifying optimal formats of activities designed to help students integrate what they are bringing to the situation, what they are learning from the in-class portion of the course, and what they are learning from their service-learning activities (Eyler & Giles, 1999; Steinke et al., 2002). Still, relatively little is known about the relationship between specific mixes of reflection techniques and observed outcomes (Steinke et al., 2002).

STUDY 1: SERVICE-LEARNING IN A BUSINESS COURSE

Half of the sections of a management information systems (MIS) department capstone course include a mandatory service-learning component. The purpose of the course is to give students the opportunity to develop and demonstrate their mastery of business strategy. They study basic theory and application, and build a document that describes a vision of how emerging technologies could transform an industry and a company.

In the context of the framework proposed here, the most pertinent student characteristic is year in school. In this case, students were in their senior year. For course variables, the class offered in the College of Business was a major requirement with a lecture/discussion format and required service-learning, although the level of integration with course objectives differed across sections of the course. Service-learning activity variables varied as well, in terms of type of service (direct or indirect) and reflection format and content. These service-learning activity variables, as well as the course variable—level of service-learning integration with course objectives—proved to have significant effects on the student outcome of civic engagement.

Students in the sections of the course where service-learning was required completed 10 to 15 hours of MIS-oriented service at local community agencies, and then drew upon their experiences to address Digital Divide issues and develop recommendations for appropriate uses of technology in nontraditional, resource-constrained settings. Most students completed their service-learning activities at recommended sites where the university had established partnerships, including homeless shelters, community centers, and emergency and social services providers. Students tutored young children and adults on the use of computing packages, developed materials for use in tutoring activities, organized and conducted mentoring programs to introduce university life to elementary school children, set up and maintained computer labs and networks, and developed databases for various office and reporting tasks. Students generally worked in teams so that they could pool their hours and achieve maximum impact in the organization. Five to ten students chose to take on leadership roles for their service-learning assignment, helping to coordinate five agencies, two professors, and 90 students per semester. In spring 2003, the authors conducted a study of the effects of service-learning on students' civic engagement and personal growth.

Participants

The present study included 135 students enrolled in one of six sections of the MIS capstone course (Table 3.1).

- **Condition 1:** 71 students were enrolled in two sections of the course where service-learning was not required (non-service-learning [NSL] condition);
- **Condition 2:** 29 students were enrolled in a section of the course where service-learning was required, but where it was minimally integrated into the classroom component of the course. There was little opportunity for reflection and integration with course readings

and little class time devoted to discussion of service activities (LowRefl condition).

- **Condition 3:** 35 students were enrolled in sections of the course where service-learning was required and where it was more thoroughly integrated into the classroom component via richer and more frequent reflection activities and more class time devoted to discussion of service activities (HiRefl condition).
- **Condition 4:** A subset of 7 students in the HiRefl section took on leadership positions to coordinate service assignments of the other students in all of the service-learning courses and to facilitate communication among faculty, students, and community partners (Leader condition).

While these "leaders" had little or no direct contact with the clients of the community organizations where they completed their service-learning, their role afforded them special planning, oversight, and managerial experiences (Hecht, 2003), activities that are arguably more closely aligned with course instructional objectives than the experiences of the students who provided more hands-on, direct services for the agency clients.

Table 3.1.   Summary of Conditions and Significant Results for Study 1

Condition	N (total = 135*)	Civic Responsibility Scale (% gains)	Involvement in Community Improvement (% gains)	Concern over Local Community Issues (% gains)
Non-Service-Learning (NSL)	71	+1.8	+2.8	+7.5
Low Reflection CSL (LowRefl)	29	−1.8	−8.6	−7.2
High Reflection CSL (HiRefl)	35	+6.1	+12.1	+7.4
Leader	7*	+5.4	+21.4	+7.1

*Note: 7 leaders are included in the count for the HiRefl condition.
($p < .05$).

Instrumentation, Procedures, and Data Analysis Plan

All 135 students completed pre-test and post-test versions of the Higher Education Service-Learning Survey (Diaz-Gallegos et al., 1999). This instrument consisted of Likert-type items asking students to rate their agreement (on a 4-point scale) with statements pertaining to Civic Engagement (9 items, $\alpha = .79$); Career Orientation and Preparedness (6 items, $\alpha = .63$); Empowerment and Efficacy (7 items, $\alpha = .61$); and Academic Orientation (6 items, $\alpha = .66$). A series of one-way analyses of variance

(ANOVAs) was conducted to compare pre-test scores as well as percent change in pre-test and post-test scores for students in each of the four service-learning conditions.

Results

No differences in baseline or percent change emerged among the four service-learning conditions for Empowerment or Academic scale scores, or for the individual survey items that comprised them (all $p > .05$). However, intriguing results emerged from the analyses pertaining to Civic Responsibility and Career Orientation and Preparedness (see Figure 3.2). More specifically, with respect to Civic Responsibility, there were no differences between student conditions on the pre-test (NSL mean = 2.95; LowRefl mean = 3.00; HiRefl mean = 2.91; and Leader mean = 3.02), but there were significant differences in how much the ratings of students in each of the four conditions changed over the course of the semester. As illustrated in Table 3.1, overall NSL students gained 1.8%, students in the LowRefl condition decreased 1.8%, students in the HiRefl condition increased 6.1%, and the Leaders increased 5.4%. ANOVA results revealed a main effect that approached conventional levels of significance ($F = 2.1333$, $p = .0991$) and post hoc comparisons indicated that the differences between the LowRefl and HiRefl and Leader means to be statistically significant. Inspection of responses to individual scale items provided more compelling evidence of the differential impact of the four service-learning conditions on students' civic engagement.

There were significant differences among the service-learning conditions in response to the item, "Being involved in a program to improve my community

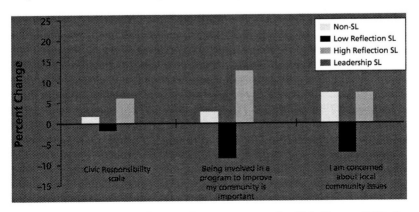

Figure 3.2.   Comparison of pre- and post-test scores for Civic Responsibility items.

is important" (F = 4.7340, p = .0036). More specifically, NSL students' rating remained relatively unchanged (increase of 2.8%). Changes in ratings from the students in the LowRefl condition revealed a disconcerting drop in civic engagement (8.6% decrease). Changes in ratings from students in the HiRefl and Leader conditions revealed significant increases in civic engagement from one end of the semester to the next (increases of 12.1% and 21.4%, respectively). Post hoc comparisons revealed the change over time for the students in the LowRefl conditions was statistically significantly different than the change for the students in the other three groups. A similar pattern emerged in response to the item, "I am concerned about local community issues." ANOVA revealed a significant main effect of service-learning condition (F = 2.6885, p = .0491) as well as significant differences between responses of students in the LowRefl groups and the other groups. Students in the NSL, HiRefl, and Leader conditions increased their agreement with this item over the course of the semester (increases of 7.5%, 7.4%, and 7.1%, respectively), while students in the LowRefl condition agreed less with this statement by the end of the semester (7.2% decrease).

Results of analyses examining change scores pertaining to Career Orientation paint a similar story, although differences do not quite reach conventional levels of statistical significance (F = 1.58, p = .1963). There were no differences at the outset between students in the four service-learning conditions in Career Orientation scale scores or in individual item scores. Comparison of pre- and post-survey scores suggested that the students in the Leader condition showed the greatest trend toward a significant increase, both overall and with respect to two scale items:

1. *I have definite career plans:* a 33.3% increase, versus less than a 10% change for students in the other conditions; and

2. *I feel well prepared for my future career:* a 31% increase, versus less than a 8% change for students in the other conditions.

While caution should be exercised so as not to over interpret these findings, taken together, they help to explicate some of the inconsistent findings reported in the literature. The data strongly suggest that not all service-learning is good, or good for all participants. The students in the LowRefl condition seemed to actually decline in civic engagement over the course of the semester. They reported seeing little connection between the service activities they were required to complete and the rest of the course, and in fact, they saw the service-learning as something of a nuisance. Their survey data also suggest they felt they gained no pragmatic career benefits to come from the experience.

These data suggest that a construct, which at first may seem very straightforward, is in actuality more complex. Elsewhere it has been reported that *indirect* service activities can have an adverse effect on students' civic engagement (e.g., Knutson Miller et al., 2002). In contrast, the results reported here suggest that indirect service *can* have positive effects on students' civic engagement. Perhaps this apparent contradiction is best explained by considering the instructional objectives in which the service-learning activities were embedded. The students in the Knutson and colleagues (2002) study were enrolled in a basic child development course, and the indirect service projects seemed like busywork to them and of marginal relevance to the course itself. In the case of the MIS course reported here, managing people and resources is central to the core objectives of the course, and so the indirect service activities that the Leaders performed were, arguably, more closely aligned with the instructional objectives of the course than were the *direct* service activities performed by the other service-learners.

For practitioners, these findings may serve to illustrate that careful attention must be paid to the design and application of service and reflection activities. When students cannot form a link between course goals and the service-learning experience and/or have not been motivated appropriately as to the civic engagement aspects of the experience, they may become frustrated with the activity, find it useless, and subsequently build negative perceptions regarding the value of supporting their communities.

STUDY 2: A FOLLOW-UP STUDY IN CHILD DEVELOPMENT

This section reports on part of a follow-up study of 477 students that completed an Introductory Child Development lecture course. For the 311 *non-service-learning* students, course requirements included a structured observation and write-up assignment but no hands-on component. For the 166 *service-learning* students, course requirements included a minimum of 20 hours of hands-on experience with children in a structured setting (a classroom, a before- or after-school program, etc.) in lieu of the observation assignment. The observation write-up was replaced with a set of "synthetic reflection" activities (Driscoll & Williams, 1997), wherein students kept a structured journal throughout the semester, and class time was intermittently dedicated to linking students' onsite experiences with course constructs. Elsewhere, it has been reported that the students in the service-learning semesters outperformed the students in the non-service-learning semesters on several measures of mastery of course content (i.e., exams), most notably in assignments where students were asked to integrate and apply core knowledge (Strage, 2000). This current analysis compares how well the students in the service-learning and non-service-learning groups have done in their subsequent child development major courses. The hypothesis is that the advantages conferred upon the students in the service-learning sections of the course, from the opportunity to gain and reflect on hands-on experience and from their superior mastery of course content, would serve as a more solid foundation for subsequent, increasingly complex and applied coursework, and that they would perform at least as well as their peers from the "non-service-learning" sections in their child development major courses.

In the context of the framework proposed here, this study looked at service-learning among students characterized as being in their senior and junior levels of undergraduate education. The courses were offered in the College of Education, were major requirements, did not require service-learning, and differed in the degree of service-learning integration with course objectives. The service-learning activity involved direct contact with clients while format and content of reflection was standardized as "synthetic reflection" (as described in the previous paragraph). Lastly, the student outcome of interest was GPA in upper-division courses for the child development major.

Participants

The records of all 477 students who participated in the original study were examined, yielding a comparison between 166 service-learning (SL) students and 311 non-service-learning (NSL) students.

Instrumentation, Procedures, and Data Analysis Plan

One-way ANOVAs were performed to compare the course grades earned by the service-learning and NSL students in four kinds of upper division courses:

1. Lecture courses (designed to build on the lower division course by delving in greater depth into research and theory, but providing little opportunity for hands-on experiences);

2. Lecture/activity courses (designed to build on the lower division course, but also providing some regular opportunity for experiential learning);

3. Lab practicum courses (where students review, integrate, and apply the core knowledge base of their academic major and where hands-

on work with children and youth make up at least half of the course requirements); and

4. The senior capstone course (where students also review, integrate, and apply the core knowledge base of their academic major, but do not engage in hands-on activities as part of the course).

Additionally, for some of the sections of the lecture/activity courses, grades on individual assignments were available, and so ANOVAs comparing the exam and activity scores for NSL and service-learning students in those classes were performed.

Differences in student performance in the upper division child development coursework favored the service-learning students, although they failed to reach conventional levels of statistical significance (see Figure 3.3.) More specifically, overall, students in the service-learning sections earned grades that were 4.8% higher than those of the NSL students (3.28 vs. 3.13 on a 4-point scale, $F = 1.9972$, $p = .1588$). In the activity courses, students in the service-learning sections earned grades that were 4.1% higher than those of the NSL students (3.52 vs. 3.38, $F = 1.8463$, $p = .1757$). In the capstone/reflection courses, students in the service-learning sections earned grades that were 4.3% higher than those of the NSL students (3.12 vs. 2.99, $F = .8045$, $p = .3710$). In the practicum courses, students in the service-learning sections earned grades that were marginally (2.4%) higher than those of the NSL students (3.43 vs. 3.35, $F = .4544$, $p = .5017$). And in the lecture courses, students in the service-learning sections earned grades that were nearly identical to those of the NSL students (3.16 vs. 3.18, $F = .0268$, $p = .8702$).

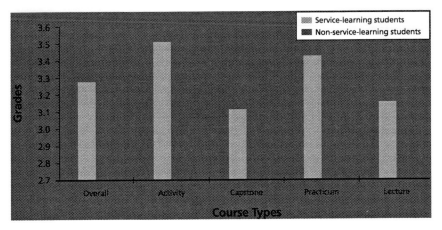

Figure 3.3.   **Grades earned in upper division child development courses.**

Results of the ANOVAs for the lecture/activity courses where grades for individual assignments were available indicated that the primary advantage for the service-learning students manifested itself in their integrative writing; whereas differences between the service-learning and NSL students' scores on descriptive assignments were negligible (less than 1%), the service-learning students outperformed the NSL students by 9.65% in midterm and final exams, which consisted of essays requiring integration and application of research and theory. This pattern of where advantages favoring the service-learning students appeared and where they did not closely parallels the findings of the original study comparing the service-learning and NSL service-learning students in their introductory child development course itself, suggesting, perhaps, that the effect of participating in the service and reflection activities continues to manifest itself most visibly when the students are called upon to think critically and integrate their research and theory knowledge base with real-world application.

Final course grades are a fairly crude index of academic outcome, and possibly as a result, the differences between service-learning and NSL students are very modest. But some preliminary conclusions can be drawn from them. The two kinds of courses where prior service-learning would seem to make the *least* difference would appear, in some ways, to fall at opposite ends of a pedagogical continuum. No significant advantages appeared in courses where students are explicitly guided to integrate in-class and real-world learning contexts through regular reflection and discussion both in class and on site (i.e., the practicum courses), or in courses where instructional objectives focus more exclusively on basic research and theory (i.e., the lecture courses). The academic arena where service-learning would appear to have the most promising long-term benefits lies somewhere in the middle of this continuum. The larger differences between service-learning and NSL students emerged in the two kinds of courses where assignments call for students to apply their disciplinary knowledge base to problems in the "real world," through simulation assignments (in the "activity" classes), or through the formulation data-driven policy recommendations (in the capstone courses).

GENERAL DISCUSSION

The introduction to the volume emanating from last year's Service-Learning Research Conference applauded the progress being made to move from narrowly focused, if carefully descriptive program evaluations, to more complex and comprehensive efforts to understand where, when, and how service-learning affects participants, and underscores the need for researchers to build upon one another's studies to show more coherently how findings from several studies relate to each other (Billig & Eyler, 2003). Such explanations are essential to building a body of knowledge that can provide practitioners with the necessary information to make informed decisions regarding the optimal design of service-learning courses.

The findings in the studies here are modest at best, as is typical of most service-learning research. The short period between pre-test and post-test surveys in the first study (MIS) limited the likelihood of observing dramatic outcomes, particularly because the survey questions did not fully control for students' tendency to provide socially desirable answers. Thus, pre-test scores were likely inflated as well, resulting in relatively small measured gains. While the second study was conducted over the long term, it used a gross measurement of outcomes—GPA—which was limited in its ability to capture all effects of the service-learning experience on student achievement and learning.

However, by placing these findings in the context of the framework proposed here, patterns can emerge among different efforts that can strengthen the value of any one study or finding. As findings and explanations for a wide range of studies are positioned in this framework, a theory can be built from consistency among multiple, albeit modest findings. Furthermore, the framework provides the necessary constructs to help researchers explore the reasons for contradictory findings across different studies. For example, contrasting the MIS study presented here with Knutson Miller and colleagues' (2002) child development study illustrates the utility of the framework for guiding systematic comparison across studies. The two studies differed in variables belonging to the service-learning experience component of the framework, specifically in terms of the course variables (MIS and child development majors) and service-learning activity variables (the MIS study involved indirect service-learning while the child development study involved direct service). The findings suggest that while indirect service-learning has no effect on student engagement in the child development discipline, it has a positive impact on student engagement in the MIS field. Differences could be attributed to the differences in a number of independent variables—the goals of each discipline, type, and intensity of reflection—whose impacts warrant further investigation in future studies. The framework also strengthens consistent findings across studies that independently can only offer findings that do not reach conventional levels of significance, or that report significant albeit small effects. In the case of the two studies reported here, integration of service-learning with course objectives, coupled with intense reflection activities, were associated with gains in civic engagement and academic achievement, as measured by GPA.

The aim is to use this framework to guide studies of service-learning activities over the long term, and to use the synergies among these studies to build practical theories on the design and conduct of service-learning courses that achieve predictable, measurable, and valued results for all constituencies involved: students, faculty, institutions, and communities. Current interdisciplinary service-learning efforts provide fertile ground for an integrative research agenda guided by the framework described in this chapter. At San José State University, the framework will be used to coordinate studies of several initiatives, including a cross-disciplinary effort among sociology, psychology, and health sciences; several collaborations between the MIS and College of Engineering supported by funding from Purdue's Engineering Projects in Community Service program and Hewlett Packard; and the infusion of service-learning in a lower division course in mathematics. Such efforts can be expected to yield valuable knowledge not only on the impacts of the service-learning pedagogies but also key recommendations for designing service-learning programs that match both within-discipline and across-discipline learning objectives.

ACKNOWLEDGMENTS

This research was partly supported by Grant No. 00LHECA072 from the Corporation for National and Community Service Learn and Serve America Higher Education Program, and by USDE Title II Teacher Quality Enhancement Grant No. P336C990077.

REFERENCES

Astin, A., & Sax, L. (1998). How undergraduates are affected by service participation. *Journal of College Student Development, 39*, 251–263.

Astin, A. W., Vogelgesang, L. J., Ikeda, E. K., & Yee, J. A. (2000). *How service-learning affects students: Executive summary.* Los Angeles: Higher Education Research Institute. Retrieved May 20, 2004, from www.gseis.ucla.edu/slc/rhowas.html

Billig, S. H., & Eyler, J. (2003). Introduction. In S. H. Billig & J. Eyler (Eds.), *Advances in service-learning research: Vol. 3. Deconstructing service-learning: Research exploring context, participation, and impacts* (pp. ix–xiii). Greenwich, CT: Information Age.

Billig, S. H., & Furco, A. (2002). Supporting a strategic service-learning research plan. In S. H. Billig & A. Furco (Eds.), *Advances in service-learning research: Vol. 2. Service-learning through a multidisciplinary lens* (pp. 217–230). Greenwich, CT: Information Age.

Boss, J. A. (1994). The effects of community service work on the moral development of college ethics students. *Journal of Moral Education, 23*, 183–198.

Bronfenbrenner, U. (1979). *The ecology of human development.* Cambridge, MA: Harvard University Press.

Campus Compact. (n.d.). Retrieved June 15, 2004 from http://www.compact.org/aboutcc/principles.html

Cohen, J., & Kinsey, D. (1994). "Doing good" at scholarship: A service-learning study. *Journalism Educator, 48,* 4–14.

Covitt, B. (2002). Motivating environmentally responsible behavior through service-learning. In S. H. Billig & A. Furco (Eds.), *Advances in service-learning research: Vol. 2. Service-learning through a multidisciplinary lens* (pp. 177–198). Greenwich, CT: Information Age.

Cruz, N., & Giles, D. E., Jr. (2000). Where's the community in service-learning research? *Michigan Journal of Community Service Learning* [Special Issue], 28–34.

Delve, C., Mintz, S., & Steward, G. (1990). Community service as values education. *New Directions for Student Services, 50.* San Francisco: Jossey-Bass.

Diaz-Gallegos, D., Furco, A., & Yamada, H. (1999). *The higher education service-learning surveys.* Berkeley: University of California, Berkeley, Service-Learning Research and Development Center.

Driscoll, A., & Williams, D. (1997). Connecting curriculum content with community service: Guidelines for student reflection. *Journal of Public Service and Outreach, 2*(1), 33–42.

Eyler, J. (2002). Stretching to meet the challenge: Improving the quality of research to improve the quality of service-learning. In S. Billig & A. Furco (Eds.), *Advances in service-learning research: Vol. 2. Service-learning research through a multidisciplinary lens* (pp. 3–14). Greenwich, CT: Information Age.

Eyler, J., & Giles, D. (1996, October). *The impact of service-learning program characteristics on student outcomes.* Paper presented at the National Society for Experiential Education conference, Snowbird, UT.

Eyler, J., & Giles, D. (1999). *Where's the learning in service-learning?* San Francisco: Jossey-Bass.

Furco, A., & Billig, S. H. (2002). Supporting a strategic service-learning research plan. In S. H. Billig & A. Furco (Eds.), *Advances in service-learning research: Vol. 2. Service-learning research through a multidisciplinary lens* (pp. 217–230). Greenwich, CT: Information Age.

Galbraith, J. (1973). *Designing complex organizations.* Reading, MA: Addison-Wesley.

Giles, D., & Eyler, J. (1998, Spring). A service-learning research agenda for the next five years. In R. A. Rhoads & J. P. F. Howard (Eds.), *Academic service-learning: A pedagogy of action and reflection: New Directions for Teaching and Learning, 73* (pp. 65–72). San Francisco: Jossey-Bass.

Gorman, M. (1994). Service experience and the moral development of college students. *Religious Education, 89*(3), 422–431.

Gray, M., Geschwind, S., Ondaatje, E., Robyn, A., Klein, S., Sax, L., Astin, A., & Astin, H. (1996). *Evaluation of Learn and Serve America, higher education: First year report, 1.* Santa Monica, CA: RAND.

Guarasci, R., Cornwell, G., & Erlandson, G. (1997). *Democratic education in an age of difference: Redefining citizenship in higher education.* San Francisco: Jossey-Bass.

Hecht, D. (2003). The missing link: Exploring the context of learning in service-learning. In S. H. Billig & J. Eyler (Eds.), *Advances in service-learning research: Vol.*

3. *Deconstructing service-learning: Research exploring context, participation, and impacts* (pp. 25–50). Greenwich, CT: Information Age.

Howard, J. (2001). *Michigan Journal of Community Service Learning: Service-learning course design workbook.* Ann Arbor: University of Michigan OCSL Press.

Howard, J. (2003). Service-learning research: Foundational issues. In S. H. Billig & A. S. Waterman (Eds.), *Studying service-learning: Innovations in education research methodology* (pp. 1–12). Mahwah, NJ: Lawrence Erlbaum Associates.

Kendrick, J. (1996). Outcomes of service-learning in an Introduction to Sociology course. *Michigan Journal of Community Service Learning, 3,* 72–81.

Knutson Miller, K., & Yen, S-C. (2003, November). *Service-learning and academic achievement: Outcomes mediated by service characteristics and reflection prompts.* Paper presented at the 3rd Annual International Conference on Advances in Service-Learning Research. Salt Lake City, UT.

Knutson Miller, K., Yen, S-C., & Merino, N. (2002). Service-learning and academic outcomes in an undergraduate child development course. In S. H. Billig & A. Furco (Eds.), *Advances in service-learning research: Vol. 2. Service-learning through a multidisciplinary lens* (pp. 199–213). Greenwich, CT: Information Age.

Kolb, D. A. (1984). *Experiential learning: Experience as the source of learning and development.* Englewood Cliffs, NJ: Prentice-Hall.

Lawrence, P., & Lorsch, J. (1967). *Organization and environment.* Cambridge, MA: Harvard University Press.

Mabry, J. B. (1998). Pedagogical variations in service-learning and student outcomes: How time, contact, and reflection matter. *Michigan Journal of Community Service Learning, 5,* 32–47.

Markus, G., Howard, J., & King, D. (1993). Integrating community service and classroom instruction enhances learning: Results from an experiment. *Educational Evaluation and Policy Analysis, 15,* 410–419.

Ostrow, J. (1995). Self-consciousness and social position: On college students changing their minds about the homeless. *Qualitative Sociology, 18,* 357–375.

Perry, W. G. (1999). *Forms of intellectual and ethical development in the college years: A scheme.* San Francisco: Jossey-Bass. (Original work published 1970)

Piaget, J. (1954). *The construction of reality in the child.* New York: Basic Books.

Rhoads, R. (1997). *Community service and higher learning: Explorations of the caring self.* Albany: State University of New York Press.

Sax, L., & Astin, A. (1997). The benefits of service: Evidence from undergraduates. *Educational Record, 78,* 25–32.

Seifer, S. D. (2002). *Discipline-specific service-learning resources for higher education.* Retrieved June 11, 2004, from http://www.servicelearning.org/article/archive/92

Steinke, P., & Burresh, S. (2002). Cognitive outcomes of service-learning: Reviewing the past and glimpsing the future. *Michigan Journal of Community Service Learning, 8*(2), 5–14.

Steinke, P., Fitch, P., Johnson, C., & Waldstein, F. (2002). An interdisciplinary study of service-learning predictors and outcomes among college students. In S. H. Billig & A. Furco (Eds.), *Advances in service-learning research: Vol. 2. Service-learning through a multidisciplinary lens* (pp. 73–122). Greenwich, CT: Information Age.

Strage, A. (2000). Service-learning as a tool for enhancing student learning outcomes in a college-level lecture course. *Michigan Journal of Community Service Learning*, 7, 5–13.

Strage, A., Baba, Y., Millner, S., Scharberg, M., Walker, E., Williamson, R., & Yoder, M. (2002). What every college professor should know: Student activities and beliefs associated with academic success. *Journal of College Student Development*, 43(2) 246–266.

Strage, A., Knutson Miller, K., Gomez, S., & Garcia, A. (2004). *Toward a more complete understanding of when service-learning is most effective*. Presentation at the 5th Carnegie Colloquium on the Scholarship of Teaching and Learning, San Diego, CA.

Vernon, A., & Foster, L. (2002). Community agency perspectives in higher education service-learning and volunteerism. In S. H. Billig & A. Furco (Eds.), *Advances in service-learning research: Vol. 2. Service-learning through a multidisciplinary lens* (pp. 153–176). Greenwich, CT: Information Age.

Vogelgesang, L., & Astin, A. (2000). Comparing the effects of community service and service-learning. *Michigan Journal of Community Service Learning*, 7, 25–34.

Votruba, J. (2003, September). Defining public engagement. Invited address, 9th Annual Conference of the Coalition of Urban and Metropolitan Universities, Ypsilanti, MI.

Vygotsky, L. S. (1978). *Mind in society: The development of higher psychological processes* (M. Cole, V. John-Steiner, S. Scribner, & E. Souberman, Eds. & Trans.). Cambridge, MA: Harvard University Press. (Original work published 1930)

Zlotkowski, E. (2001). Mapping new terrain: Service-learning across the disciplines. *Change, 33*(1), 25–33.

CHAPTER 4

THE IMPACT OF K–12 SCHOOL-BASED SERVICE-LEARNING ON ACADEMIC ACHIEVEMENT AND STUDENT ENGAGEMENT IN MICHIGAN

Stephen J. Meyer, Shelley H. Billig, and Linda Hofschire

ABSTRACT

This quasi-experimental study examined the impact of service-learning on academic achievement and student engagement outcomes and the extent to which service-learning quality moderated impact on students. Outcomes for service-learning participants and a comparison group were compared, based on data from a sample of nearly 2,000 students in Michigan collected during the 2001–2002 school year. Surveys were used to collect data about student engagement and state achievement test data were also collected for students who participated in the study. A teacher survey included detailed measures of service-learning quality. Findings revealed statistically significant, but small differences in 5th-grade social studies and science achievement scores that favored service-learning participants. While differences in student engagement ratings between service-learning participants and a comparison group were

New Perspectives in Service-Learning: Research to Advance the Field, pages 61–85
Copyright © 2004 by Information Age Publishing

mixed, service-learning student ratings of engagement in service-learning activities were consistently higher than ratings of engagement in school in general. The moderating effect of service-learning quality on the relationship between service-learning participation and student engagement was mixed.

INTRODUCTION

Service-learning is a teaching and learning strategy that involves students in service projects that are connected to academic curricula. Service-learning has its roots in the ideas of philosophers, such as Piaget (e.g., Gruber & Voneche, 1995) and Dewey (e.g., 1902), who argued that students learn more when they are actively involved in their own learning and when learning has a distinct purpose (Anderson, Kinsley, Negroni, & Price, 1991; Conrad & Hedin, 1991; Kinsley, 1997). A body of evidence is building in support of the positive academic outcomes of service-learning (see Billig, 2000, 2004, for a review), and the emphasis on identifying these academic outcomes has grown in the current K–12 educational context that strongly stresses school accountability and standards-based education.

Studies have documented positive effects of service-learning on standardized test scores (Anderson et al., 1991; Klute, 2002; Meyer & Billig, 2003; Santmire, Giraud, & Grosskopf, 1999) and grades (Dean & Murdock, 1992; Follman, 1998; Laird & Black, 2002; O'Bannon, 1999; Shaffer, 1993; Shumer, 1994). Some research has reported positive results of service-learning in particular academic areas, such as:

- Mathematics (Akujobi & Simmons, 1997; Melchior, 1999; Morgan, 2000; Rolzinski, 1990; Santmire et al., 1999; Supik, 1996);
- Language arts (Akujobi & Simmons, 1997; Morgan, 2000; Rolzinski, 1990; Supik, 1996; Weiler, LaGoy, Crane, & Rovner, 1998);
- Science (Melchior, 1999; Melchior & Bailis, 2002); and
- Social studies (Melchior & Bailis, 2002).

Service-learning has also been shown to be positively associated with outcomes such as attendance, school engagement, attitudes toward school, motivation, and educational aspirations (Follman, 1998; Loesch-Griffin, Petrides, & Pratt, 1995; Melchior, 1999; Melchior & Bailis, 2002; Meyer & Billig, 2002; Meyer, Billig, & Hofschire, 2004; O'Bannon, 1999; Scales, Blyth, Berkas, & Kielsmeier, 2000; Shaffer, 1993; Shumer, 1994; Supik, 1996; Weiler et al., 1998).

However, the conclusions that can be drawn from much of the service-learning research literature are limited by methodological problems. In particular, many studies do not pay adequate attention to the nature and quality of the service-learning programming (Billig, 2000). Numerous definitions of service-learning exist and programs vary tremendously in quality. Melchior (1999) and Weiler and colleagues (1998) even found a great deal of variation among service-learning programs initially identified as being "high quality." Research indicates that the quality of service-learning matters in terms of the relative impact of service-learning. For example, in a study of the Philadelphia Need in Deed program, Meyer and Billig (2003) found that the quality of services and fidelity to the model made a difference in the impacts that were found. Focus groups revealed that in some of the cases where the impact was lowest, teachers did not implement all of the service-learning activities or did so without allowing adequate student voice in the process or time for reflection.

Melchior and Bailis (2002) also found that program quality had a positive effect on outcomes in their study comparing outcomes of high-quality Learn and Serve programs with Serve America and Active Citizenship Today (ACT) programs. Ammon (2002) also found that quality, as measured by clarity of teacher goals, dialogue between the teacher and student about goals, and teachers' roles as facilitators in understanding during reflection processes, had a positive impact on outcomes.

THE ROLE OF ENGAGEMENT IN STUDENT LEARNING

Many researchers attribute poor educational performance to a lack of student engagement in schools (Kelly, 1989; Merchant, 1987; Natriello, 1984; Rumberger, 1987; Voelkl, 1995; Wlodkowski & Jaynes, 1990). Engagement in learning has been linked to reduced dropout rates and increased levels of student success (Blank, 1997; Dev, 1997; Dryfoos, 1990; Kushman, Sieber, & Heariold-Kinney, 2000; Woods, 1995). Research also indicates that students are becoming increasingly disengaged. In a 4-year study of more than 20,000 high school students, Steinberg (1996) found that over one third of students did not take school seriously and got through the day by fooling around with classmates; half said their classes were boring; two thirds said they cheated on a school test; 90% copied homework from someone else; and 20% said disengagement was a result of confusion or difficulty of subject matter. Steinberg's findings also indicated that to be engaged in schools, students needed to believe that what they were learning was both interesting and valuable.

Research indicates that students' interest in challenging subjects can decline due to the lack of active learning experiences (Reyes & Laliberty, 1992), and that students who are not given opportunities to experience academic success are more likely to become disengaged (Wagenaar, 1987). Student engagement and disengagement have also been shown to affect teachers' expectations (Brophy, 1987; Stipek, 1988).

In a 1999 interdisciplinary meeting, Bartko (1999) identified three components of engagement: behavioral, affective, and cognitive. *Behavioral engagement* (active participation, persistence, concentration, and so on) and *affective engagement* (level of interest, "flow," enjoyment of learning) have been highly correlated with learning. Less is known, however, about *cognitive engagement*, defined as incorporating the information into one's knowledge base, seeking out information from other sources, and persistently trying to understand phenomena.

The concept of engagement has great utility for understanding educational outcomes. It is easily understood by practitioners, integrates psychological and sociological perspectives, is measurable, and is predictive of policy-relevant outcomes such as graduation from school, community involvement, and economic self-sufficiency in adulthood. Bartko (1999) linked the need for engagement to structural changes, such as reducing teacher–student ratio, standards, resource allocation, and supports (so-called "top-down" reform); and changes in curricula to include project-based learning and authentic tasks (so-called "bottom-up reform"). They specifically called for the development of instruction that entices students into learning through the use of more authentic tasks.

Strategies to Increase Engagement

Maehr and Midgley (1991) identified several strategies to increase engagement and student motivation to learn. These include:

- Stressing goal setting and self-regulation/management;
- Offering students choices in instructional settings;
- Rewarding students for attaining "personal best" goals;
- Fostering teamwork through group learning and problem-solving experiences;
- Replacing social comparisons of achievement with self-assessment and evaluation techniques; and
- Teaching time management skills and offering self-paced instruction when possible.

Eccles, Midgley, and Adler (1984) argued that motivation increases when students are asked to "assume greater autonomy and control over their lives and learning," and recommend that schools create environments that stress task involvement rather than ego involvement. Ames (1992), Anderman and Midgley (1998), and Strong, Silver, and Robinson (1995) found that teachers who are most successful in engaging students develop activities that:

- Address intellectual and psychological needs, including work that develops their sense of competency;
- Encourage self-expression and originality;
- Allow them to develop connections with others; and
- Give them some degree of autonomy.

Several researchers who have studied curricular components related to dropout prevention have also found that a mix of academic instruction and experiential learning is particularly effective (e.g., Dryfoos, 1990). Service-learning is an especially promising expression of experiential learning because it has all of the factors that lead to engagement embedded within it, and it provides a direct link to curriculum. This research suggests that if service-learning does impact academic outcomes, it may do so at least in part because it increases students' engagement in school.

To gain a deeper understanding of the impact of service-learning on student engagement and academic achievement, the Michigan Community Service Commission (MCSC) partnered with RMC Research to conduct a study in schools that received Learn and Serve Michigan funding. Particular attention was paid to examining the role of service-learning quality in moderating outcomes.

CONCEPTUAL MODEL

Figure 4.1 presents the conceptual model guiding the study. The model suggests that participation in service-learning has an impact on academic outcomes (arrow c) and on student engagement in school (arrow a), which, in turn, has an impact on academic achievement (arrow b). In other words, these arrows reflect the hypothesis that the impact of service-learning on academic outcomes is mediated, in part, through its impact on

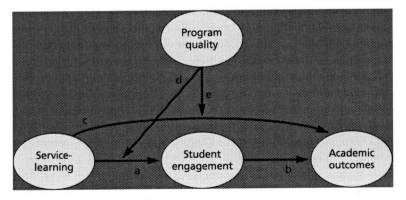

Figure 4.1.   **Conceptual Model.**

student engagement. Arrows d and e depict program quality as a moderator of the effect of service-learning on engagement in school and academic outcomes. These arrows reflect the hypothesis that the impact of service-learning on student outcomes will be greatest when students participate in high-quality service-learning programming.

RESEARCH QUESTIONS

The analyses presented in this chapter examine the relationships depicted by arrows a, c, and d in the model in Figure 4.1. Specifically, findings are presented to address the following three research questions:

1. What is the association between participation in service-learning and academic achievement, as measured by the Michigan Educational Assessment Program (MEAP) assessments for students in Learn and Serve Michigan schools?
2. What is the association between participation in service-learning and student engagement in school?
3. Do aspects of program quality moderate the association between participation in service-learning and student engagement in school? Which program characteristics are most important for predicting student engagement in school?

Because MEAP data cannot be compared across grade levels, analytic samples were too small to examine two questions posited by the conceptual model. Specifically, questions about the extent to which program quality moderated the impact of service-learning on academic achievement (arrow b) and the extent to which student engagement mediated the impact of service-learning on academic achievement (arrow e) could not be examined using data collected for this study.

Sample

Each of the 27 Michigan Learn and Serve grantees that received funding during the 2001–2002 school year was invited to participate in the study, and 16 grantees (59%) participated. Reasons for nonparticipation included lack of administrative approval (e.g., by a superintendent); failure to recruit teachers; and external conditions, such as building renovations. Each participating site was asked to recruit a minimum of two service-learning classrooms and two comparison classrooms, focusing on grades in which the MEAP assessment was administered (Grades 4, 5, 7, 8, and high school). Recruitment of comparison classrooms was a challenge in several sites. Over half (9 of 16) of the grantees were unable to recruit comparison classrooms, in most cases because all students in a given school or district participated in service-learning.

In April and May 2002, teachers who volunteered to participate in the study were sent surveys to administer to their students. There were two versions of the surveys, one for students in Grades 3 through 6 and one for students in Grades 7 through 12. Student surveys were primarily designed to collect information about student engagement in school. Teachers in the service-learning group were also asked to complete a survey designed to collect information about the nature and quality of their service-learning activities. In spring 2002, district and school staff collected achievement data for students who had completed surveys.

A total of 70 teachers and 1,988 students participated in the study. Approximately three fourths of the teacher and student samples (52 teachers and 1,437 students) were from service-learning classrooms. The student sample was roughly equal in terms of gender. Background information collected for students in Grades 7 through 12 indicated that the sample was predominantly Caucasian and consisted mostly of students who had prior experience with service. Based on the number of teachers recruited and the number of students teachers expected to participate in the study at the time of recruitment, response rates for the surveys were as follows:

- Service-learning teacher survey (72%);
- Service-learning student survey (68%);
- Comparison student survey (52%).

MEAP achievement scores were received for 36 participating classrooms and 1,012 students. Where required by schools and districts, parental consent was obtained for the release of MEAP scores. Sites that did not provide MEAP data were unable to secure district or superintendent approval, had too small a group of students who took the MEAP assessment to preserve student confidentiality, or failed to return data within the data collection period. Based on the number of students who completed surveys, the response rate for MEAP data collection was 51%.

Measures of Academic Achievement

Scores from the MEAP were collected for students who completed surveys. MEAP scores for different subject areas were collected, as well as scores for individual "strands" or subtests within each subject area. The MEAP assessment was administered to students in Grades 4, 5, 7, 8, and high school. The number of students for whom achievement data were collected in Grade 4 and high school were too small to conduct reliable analyses; therefore, this chapter presents results only for students in Grades 5, 7, and 8. Scores for 5th-grade students included:

- Total writing;
- Total science and five science strand scores; and
- Total social studies and five social studies strand scores.

Scores for 7th-grade students included total writing and two strand scores for reading. Grade 8 scores included:

- Total science and five science strand scores;
- Total social studies and five social studies strand scores; and
- Total mathematics and six mathematics strand scores.

Descriptive statistics for the student achievement measures are presented in Table 4.1.

Table 4.1.   Descriptive Statistics for Student Achievement Measures

MEAP Score	N	Mean	SD*	Range
Grade 5				
Writing: Points earned	417	2.35	0.52	1–4
Science: Constructing new scientific knowledge	419	8.47	1.90	3–11
Reflecting on scientific knowledge	419	7.37	2.07	2–12
Using life science	418	6.97	1.05	3–8
Using physical science	419	6.72	1.79	1–9
Using earth science	419	8.09	1.86	1–11
Science: Total Score	418	37.64	6.33	18–50
Social Studies: Historical perspective	417	6.97	1.92	1–10
Geographic perspective	417	7.48	2.00	1–10
Civic perspective	417	5.41	2.01	0–10
Economic perspective	417	5.18	2.03	0–10
Inquiry and decision making	310	2.29	0.88	0–5
Social Studies: Total Score	310	27.25	6.54	7–40.5
Grade 7				
Writing: Points earned	220	2.53	0.57	1–4
Reading: Story selection score	221	307.59	20.36	233–338
Informational selection score	221	307.01	24.92	216–395

* Standard deviation

Table 4.1.   Descriptive Statistics for Student Achievement Measures

MEAP Score	N	Mean	SD*	Range
Grade 8				
Science: Constructing new scientific knowledge	249	9.41	1.93	2–13
Reflecting on scientific knowledge	249	6.44	1.68	1–9
Using life science	249	7.63	2.22	1–12
Using physical science	249	6.56	1.96	1–11
Using earth science	249	9.65	1.73	4–12
Science: Total Score	249	39.69	7.20	15–54
Social Studies: Historical perspective	249	6.94	1.91	2–10
Geographic perspective	249	5.97	2.23	1–10
Civic perspective	249	6.12	2.18	1–10
Economic perspective	249	7.44	1.85	0–10
Inquiry and decision making	248	2.39	0.73	0.5–4
Social Studies: Total Score	248	28.83	6.88	11–42
Math: Patterns, relationships, and functions	248	5.92	2.04	1–9
Geometry and measurement	248	6.56	2.21	1–10
Data analysis and statistics	248	6.79	1.74	0–9
Number sense and numeration	248	3.75	1.12	0–5
Numerical and algebraic operations and analytical thinking	248	5.87	2.69	0–10
Probability and discrete mathematics	248	3.02	1.26	0–5
Math: Total Score	248	31.90	8.43	7–48

* Standard deviation

Measures of Student Engagement

The student surveys were used to assess three primary dimensions of student engagement: (1) behavioral, (2) affective, and (3) cognitive, based on a scale developed by Blumenfeld, Secada, Modell, Bartko, and Fredericks (1999). The Behavioral Engagement scale assessed the degree to which students actively participated in school and consisted of seven items such as *I pay attention in class.* The Affective Engagement scale measured the emotional component of engagement in school using seven items such as *I feel excited by the work in school.* The Cognitive Engagement scale measured activities through which students were likely to incorporate information into their knowledge base, using seven items such as *I talk with people outside of school about what I am learning in class.* All items for the three scales were rated on a 5-point scale ranging from "never" to "always." A version of the survey administered to students in Grades 3 through 5 included fewer items and a 3-point response scale with the categories "no," "sometimes," and "yes."

Surveys administered to students in Grades 7 through 12 assessed additional dimensions of student engagement. An academic engagement measure was adapted from a scale developed by Newmann (1981) to assess student effort in the classroom. The index consisted of four items such as *How often do you find yourself concentrating so hard that time passes quickly?* Student responses to a 5-point scale, ranging from "never" to "always," were averaged to create a measure of overall academic engagement as well as engagement measures in each of four subject areas (math, English, social studies, and science). A valuing school scale was adapted from a scale developed by Wehlage, Rutter, Smith, Lesko, and Fernandez (1989) and a scale developed by Blumenfeld and colleagues (1999). This scale consisted of 10 items rated on a 4-point scale ranging from "strongly agree" to "strongly disagree" and included items such as *Success in life does not have much to do with the things studied in school.* Cronbach's alpha coefficients for scales on the older student survey ranged from .74 to .86. For the younger student survey, which had fewer items, Cronbach's alpha coefficients ranged from .51 to .82. Descriptive statistics for the student engagement measures are presented in Table 4.2.

Table 4.2.   Descriptive Statistics for Student Engagement Measures

Measure	n	Mean	SD*	Range
Survey for Grade 3–6 Students				
Behavioral Engagement	1107	2.53	.37	1–3
Affective Engagement	1109	2.18	.48	1–3
Cognitive Engagement	1109	2.09	.48	1–3
Survey for Grade 7–12 Students				
Behavioral Engagement	880	3.92	.61	1–5
Affective Engagement	881	3.01	.82	1–5
Cognitive Engagement	878	2.74	.69	1–5
Academic Engagement	879	3.68	.73	1–5
Math Engagement	877	3.72	.93	1–5
English Engagement	877	3.57	.90	1–5
Social Studies Engagement	831	3.68	.90	1–5
Science Engagement	873	3.77	.89	1–5
Valuing School	878	3.03	.48	1–4

* Standard deviation

Response categories on the survey for Grade 3–6 students were 1 = no, 2 = sometimes, and 3 = yes. Response categories on the survey for Grade 7–12 students were 1 = never, 2 = seldom, 3 = fairly often, 4 = usually, and 5 = always for all items except those for the valuing school measure, which had the following response categories: 1 = strongly disagree, 2 = disagree, 3 = agree, and 4 = strongly agree.

Measures of Service-Learning Quality

The teacher survey included a 43-item measure of the service-learning, based on the 11 Essential Elements of Service-Learning as defined by the National Service-Learning Cooperative (1998). Items, such as *Service-learning activities have clear educational goals*, were rated on a 4-point scale, ranging from "never or almost never" to "always or almost always." Responses to all items were averaged to construct an overall quality index, and indices for each of the 11 Essential Elements were also created. Cronbach's alpha coefficients for these scales ranged from .67 to .95. The teacher survey also recorded service-learning duration (total number of hours), an indicator of whether service-learning activities were linked to state curriculum frameworks, and an indicator of whether activities were required or voluntary. Among the 49 teachers who responded to these items, 91.8% reported that service-learning activities were linked to state curriculum frameworks and 77.5% reported that service-learning activities were required. Descriptive statistics for the remaining service-learning quality measures are presented in Table 4.3.

Table 4.3.   Descriptive Statistics for Service-Learning Quality Measures

Measure	n	Mean	SD*	Range
Overall Quality of Service-Learning	50	3.10	.49	1.7–4.0
Essential Element				
Clear educational goals.	50	3.33	.57	1.8–4.0
Involve students in cognitively challenging tasks.	51	3.30	.58	2.0–4.0
Assessment used to enhance student learning and evaluate how well students have met content and skill standards.	51	2.89	1.00	1.0–4.0
Students are engaged in service tasks with clear goals that meet genuine community needs and have significant consequences.	51	3.15	.57	1.8–4.0
Use of evaluation.	48	2.73	.76	1.3–4.0
Youth voice in selecting, designing, implementing, and evaluating service-learning projects.	51	2.88	.74	1.0–4.0
Valuing diversity.	50	3.13	.73	1.5–4.0
Communication, interaction, partnerships, and collaboration with the community.	48	2.85	.55	1.4–4.0
Students are prepared for all aspects of their service work.	51	3.44	.49	2.0–4.0
Use of reflection.	50	3.16	.72	1.0–4.0
Celebration and acknowledgment of service work.	50	3.06	.85	1.0–4.0
Duration of Service-Learning (in hours)	52	54.33	79.60	2.0–300

* Standard deviation
Response categories for teacher survey items used to create the overall quality measure and measures corresponding to each Essential Element were 1 = never or almost never, 2 = sometimes, 3 = often, and 4 = always or almost always.

ANALYSIS STRATEGY

Hierarchical linear modeling (HLM) was used to analyze the data (Bryk & Raudenbush, 1992). Because students in a given classroom are likely to be more similar to each other than they would be to students in other classrooms, an assumption of most traditional statistical techniques (the independence of observations) is violated. HLM addresses this problem by modeling variation in student outcomes at multiple levels. In this case, models consisted of students at level 1, nested within classrooms at level 2. Separate models were run for each student engagement and student achievement variable. Student engagement analyses were conducted separately for students in Grades 3 through 6 and for students in Grades 7 through 12. Analyses of achievement on the MEAP were conducted separately for grade levels 5, 7, and 8.

Initial unconditional models were run to determine the variability in outcomes within and across classrooms. All level 1 models included gender as an independent variable, and models for students in Grades 7 through 12 included an additional variable indicating whether or not the student had prior service experience. When it was determined that there was significant variation across classrooms, level 2 models were developed that included a variable identifying classrooms as service-learning or comparison and included variables for each indicator of service-learning quality. Level 2 models also included grade level as a control variable in models that predicted student engagement.

To assess the moderating impact of service-learning quality on student engagement, service-learning programs were divided into groups based on each measure of quality (overall quality, and each of the 11 Essential Elements' indicators). Service-learning classrooms were assigned to a low-quality or high-quality group for each quality variable by splitting the sample of classrooms at the variable's median. Classrooms with scores at or below the median were assigned to the low-quality group and those with scores above the median were assigned to the high-quality group. Each of the engagement outcomes was reexamined by comparing the low-and high-quality service-learning classrooms separately to the comparison group. If the relationship between service-learning and student engagement were moderated by service-learning quality, these analyses would show that only one group (e.g., the high-quality service-learning classrooms) scored significantly differently than the comparison group. Additional level 2 models examined the impact of service-learning duration, whether service-learning was linked to curriculum frameworks, and whether service-learning was required or voluntary.

THE IMPACT OF SERVICE-LEARNING PARTICIPATION ON STUDENT ACHIEVEMENT

Student achievement scores on the MEAP were compared for service-learning and comparison students in Grades 5, 7, and 8. Table 4.4 presents coefficients for the Grade 5 student achievement models. All models control for student gender, and positive coefficients correspond to higher average achievement among service-learning students. Table 4.4 shows that statistically significant differences were found indicating higher average achievement among service-learning students in social studies. Differences favoring service-learning students were found for the total social studies score and for three of the five social studies strands (historical perspective, geographic perspective, and inquiry and decision making). Differences at the level of a trend ($p < .10$) were also identified for the total writing score and the using earth science strand of the science test. While these findings should be viewed with caution, they also suggest higher average achievement for service-learning students.

Table 4.4.   Effect of Service-Learning Participation on Student Achievement, Grade 5

	Point Range	Effect	t	df
Social Studies				
Historical Perspective	1–10	0.52*	2.60	14
Geographic Perspective	1–10	0.79*	2.72	14
Civic Perspective	0–10	0.45	1.59	14
Economic Perspective	0–10	0.29	0.73	14
Inquiry and Decision Making	0–5	0.37*	3.23	9
Social Studies Total	7–40.5	3.09*	2.27	9
Writing	1–4	0.20~	1.84	14
Science				
Constructing New Scientific Knowledge	3–11	0.46	1.53	14
Reflecting on Scientific Knowledge	2–12	0.30	0.78	14
Using Physical Science	1–9	0.50	1.73	14
Using Earth Science	1–11	0.60~	1.79	14
Science Total	18–50	1.87	1.49	14

Note: $\sim p < .10$; $*p < .05$; $**p < .01$; $***p < .001$. The unconditional HLM model for cognitive engagement indicated that "using life science" scores did not vary significantly across classrooms; therefore, this variable was not included in the analysis. All models control for gender. Coefficients presented in this table correspond to a dummy variable in the classroom (level 2) models, with a value of "0" for comparison classrooms and a value of "1" for service-learning classrooms.

The Grade 7 MEAP assessments included an overall writing score and two reading scores. Analysis of 7th-grade student scores showed that the service-learning and comparison groups did not differ significantly on writing achievement scores. Because the unconditional models indicated that there was no significant variation in reading scores among classrooms, reading scores could not be compared.

Analysis of MEAP achievement data for students in Grade 8 revealed that differences between the service-learning and comparison group were not significant for scores in:

- Science (overall score and using physical science strand);
- Social studies (overall score, historical perspective, geographic perspective, civic perspective, and inquiry and decision-making strands); and
- Math (overall score, patterns, relationships, and functions strand, geometry and measurement, data analysis and statistics, numerical and algebraic operations and analytical thinking, and probability and discrete mathematics strands).

The remaining strand scores could not be compared due to nonsignificant variation among classrooms, as indicated by initial unconditional models.

THE IMPACT OF SERVICE-LEARNING PARTICIPATION ON STUDENT ENGAGEMENT

Nine engagement variables were used to test for differences between the service-learning and comparison groups. Behavioral and affective engagement outcomes were compared for all students. Cognitive engagement could be compared only for students in Grades 3 through 6. The remaining variables (academic, math, English, social studies, science engagement, and valuing school) were compared only for students in Grades 7 through 12, who took the version of the survey that included these measures. All models controlled for gender and grade level. Models for older students also controlled for students' prior service experience.

Table 4.5 presents coefficients for the student engagement models. Positive coefficients correspond to higher average engagement among service-learning students. The figure shows that, among younger students, the service-learning and comparison groups differed significantly on one of the three engagement variables. Service-learning students had significantly higher Cognitive Engagement scores than the comparison group, after controlling for gender and grade level. Among older students, the service-learning and comparison group differed significantly on two of eight engagement measures that were compared. Contrary to what was hypothesized, the service-learning group had slightly lower Behavioral Engagement scores than the comparison group, after controlling for gender, prior experience with service, and grade level. The service-learning group had significantly higher English Engagement scores than the comparison group, after controlling for gender, prior experience with service, and grade level.

Table 4.5.   Effect of Service-Learning Participation on Student Engagement

	Younger Students (Grades 3–6)			Older Students (Grades 7–12)		
	Effect	t	df	Effect	t	df
Affective Engagement	0.07	1.42	38	0.05	1.31	26
Behavioral Engagement	0.00	0.14	38	−0.11*	2.71	26
Cognitive Engagement	0.21**	3.72	38	Not tested †		
Academic Engagement				0.01	0.14	26
Math Engagement	Not measured on the younger student survey			−0.01	−0.09	26
English Engagement				0.23***	2.26	26
Social Studies Engagement				−0.03	−0.27	26
Science Engagement				−0.12	−1.17	26
Valuing School				0.03	0.70	26

Note: ~p < .10; *p < .05; **p < .05; ***p < .01. † The unconditional HLM model indicated that cognitive engagement scores for older students did not vary significantly across classrooms; therefore, this variable was not included in the analysis. Coefficients in this table correspond to a dummy variable in the classroom (level 2) models, with a value of "0" for comparison classrooms and a value of "1" for service-learning classrooms.

Student engagement was also assessed by comparing student ratings of engagement in school activities relative to overall engagement in school. Nine pairs of items on the survey administered to service-learning students in Grades 3 through 6 measured engagement both in terms of school in general, and in terms of service-learning activities specifically. Paired t tests were used to compare student ratings on each pair of items. Table 4.6 shows that statistically significant differences were found for students in Grades 3 through 6 for all of the indicators of engagement. In every case, average ratings of service-learning engagement were significantly higher than those for school engagement in general.

The survey administered to service-learning students in Grades 7 through 12 included 13 pairs of items that measured engagement both in terms of school in general, and in terms of service-learning activities specifically. Again, paired t tests were used to compare student ratings on each pair of items. Table 4.7 shows that statistically significant differences (at the p < .05 level) were found for 9 of the 13 indicators of engagement. In all but one case, average

Table 4.6. Student Ratings of School and Service-Learning Engagement, Grades 3–6

School Engagement			Service-Learning Engagement				
Item	*Mean*	*SD**	*Item*	*Mean*	*SD*	*n*	*Difference*
I pay attention in class.	2.46	0.51	I pay attention when planning or working on my service-learning activities.	2.76	0.46	793	0.30***
I feel happy in school.	2.36	0.58	I feel happy when I am doing service-learning.	2.62	0.56	790	0.26***
When I am in class, I just act as if I am working.	2.59	0.59	When I am doing service-learning, I just act as if I am working.	2.70	0.59	792	0.11***
I feel bored in school.	2.10	0.63	I feel bored when I am doing service-learning.	2.56	0.62	790	0.46***
When work is hard, I either give up or do the easy parts.	2.37	0.72	When my service-learning activities are hard, I either give up or do the easy parts.	2.60	0.66	794	0.23***
I feel excited by the work in school.	2.04	0.63	I feel excited by my service-learning activities.	2.51	0.61	797	0.47***
I like being at school.	2.34	0.66	I like doing service-learning.	2.62	0.58	790	0.28***
I talk with people outside of school about what I am learning in class.	2.19	0.74	I talk with people outside of school about my service-learning activities.	2.25	0.76	792	0.06*
I am interested in the work at school.	2.25	0.62	I am interested in the service-learning projects we do at school.	2.62	0.58	793	0.37***

* Standard deviation

Note: ~p < .10; *p < .05; **p < .05; ***p < .01. 1 = never; 2 = seldom; 3 = fairly often; 4 = usually; and 5 = always. Ratings on italicized items were reversed for analysis.

Table 4.7. Student Ratings of School and Service-Learning Engagement, Grades 7–12

School Engagement			Service-Learning Engagement				
Item	Mean	SD*	Item	Mean	SD	n	Difference
I pay attention in class.	3.87	0.73	I pay attention when planning or working on my service-learning activities.	3.68	1.03	606	-0.19***
I feel happy in school.	3.39	1.07	I feel happy when I am doing service-learning.	3.39	1.11	604	0.00
When I am in class, I just act as if I am working.	3.43	1.10	When I am doing service-learning, I just act as if I am working.	3.33	1.14	584	-0.10~
I feel bored in school.	2.90	1.19	I feel bored when I am doing service-learning.	3.68	1.04	592	0.78***
When work is hard, I either give up or do the easy parts.	3.66	1.08	When my service-learning activities are hard, I either give up or do the easy parts.	3.99	1.00	599	0.33***
I find myself focusing so hard at school that time passes quickly.	2.97	1.04	When I am working on service-learning, I find myself focusing so hard that time passes quickly.	3.09	1.17	603	0.12*
I feel excited by the work in school.	2.23	1.03	I feel excited by my service-learning activities.	3.05	1.13	598	0.82***
Besides my homework, I do more work than the teacher says that I have to do.	2.10	0.96	When I am working on service-learning projects, I do more work than the teacher says that I have to do.	2.63	1.11	604	0.53***
I like being at school.	3.06	1.22	I like doing service-learning.	3.34	1.19	600	0.28***
I talk with people outside of school about what I am learning in class.	2.78	1.18	I talk with people outside of school about my service-learning activities.	2.85	1.30	605	0.07
I feel frustrated in school.	3.44	1.09	I feel frustrated when I am working on service-learning.	3.80	0.97	593	0.36***
I don't try very hard in school.	3.89	1.02	I don't try very hard when I am working on service-learning activities.	3.97	1.03	604	0.08~
I am interested in the work at school.	2.84	1.03	I am interested in the service-learning projects we do at school.	3.31	1.19	606	0.47***

* Standard deviation

Note: $\sim p < .10$; $*p < .05$; $**p < .05$; $***p < .01$. 1 = never; 2 = seldom; 3 = fairly often; 4 = usually; and 5 = always. Ratings on italicized items were reversed for analysis.

ratings of service-learning engagement were significantly higher than those for school engagement in general. The exception was for student ratings of paying attention in school relative to during service-learning activities, which showed that ratings of school engagement were higher than those for service-learning engagement. Two additional items were significant at the level of a trend ($p <$ .10) and indicated small differences between service-learning engagement and overall school engagement. Differences showed higher School Engagement in one case and higher service-learning engagement in the other.

THE MODERATING EFFECT OF SERVICE-LEARNING QUALITY ON THE RELATIONSHIP BETWEEN SERVICE-LEARNING ON STUDENT ENGAGEMENT

Fifteen program quality variables were examined to assess the extent to which service-learning quality moderated the relationship between service-learning participation and student engagement. Table 4.8 summarizes the results of a series of HLM models that examined the moderating effect of quality indicators on each of 10 student engagement indicators (three for younger students and seven for older students). This table presents statistically significant coefficients from each model that reflect differences between service-learning and comparison students. Coefficients that were significant at the level of a trend ($p < .10$) are also reported. All models control for gender and grade level, and models for students in Grades 7 through 12 also control for students' prior service experience.

Quality indicators are presented in the left column of Table 4.8 and include:

- A measure of duration;
- An overall quality measure;
- Measures of each of the 11 Essential Elements of Service-Learning;
- An indicator of whether service-learning was linked to curriculum frameworks; and
- An indicator of whether service-learning activities were required.

With the exception of duration, which was treated as a continuous variable, each quality variable was used to divide service-learning classrooms into low- and high-quality groups. Student engagement measures for each of the groups were compared to those for students in the comparison group. A positive coefficient corresponds to higher average student engagement in the service-learning group and a negative coefficient corresponds to higher average student engagement in the comparison group. The hypotheses about the moderating effect of service-learning quality would lead one to expect significant positive coefficients for the high-quality groups and nonsignificant or significant negative coefficients for the low-quality groups.

The pattern of effects shown in Table 4.8 reveals the following:

- Two quality variables emerged as moderators more than once in the expected direction. Essential Element 8 (communication and interaction with the community) emerged as a moderator for both younger and older students. Only those students who participated in service-learning characterized by more involvement with the community had significantly higher affective, cognitive, and English engagement than students in the comparison group. In addition, only those students who participated in service-learning activities that were linked to the Michigan Curriculum Frameworks had higher affective engagement than the comparison group at the level of a trend ($p < .10$).
- Three quality variables emerged as moderators more than once, with the direction of the effect being opposite of what was expected. For the measure of overall quality and Essential Elements 1 (clear educational goals) and 5 (use of evaluation), students who were exposed to lower quality service-learning reported higher average student engagement. These effects were predominantly for older students.
- Four quality variables emerged as moderators in mixed directions. Essential Elements 6 (use of youth voice), 9 (preparation for service work), and 11 (celebration of service work), and whether service-learning was required or voluntary, emerged as moderators in both expected and unexpected directions.
- Six quality variables rarely or never moderated the association between participation in service-learning and student engagement. Essential Element 2 (involving students in challenging tasks) never moderated the association between participation in service-learning and student engagement. Essential Elements 3 (use of assessment), 4 (meaningful service tasks), 7 (valuing diversity), 10 (use of reflection), and duration of service-learning moderated the association between service-learning and student engagement for only one of the 11 student engagement outcomes.

LIMITATIONS AND DIRECTIONS FOR FUTURE RESEARCH

The generalizability of this study is limited due to the sample size, response rate, and the fact that findings are based on data collected at only one point in time. However, the results suggest positive impacts of service-learning and suggest elements of service-learning programs that may moderate effects on students. While the impact of service-learning participation on student engagement relative to students in a comparison

Table 4.8. Moderating Effect of Service-Learning Quality on Student Engagement

	Younger Students (Grades 3–6)			Older Students (Grades 7–12)							Evidence of Moderation
	Affective	Behavioral	Cognitive	Affective	Behavioral	Math	English	Social Studies	Science	Valuing School	
Duration (in hours)						0.001~					None
Overall Quality Low			0.23**				0.37**				
Overall Quality High			0.25**		-0.13**						Unexpected Direction
1. Clear goals Low	0.14*		0.22**				0.28*				
Clear goals High			0.25**		-0.11*						Unexpected Direction
2. Cognitively challenging tasks Low			0.29*		-0.17		0.21~				
Cognitively challenging tasks High			0.26**		-0.09*		0.22*				None
3. Assessment Low			0.23*				0.27~				
Assessment High			0.25**		-0.12**		0.21~				None
4. Meaningful service tasks Low			0.21*		-0.15~						
Meaningful service tasks High			0.27**		-0.08~		0.29**				None
5. Use of evaluation Low			0.23**	0.22~			0.22~				
Use of evaluation High			0.24*		-0.15***		0.22~			0.09~	Unexpected Direction
6. Youth voice Low			0.19**				0.29**				
Youth voice High	0.14*		0.30**		-0.16***				-0.22~		Mixed
7. Valuing diversity Low			0.35***		-0.11~		0.35**				
Valuing diversity High			0.20**		-0.12~						None

Table 4.8. Moderating Effect of Service-Learning Quality on Student Engagement (Cont.)

| | | Younger Students (Grades 3–6) | | | Older Students (Grades 7–12) | | | | | | | |
		Affective	Behavioral	Cognitive	Affective	Behavioral	Math	English	Social Studies	Science	Valuing School	Evidence of Moderation
8.	Community interaction											
	Low			0.22**		-0.13*						Expected Direction
	High	0.13*		0.27**		-0.13**		0.35**				
9.	Student preparation											
	Low				0.23~							Mixed
	High	0.10~		0.26***		-0.12*		0.56***	-0.28*		0.10~	
10.	Reflection											
	Low			0.28***		-0.09~		0.31*				None
	High	0.13*		0.22**		-0.14*						
11.	Celebration/ acknowledgment											
	Low			0.15*							0.10~	Mixed
	High	0.13*		0.29***		-0.16***		0.27*				
	Link to standards											
	Yes	0.10~		0.24**			Not tested †					Expected Direction
	No			0.36***								
	Required											
	Yes		0.17**	0.24***		-0.11*		0.22*				Mixed
	No	0.35~		0.21*								

Note: ~p < .10; *p < .05; **p < .05; ***p < .01. The unconditional HLM model indicated that cognitive engagement scores for older students did not vary significantly across classrooms; therefore, this variable was not included in the analysis. †All teachers in Grades 7–12 reported that service-learning was linked to curriculum standards, therefore this variable was not included in analyses for older students. Coefficients in this table correspond to a dummy variable in the classroom (level 2) models, with a value of "0" for comparison classrooms and a value of "1" for service-learning classrooms.

group was mixed, students who participated in service-learning gave consistently higher ratings of engagement in service-learning activities relative to engagement in school more generally. Small, but statistically significant differences in social studies and science achievement outcomes for students in 5th-grade also suggest positive effects of service-learning participation. More rigorous research, especially in the form of experimental or quasi-experimental longitudinal designs, is needed to test hypotheses and the robustness of the results that emerged here. These findings showed that service-learning is, at the very least, worth examining as a vehicle for improving student engagement and academic achievement.

ACKNOWLEDGMENT

This project was funded by the Michigan Community Service Commission Contract No. 801P3000345. We gratefully acknowledge the personal and financial support of the Michigan Commission and its wonderful staff.

REFERENCES

Akujobi, C., & Simmons, R. (1997). An assessment of elementary school service-learning teaching methods: Using service-learning goals. *NSEE Quarterly*, *23*(2), 19–28.

Ames, C. (1992). Classroom goals, structures, and student motivation. *Journal of Educational Psychology, 84*(3), 261–271.

Ammon, M. S. (2002). Probing and promoting teachers' thinking about service-learning: Toward a theory of teacher development. In S. H. Billig & A. Furco (Eds.), *Advances in service-learning research: Vol. 2. Service-learning through a multidisciplinary lens* (pp. 33–84). Greenwich, CT: Information Age.

Anderman, L. H., & Midgley, C. (1998). *Motivation and middle school students.* Champaign, IL: ERIC Clearinghouse on Elementary and Early Childhood Education. (ERIC Document Reproduction Service No. ED 421 281)

Anderson, V., Kinsley, C., Negroni, P., & Price, C. (1991, June). Community service-learning and school improvement in Springfield, Massachusetts. *Phi Delta Kappan, 72,* 761–764.

Bartko, W. T. (1999). *Student engagement and development.* Ann Arbor: University of Michigan.

Billig, S. H. (2000, May). Research on K–12 school-based service-learning: The evidence builds. *Phi Delta Kappan, (81)*9, 658–664.

Billig, S. H. (2004). Heads, hearts, hands: The research on K–12 service-learning. In J. Kielsmeier, M. Neal, & M. McKinnon (Eds.), *Growing to greatness: The state of service-learning project* (pp. 12–25). St. Paul, MN: National Youth Leadership Council.

Blank, W. (1997). Authentic instruction. In W. E. Blank & S. Harwell (Eds.), *Promising practices for connecting high school to the real world* (pp. 15–21). Tampa: University of South Florida. (ERIC Document Reproduction Service No. ED407586)

Blumenfeld, P., Secada, W., Modell, J., Bartko, T., & Fredericks, J. (1999). *The MacArthur school engagement survey.* Ann Arbor: University of Michigan.

Brophy, J. (1987). *On motivating students.* Occasional Paper No. 101. East Lansing: Institute for Research on Teaching, Michigan State University. (ERIC Document Reproduction Service No. ED276724)

Bryk, A. S., & Raudenbush, S. W. (1992). *Hierarchical linear models: Applications and data analysis methods.* Newbury Park, CA: Sage.

Conrad, D., & Hedin, D. (1991, June). School–based community service: What we know from research and theory. *Phi Delta Kappan,* 743–749.

Dean, L., & Murdock, S. (1992, Summer). The effect of voluntary service on adolescent attitudes toward learning. *Journal of Volunteer Administration,* 5–10.

Dev, P. C. (1997). Intrinsic motivation and academic achievement: What does their relationship imply for the classroom teacher? *Remedial and Special Education, 18*(1), 12–19.

Dewey, J. (1902). *The child and the curriculum.* Chicago: University of Chicago Press.

Dryfoos, J. G. (1990). A*dolescents at risk: Prevalence and prevention.* New York: Oxford University Press.

Eccles, J., Midgley, C., & Adler, T. F. (1984). Grade-related changes in school environment: Effects on achievement motivation. In J. G. Nicholls (Ed.), *The development of achievement and motivation,* (Vol. 3, pp. 282–331). Greenwich, CT: JAI Press.

Follman, J. (1998, August). *Florida Learn and Serve: 1996–97 outcomes and correlations with 1994–95 and 1995–96.* Tallahassee: Florida State University, Center for Civic Education and Service.

Goldschmidt, P., & Wang, J. (1999). When can schools affect dropout behavior? A longitudinal multilevel analysis. *American Educational Research Journal; 36*(4), 715–738.

Gruber, H. E., & Voneche, J. J. (1995). *The essential Piaget.* Northvale, NJ: Aronson.

Kelly, D. (1989, March). *Slipping in and out of the system: Continuation high schools and the process of disengagement.* Paper presented at the annual meeting of the American Educational Research Association, San Francisco.

Kinsley, C. W. (1997, October). Service-learning: A process to connect learning and living. *National Association of Secondary School Principals (NASSP) Bulletin, 81*(591), 1–7.

Klute, M. M. (2002, December). *Antioch's Community-Based School Environmental Education (CO-SEED): Quantitative evaluation report.* Denver, CO: RMC Research Corporation.

Kushman, J. W., Sieber, C., & Heariold-Kinney, P. (2000). This isn't the place for me: School dropout. In D. Capuzzi & D. R. Gross (Eds.), *Youth at risk: A prevention resource for counselors, teachers, and parents* (3rd ed., pp. 471–507). Alexandria, VA: American Counseling Association.

Laird, M., & Black, S. (2002, October). *Service-learning evaluation project: Program effects for at risk students.* Presentation at 2nd International Service-Learning Research conference, Nashville, TN.

Loesch-Griffin, D., Petrides, L. A., & Pratt, C. (1995). *A comprehensive study of Project YES–Rethinking classrooms and community: Service-learning as educational reform.* San Francisco: East Bay Conservation Corps.

Maehr, J. L., & Midgley, C. (1991). Enhancing student motivation: A schoolwide approach. *Educational Psychologist, 26*(3/4), 399–427.

Melchior, A. (1999). *Summary report: National evaluation of Learn and Serve America.* Waltham, MA: Brandeis University, Center for Human Resources.

Melchior, A., & Bailis, L. N. (2002). Impact of service-learning on civic attitudes and behaviors of middle and high school youth: Findings from three national evaluations. In A. Furco & S. H. Billig (Eds.), *Advances in service-learning research: Vol. 1. Service-learning: The essence of the pedagogy* (pp. 201–222). Greenwich, CT: Information Age.

Merchant, B. (1987). *Dropping out: A preschool through high school concern.* Berkeley: Policy Analysis for California Education.

Meyer, S., & Billig, S. H. (2003). *Evaluation of Need in Deed.* Denver, CO: RMC Research Corporation.

Meyer, S., Billig, S. H., & Hofschire, L. (2004). *Wai'anae High School Hawaiian studies program.* Denver, CO: RMC Research Corporation.

Morgan, W. (2000). *Standardized test scores improve with service-learning.* Bloomington, IN: Civic Literacy Project.

National Service-Learning Cooperative. (1998, April*). Essential elements of service-learning.* St. Paul, MN: National Youth Leadership Council.

Natriello, G. (1984). Problems in the evaluation of students and student disengagement from secondary schools. *Journal of Research and Development in Education, 17,* 14–24.

Newmann, F. M. (1981). Reducing student alienation in high schools: Implications of theory. *Harvard Educational Review, 51,* 546–564.

O'Bannon, F. (1999). Service-learning benefits our schools. *State Education Leader, 17*(3). Retrieved June 15, 2004, from http://www.ecs.org/clearinghouse/16/56/1656.htm#Benefits

Reyes, M. de la Luz, & Laliberty, E. A. (1992). A teacher's "pied piper" effect on young authors. *Education and Urban Society, 24*(2), 263–278.

Rolzinski, C. (1990). *The adventure of adolescence: Middle school students and community service,* Washington, DC: Youth Service America.

Rumberger, R. W. (1987). High school dropouts: A review of issues and evidence. *Review of Educational Research, 57*(2), 101–122.

Santmire, T., Giraud, G., & Grosskopf. K. (1999). *Furthering attainment of academic standards through service-learning.* Presentation at the National Service-Learning Conference, San José, CA.

Scales, P. C., Blyth, D. A., Berkas, T. H., & Kielsmeier, J. C. (2000). The effects of service-learning on middle school students' social responsibility and academic success. *Journal of Early Adolescence, 20*(3), 332–358.

Shaffer, B. (1993). Service-learning: An academic methodology. In R. Bhaerman, K. Cordell, & B. Gomez (Eds.), *The role of service-learning in educational reform.*

Raleigh, NC: National Society for Experiential Education and Needham, MA: Simon & Schuster.

Shumer, R. (1994). Community–based learning: Humanizing education. *Journal of Adolescence, 17*(4), 357–367.

Steinberg, L. (1996). *Beyond the classroom: Why school reform has failed and what parents need to do.* New York: Simon & Schuster.

Stipek, D. J. 1988. *Motivation to learn: From theory to practice.* Englewood Cliffs, NJ: Prentice Hall.

Strong, R., Silver, H. F., & Robinson, A. (1995). What do students want? *Educational Leadership, 53*(1), 8–12.

Supik, J. (1996). *Valued youth partnerships: Programs in caring.* San Antonio, TX: Intercultural Research and Development Association.

Voelkl, K. E. (1995). School warmth, student participation, and achievement. *Journal of Experimental Education, 63*(2), 127–138.

Wagenaar, T. C. (1987). *Changes in postsecondary educational choices: 1972 to 1980.* Contractor Report. (ERIC Document Reproduction Service No. ED 284 481)

Wehlage, G., Rutter, R., Smith, G., Lesko, N., & Fernandez, R. (1989). *Reducing the risk: Schools as communities of support.* Philadelphia and New York: Falmer Press.

Weiler, D., LaGoy, A., Crane, E., & Rovner, A. (1998). *An evaluation of K–12 service-learning in California: Phase II Final Report.* Emeryville, CA: RPP International with the Search Institute.

Wlodkowski, R. J., & Jaynes, J. H. (1990). *Eager to learn: Helping children become motivated and love learning.* San Francisco: Jossey-Bass.

Woods, E. G. (1995). Reducing the dropout rate. In *School Improvement Research Series (SIRS): Research you can use* (Close-Up #17). Portland, OR: Northwest Regional Educational Laboratory. Retrieved October 29, 2001, from http://www.nwrel.org/scpd/sirs/9/c017.html

CHAPTER 5

THE LONG-TERM EFFECTS OF UNDERGRADUATE SERVICE-LEARNING PROGRAMS ON POSTGRADUATE EMPLOYMENT CHOICES, COMMUNITY ENGAGEMENT, AND CIVIC LEADERSHIP

Judith Warchal and Ana Ruiz

ABSTRACT

In the past 15 years, there has been a proliferation of service-learning experiences developed on college campuses across the country. Surprisingly, there has been little research on the long-term outcomes of service-learning programs, despite the general movement toward accountability and assessment in the accreditation process in higher education. The goals of this project consisted of determining (a) the relationships between the undergraduates' participation in a service-learning experience in college and their postgraduate employment choices, and (b) whether different types

New Perspectives in Service-Learning: Research to Advance the Field, pages 87–106
Copyright © 2004 by Information Age Publishing

of service requirements had an effect on job placement, community engagement, and civic leadership. The methods allowed for analysis of responses that spanned 41 years of postgraduation experiences and represented 21 different majors with four different types of service. The results of this study suggest that service-learning experiences are a significant factor in the employment choices of students after graduation. Correlational analysis indicated that students involved in service-learning experiences frequently receive an offer of employment related to the experience. In addition, the quality of the service-learning experience is related to employment after graduation. Analysis of variance (ANOVA) indicated that students involved in service-learning experiences accepted employment offers in service-related fields. ANOVA also indicated that the number of postgraduate community service hours per year increased with age and were a significant factor in civic leadership activities. The importance of these findings and recommendations for future research are also discussed.

INTRODUCTION

In the past 15 years, there has been a proliferation of service-learning experiences developed on college campuses across the country (Gray, Ondaatje, & Zakaras, 1999). Surprisingly, there has been little empirical research on the long-term effects of these programs, despite the general movement toward accountability and assessment in the accreditation process in higher education. The evidence has focused on the impact of service-learning on the students, community, and institutions (Eyler, Giles, & Gray, 1999; Gray et al., 1999). However, these studies have usually been conducted immediately following the service-learning experience.

Research agendas have recommended increased attention to the presumed long-term outcomes of the service-learning experiences (Eyler & Giles, 1999; Furco & Billig, 2002). However, the lasting effects of service-learning on students and communities have yet to be studied systematically (Bringle & Hatcher, 2000). Assessment of long-term service-learning outcomes is a difficult endeavor due to the complex nature of the experience. It is difficult to establish cause-and-effect relationships because students who select service-learning courses are known to be fundamentally different from those who do not on several measures (Eyler, Giles, & Braxton, 1997). Long-term outcomes can be attributed to factors other than service-learning directly (i.e., impact of the college experience).

THEORETICAL FRAMEWORK

A major challenge in service-learning research is the lack of a well-developed theory that addresses the multifaceted nature of the experience. Because experience is the cornerstone of both Dewey (1916, 1938) and Kolb's (1984) theories, Bringle and Hatcher (2000) suggested that they form the theoretical foundation of the service-learning movement. In the absence of a theoretical framework, researchers often apply discipline-specific theory to the examination of the problem. Two different perspectives will be used in this chapter to explore two distinct aspects of the long-term effects of undergraduate service-learning programs. Postgraduate employment choices will be examined using Krumboltz's (1994) Social Learning Theory of Career Decision Making. Citizenship will be investigated through the lens of Dewey (1916), his vision for a democratic society, and the work of more recent proponents of civic responsibility.

Career Development and Employment Choices

The field of career development offers a point of convergence with educational experiential learning theories and may provide a set of theoretical propositions to test through the service-learning experience. Boyte and Farr (2000) suggested that work "is and should be at the center of citizenship, and this should be the problem for service-learning" (p. 9). Billig (2000) reported, "Service-learning helps students become more knowledgeable and realistic about careers" (p. 661). Krumboltz, Mitchell, and Gelatt (1975), Mitchell and Krumboltz (1984, 1990), and Krumboltz (1994) developed and refined a theory of career development and career decision making based on social learning, environmental conditions and events, genetic influences, and learning experiences. Mitchell and Krumboltz (1984) indicated that the Social Learning Theory of Career Decision Making, also known as SLTCDM,

> assumes that the individual personalities and behavioral repertoires that persons possess arise primarily from their unique learning experiences rather than from innate developmental or psychic processes. These learning experiences consist of contact with and cognitive analysis of positively and negatively reinforcing events. (p. 235)

Krumboltz (1994) identified four categories of influence in career choice:

1. Genetic endowment (race, sex, physical appearance, intelligence, and special abilities);

2. Environmental conditions and events (the number and variety of job and training opportunities; neighborhood and community influences; labor and union laws; physical events, such as earthquakes and floods; and family characteristics);

3. Learning experiences of two distinct types. Instrumental learning experiences (ILEs) in which antecedents and covert and overt behavioral responses and consequences lead to the development of skills necessary for career planning and other occupational and educational performances. Associative learning experiences (ALEs) where the learner pairs a previously neutral situation with some emotionally positive or negative reaction (i.e., observational learning); and

4. Task approach skills, such as problem-solving skills, work skills, mental sets, work habits, and cognitive processes that both influence outcomes and are outcomes themselves. (p. 18)

These four sources of influence lead to self-observation generalizations, task approach skills, and actions that involve direct steps in the career progression. Krumboltz and colleagues (1975) stated,

> It is the sequential cumulative effects of numerous learning experiences affected by environmental circumstances that cause a person to make decisions to enroll in a certain educational program or become employed in a particular occupation. (p. 75)

Well-designed service-learning experiences involve the kinds of affective, cognitive, and behavioral components discussed in SLTCDM. Interactive learning is at the heart of both the service-learning experience and the theory of career development (Krumboltz et al., 1975; Mitchell & Krumboltz, 1984, 1990). Skills, interests, beliefs, values, work habits, and personality characteristics are all subject to change as a result of learning experiences (Krumboltz & Worthington, 1999). Service-learning experiences may help students adapt to the ever-changing world of work, develop an attitude of flexibility, and expand awareness of career opportunities. Existing research has shown that service-learning affects behavioral choices such as attendance at graduate school and acquisition of higher degrees (Astin, Sax, & Avalos, 1999).

Mitchell and Krumboltz (1984, 1990) and Krumboltz (1994) and his colleagues (1975) advanced several testable hypotheses that are applicable to this study. He proposed that people will prefer an occupation if (a) they succeed at tasks they believe are performed by members of that occupation and (b) they have observed a valued model being reinforced for activities like those performed by members of that occupation. Service-learning may offer students the opportunity to experience success in career settings and make informed choices about employment options. However, the variety of service-learning experiences and the evolving understanding of the elements necessary for a high-quality service-learning experience make it difficult to assess such outcomes effectively (Furco, 2002).

For the purposes of this study, four types of undergraduate service requirements and the potentially different long-term effects were considered:

- Group 1: No service requirement;
- Group 2: Service-learning experience;
- Group 3: 40-hour community service requirement; and
- Group 4: Combination of 40-hour community service requirement and service-learning experience.

To expand on the framework of Mitchell and Krumboltz (1984, 1990) and Krumboltz (1994) and his colleagues (1975, 1994), the following hypotheses were designed to investigate the long-term effect of different types of service experiences on employment choices.

- A positive relationship exists between having the service-learning experience and an offer of postgraduate employment related to the experience;
- A positive relationship exists between the quality of the service-learning experience and the first job after graduation;
- A positive relationship exists between a student's service-learning experience and the choice of state of the country for the first job;
- A positive relationship exists between the number of hours a student spends in a service-learning experience and the choice of employment site; and
- More alumni engaged in service-learning experiences (groups 2 and 4) choose an employment site related to the experience than alumni that participated in a 40-hour community service requirement (group 3) or had no service requirement (group 1).

Citizenship, Community Engagement and Civic Leadership

Dewey (1916) wrote in *Democracy and Education*, "A democracy is more than a form of government; it is primarily a mode of associated living, of conjoint communicated experiences" (p. 101). He believed that the educational system should be responsible for nurturing young people to become active engaged citizens in a democratic society, but he did not provide an operational definition of civic engagement nor a blueprint for achieving this goal. At its most basic element, as Dewey proposed, civic engagement is the interaction of citizens with their society and the government (Patrick, 1998). Kirlin (2003) defined civic engagement as "a combination of activities in political and community arenas that facilitate collective decision making and through which individuals help to improve their communities" (p. 1) and suggested that education and involvement in certain types of extracurricular activities during high school are two important predictors of future civic engagement.

Different models of citizenship have been proposed. Westheimer and Kahne (2003) suggested that three visions of citizenship drive different educational program designs. The first is the *personally responsible citizen* who acts responsibly in his community by contributing to food drives, recycling, and picking up litter. The second is the *participatory citizen* who engages in the civic affairs and social life of the community by planning and organizing service activities. The third is the *justice-oriented citizen* who calls attention to matters of injustice and pursues social change.

Andolina, Keeter, Zukin, and Jenkins (2003) presented another model of civic engagement. They described four categories of citizenship based on activities in the civic and electoral domain. Individuals are grouped as:

1. *Electoral Specialist*: Voting, wearing campaign buttons, donating money to a political campaign;

2. *Civic Specialist*: Volunteering for a nonelectoral organization, having active group membership, working with others to solve a community problem;

3. *Dual Activist*: Having elements of both civic and electoral dimensions; and

4. *Disengaged*: Not participating in either the electoral or civic dimension. (p. 12)

A survey of 3,246 individuals aged 15 and up indicated that 48% of respondents fell into the disengaged category, 20% into the electoral specialist category, 16% into the civic specialist category, and another 16% qualified as dual activists.

Independent of the models, Sax (2000) and Lopez (2003) identified a disturbing trend in citizenship activities among recent college graduates. While younger people appear to be more involved in volunteerism and community service, having performed many hours of community service as graduation requirements in high school and college, as a group their interest in politics has declined significantly. Another interesting finding of Sax's research is that while many measures of civic responsibility increase during the college years, many of these gains disappear in the first few years after graduation, suggesting that the effects of college on students' commitment to the community may be temporary. Lopez reported that the rise in volunteering in college-aged individuals appears to be more episodic than sustained activity.

In an attempt to address the effects of service activities in the undergraduate years, Astin and colleagues (1999) studied the relationship of student involvement in community service activities based on the number of hours devoted to volunteer work in the last year of college and the number of hours spent in volunteer work after college. They found a modest correlation between the number of hours spent in volunteer activities in college and the number of hours spent volunteering after college. Korn (1999) found similar results in a study of the University of Washington alumni. Astin, Vogelgesang, Ikeda, and Yee (2000) reported that collective qualitative evidence exists suggesting that students who engage in service-learning courses are more likely to have a heightened sense of civic responsibility after graduation. Very little longitudinal data on the civic outcomes of service experiences in general, as well as service-learning specifically, exists.

This study investigated the long-term effects of different types of service at the undergraduate level on postgraduation community engagement and civic leadership by testing the following hypotheses:

(a) The more alumni engaged in service-learning experiences in college (groups 2 and 4), the more likely they were to participate in community service after graduation than alumni who participated in a 40-hour community service requirement (group 3) or alumni who had no service requirement (group 1).

(b) The more alumni engaged in service-learning experiences in college (groups 2 and 4), the more likely they were to participate in civic leadership activities after graduation than alumni who participated in a 40-hour community service requirement (group 3) or alumni who had no service graduation requirement (group 1).

RATIONALE FOR THE STUDY

These hypotheses can be tested because of the change in graduation requirements that occurred in 1991 at a participating small, Catholic college in southeastern Pennsylvania. The history of the college dates back to 1926 when the Bernardine Sisters of the Third Order of Saint Francis established a Teacher's Seminarium for the education of the Sisters. The college then opened its doors to female students from the laity and then later to male students. The mission statement of the college (Alvernia College, 2003) emphasizes the college's commitment to service. It states:

Its purpose is to provide affordable quality education that combines liberal arts with career and professional opportunities. The goal is to prepare learners for personal achievement, for social responsibility, for moral integrity, and for spiritual fullness.... True to the Judeo-Christian tradition, to the Catholic faith, and to the Franciscan heritage, (the college) seeks to foster a community of faith, reverence for the dignity of all life, commitment to peace and justice, and devotion to service—particularly to the materially and spiritually disadvantaged. (pp. 7–8)

In 1991, the college instituted a community service graduation requirement. As stated in the college catalog:

As a college whose mission is rooted in the Franciscan tradition, [the college] seeks to foster in its students a reverence for the dignity of all life, a commitment to peace and justice, and a devotion to the service of others, particularly the materially and spiritually disadvantaged. Therefore, all baccalaureate students must complete 40 clock hours of approved service to others. (p. 80)

In 1997, the college was placed on the Templeton Foundation's Honor Roll of Character-Building Colleges, a national recognition for the college's service requirement as an outstanding contribution to the community.

In the 45-year time span from 1958 to 2003, students at the college had a chance to participate in different types of service. Prior to 1991, any community service activity was strictly voluntary and initiated by either an individual student or a student club (group 1). Before 1991, some students were involved in internships, field experiences, practica, and student teaching with reflection (group 2). After 1991, students were required to complete a minimum of 40 hours of community service as a graduation requirement (group 3). From 1991 to 2003, students might also have been involved in a service-learning internship, field experience, practicum, or student teaching experience in addition to the 40-hour community service requirement (group 4).

For the purpose of this study, the service-learning experiences were identified using the Bringle and Hatcher (1995) definition that service-learning is a "course-based, credit-bearing educational experience that allows the students to

(a) participate in an organized service activity that meets identified community needs and (b) reflect on the service activity in such a way as to gain further understanding of course content, a broader appreciation of the discipline, and an enhanced sense of civic responsibility. (p. 112)

The Franciscan tradition of the college has always stressed service to the community as its mission. Consistent with that mission, reflection on civic responsibilities was an integral part of every experiential course. Even though the term "service-learning" was not in use during the earlier years covered by this study, these authors asserted that any internship, field experience, practicum, or student teaching activity that included equally balanced, structured time for reflection, academic learning goals, and service to the recipients was in fact service-learning. These activities are in contrast to volunteers as people who serve the community on their own free will and without pay (Toole & Toole, 1992). In this study, the above definition of volunteerism is applicable to the number of postgraduation community service hours and the civic leadership activities of alumni.

In summary, this study will test seven hypotheses regarding the long-term effects of four different types of service requirements on postgraduate job placement, employment choices, community engagement, and civic leadership.

METHODS

Participants

The sample for this study was composed of 124 alumni. The participants graduated between 1961 and 2002, covering a range of 41 years of postgraduation experiences. The participants graduated from 21 different majors (54.7% of those 21 majors did not require a service-learning experience, 35.9% of the 21 majors required a service-learning experience, and 9.4% of the respondents listed "other").

Four groups were created to identify the different types of service requirements:

- Group 1: No service requirement ($N = 25$);
- Group 2: Service-learning experience only ($N = 49$);
- Group 3: 40 hours of community service only ($N = 24$); and
- Group 4: Combination 40 hours of community service and service-learning experience ($N = 26$).

Participants ranged in age from 23 to 79 years old (mean age = 42 years; mode = 26 years, SD = 13.26). The average age of Group 1 alumni was 46; the average age of Group 2 was 48. In Group 3, the average age was 33; and in Group 4, the average age was 30. Males comprised 24% of the sample and females 75.2% (0.8% did not answer). Other demographic measures, such as socioeconomic status, grade point average, and race, were not included in the survey.

**Table 5.1.   Number of Participants, Age, and Gender
by Type of Service Experience**

| | *Type of Service* | | | | |
	No Service Requirement	*Service-Learning*	*40 Hours of CS**	*40 Hours of CS* and Service-Learning*	*Total*
N	25	49	24	26	124
Average Age	46	40	33	30	42
Gender					
Male	18	39	15	22	94
Female	7	10	8	4	29

* Community Service

Materials

For this study, an alumni survey was developed by the principal investigators. The survey consisted of four sections:

1. Demographic information included questions about date of birth and gender;
2. Education asked the participants about their academic degree, date of graduation, major, and several questions regarding the type and quality of the service-learning experience they had during the college years;
3. Employment focused on questions related to the first employment position after graduation and the current position; and
4. Community service experience addressed questions related to civic leadership activities, community service hours and activities, and whether the community service was a requirement for college education.

A pilot study tested the effectiveness of the survey. Feedback was used to adjust and clarify ambiguous questions. Administration time was approximately 15 minutes.

Procedures

The survey and a letter outlining the purpose of the study and procedures for completing the survey were reviewed and approved by the Institutional Review Board of the participating college. The survey and letter were mailed to 775 alumni based on information provided by the Office of Institutional Advancement. Of the 775 surveys mailed to alumni, 139 (17.9%) were returned, of which 124 were used in the data analysis.

RESULTS

The number of participants in each of the groups was equally balanced, χ^2 = 14.00, df = 3, $p < .005$. There was a significant difference among the groups regarding their age, $F(42,122)$ = 4.77, $p < .0001$. There was no significant difference between the groups regarding gender, χ^2 = 3.116, $df = 3, p > .5$.

Analysis of Career Development and Employment Choices

Correlational analyses were used to test the hypotheses on employment choices and job placement (Hypotheses 1 through 5). Hypothesis #1, that a relationship exists between *having the service-learning experience* and *the offer of postgraduate employment related to the experience*, was supported by the findings (r = .396, $p < .001$, $N = 109$). Thirty-two percent of the alumni who participated in a service-learning experience received offers from a placement, and 62.5% of them accepted the offer to work at that placement. Participation in the service-learning experience was related to being offered jobs from such experiences (compared to other types of service).

The results supported Hypothesis #2 that a positive relationship exists between the *quality of the service-learning experience* and accepting *the first job after graduation* (r = .440, $p < .05$, $N = 24$). Fifty-eight percent of all of the alumni who rated the service-learning experience *very good* accepted the offers from the placement, while 18% of the alumni who rated the service-learning experience poor, neutral, or good accepted postgraduation positions that they felt were unrelated to their service-learning experiences. The quality of the service-learning experience had an impact on a graduate's acceptance of the first postgraduation job related to such an experience.

Hypothesis #3, that a positive relationship exists between a *student service-learning experience* and *the choice of state for the first job*, was supported (r = .447, $p < .001$, $N = 76$). Eighty-four percent of all the alumni had their service-learning experiences in Pennsylvania and their first employment position in Pennsylvania. The relationship between the *choice of state of present employment* and th*e state where alumni service-learning experience occurred* was also significant ($r = .244, p < .05, N = 67$). Seventy-seven percent of all of the alumni who had their service-learning experience in Pennsylvania were employed in Pennsylvania at the time of the survey. Alumni who participated in service-learning experiences accepted more jobs in the state of Pennsylvania than alumni with other service experiences.

Hypothesis #4, that a relationship exists between *the number of hours a student spends in a service-learning experience* and *the choice of employment site,* was not fully supported by these findings. There was no significant relationship between *the number of hours spent in a service-learning experience* and *receiving an offer of employment,* $r = .118$, $p > .50$, $N = 34$ or *accepting that position,* $r = .042$, $p < .10$, $N = 12$. However, for a small group of alumni, a significant relationship was identified between *the number of hours in the second service-learning experience* and *choice of employment site,* $r = .954$, $p < .005$, $N = 6$. The number of hours spent in the service-learning experience did not seem to affect the offers of employment available postgraduation.

Table 5.2.   Correlations between Major Study Variables

Variables correlated	r	N
Type of service *and* Offer of employment	.396**	109
Quality of service *and* 1st job after graduation	.440*	24
State where service took place *and* State of first job	.447**	76
State where service took place *and* State of current job	.244*	67
Number of hours *and* Offer of employment	.118	34
Number of hours *and* Acceptance of offer	.042	12

Note: * $p < .05$, ** $p < .001$

Analyses of Job Placement, Community Engagement, and Civic Leadership

The goal of the second set of analyses was to determine whether the different types of service requirements as represented by the four groups had an effect on job placement, community engagement, and civic leadership.

The results of ANOVA supported Hypothesis #5, that more graduates with a service-learning experience (groups 2 and 4) choose an employment site related to the experience than those in group 3 who participated in 40-hour community service or those in group 1 who had no service requirement. One ANOVA was conducted with the first postgraduation job placement of respondents as the dependent variable and the type of service requirement as the independent variable. The main effect for the type of service requirement was significant, $F(3, 105) = 6.625$, $p < .0001$. Post-hoc analysis indicated a significant difference regarding the choice of first employment site and service-learning experience among alumni in group 4 with a combination 40 hours of community service and service-learning experiences when compared to group 1 alumni with no service requirement and those in group 3 with 40 hours of service requirement.

Another ANOVA was conducted with present job placement as dependent variable and the type of service requirement as independent variable. The main effect for the relationship between the present job placement and type of service requirement was significant, $F(3,88) = 9.052$, $p < .001$. Post hoc analysis identified significant differences among all of the four different types of service. These results, combined with previous correlational analysis (Hypothesis #2), indicated that first and present employment were more related to service-learning experiences than other types of service.

The results of this study partially supported Hypothesis #6, that alumni with a service-learning experience (groups 2 and 4) engaged in more community service postgraduation than alumni in group 3 who participated in a 40-hour community service requirement or those in group 1 who had no service requirement. Three measures were used to identify engagement: rate of participation, number of postgraduate community service hours per year, and type of activity. Regarding rate of participation, in this sample, 72.6% of the alumni participated in community service, while 27.4% of the respondents did not engage in service in the community. The number of postgraduate community service hours per year varied from (0) none (28.4%), (1) between 1 and 40 hours (22%), (2) from 50 to 200 hours (18.3%), (3) from 300 to 600 hours (14.7%), (4) from 700 to 1,500 hours (5.5%), and (5) more than 1,500 hours (11%).

An ANOVA was conducted with the number of postgraduate community service hours per year as dependent variable and the type of service requirement as the independent variable. The main effect for the type of service requirement was significant, $F(3,105) = 5.429$, $p < .005$. Post hoc analysis indicated that the group with the highest number of postgraduate community service hours per year was group 1 who had no service requirement ($M = 549$ hours/year), followed by group 2 with the service-learning experience only ($M = 419$ hours/year), then group 4 with the 40-hour community service requirement and the service-learning experience ($M = 374.4$ hours/year), and finally group 3 with the 40-hour community service requirement ($M = 142.5$ hours/year).

As indicated in the demographic section, the age of the participants was significantly different for each group. An ANOVA was conducted with the number of postgraduate community service hours per year as dependent variable and type of service requirement and age of the alumni as independent variables. The main effect for the type of service requirement was significant, $F(3,105) = 2.962$, $p < .05$, and the interaction between the type of service requirement and age was also significant, $F(8,105) = 2.017$, $p < .01$. Post-hoc analysis indicated that the older alumni listed more postgraduate community service hours per year than the younger alumni. Alumni in group 1, who had no service requirement, reported $M = 549$ hours/year, and the alumni with service-learning experience (group 2) reported $M = 419$ hours/year. However, for the younger alumni, the group with the combination community service and service-learning experience (group 4) reported more postgraduate community service hours per year ($M = 374.4$ hours) than the group with the 40-hours of community service requirement only (group 3, $M = 142.5$ hours/year). This hypothesis was partially supported; even though the service-learning experience did not have a significant impact on the number of postgraduate community service hours for the older alumni, it made a difference for the younger ones.

Another measure of community engagement used in this study was the type of community service activity reported by the alumni. A list of 32 activities was provided in the survey, of which the alumni selected 13 (the mode was "other" with 50.4% of the responses, which consisted of a combination of activities, followed by recreation with 4.8%, ministry with 3.6%, and others).

An ANOVA with community service activities as dependent variable and the type of service requirement as the independent variable indicated no significant main effect for the type of service requirement, $F(3,81) = 1.84$, $p = .146$.

The findings of this study did not support Hypothesis #7, that alumni with a service-learning experience (groups 2 and 4) are more likely to engage in civic leadership activities after graduation than group 3 alumni who participated in a 40-hour community service requirement or group 1 alumni who had no service requirement. An ANOVA with civic leadership as the dependent variable and the type of service requirement as independent variable indicated no significant main effect for the type of service requirement, $F(3,118) = 1.00$, $p > .10$. No main effect was identified for age ($F(5,118) = .514$, $p > .5$) and no interaction was identified for age ($F(8,118) = 1.265$, $p > .10$).

An ANOVA with civic leadership as the dependent variable and the number of postgraduate community service hours per year as the independent variable revealed a significant main effect of number of hours of community service, $F(5,107) = 2.88$, $p < .05$. The alumni with more postgraduate community service hours per year indicated participation in more civic leadership activities listed. In summary, the older alumni reported more postgraduation community service hours and more leadership activities.

Table 5.3.   Analysis of Variance for Major Study Variables

Independent and Dependent Variables	F	df
Type of service and first job placement	6.625**	3, 105
Type of service and present job placement .	9.052**	3, 88
Type of service and number of postgraduate CS[a] hours/year	5.429*	3, 105
Type of service, age, and number of postgraduate CS hours/year		
Main effect	2.962*	3, 105
Interaction	2.017*	8, 105
Type of service and CS activity	1.84	3, 81
Type of service and civic leadership	1.00	3, 118
Number of hours of CS and leadership activities	2.88	5, 107

Note: * $p < .05$, ** $p < .001$. [a] Community Service

DISCUSSION

The results of this study suggested that service-learning experiences are a significant factor in alumni postgraduate employment choices and the type of postgraduate community engagement. The results supported several of the hypotheses proposed. Interestingly, the strongest and most significant results were found in testing the hypotheses related to Krumboltz's (1994) theory of career development.

First, students involved in service-learning experiences frequently received an offer of employment from the experience. Second, the quality of the service-learning experience, as rated by the alumni, was directly related to the acceptance of an offer of employment (see also Eyler & Giles, 1999). These findings are consistent with Krumboltz's (1994) position that environmental factors, such as the number and variety of job and training opportunities, influence career choice through positive learning experiences with models in the occupation.

Third, students involved in service-learning experiences were more likely to accept employment positions in service-related areas. While it can be argued that these students were already interested in a service-related occupation prior to the service-learning experience, the Krumboltz (1994) theory suggests that students' skills, values, and interests can change as a result of the reinforcements or lack of positive reinforcements they receive in the work environment. If students are positively reinforced for their efforts and observe valued role models being positively reinforced for their work activities, they are more likely to choose to accept rather than reject a position in a service-related field. Additionally, this finding may be of interest to institutions with a commitment to service as an outcome measure of the effectiveness of their mission statement. The personal, social, and educational outcomes of service-learning validate the mission statements of most colleges with a tradition of service.

Fourth, another interesting result of this study was that students who were involved in a service-learning experience in Pennsylvania took positions in the state. Tom Ridge, the former governor of Pennsylvania, developed an initiative called the Brain Gain that supported internship experiences in an attempt to reverse the loss of young professionals in the state each year. Our data suggest that adding the social reflection component to internship experiences could be an important component in reducing the *brain drain* on state resources and a way to encourage highly trained professionals to remain in the state where they received their education.

Fifth, the findings also indicated that alumni do increasingly more community service per year as the postgraduation time increases. There are several probable explanations for these findings. First, consistent with prior research in the area, it may simply be a function of having more time as the pressures of early professional career life diminish. Second, it could also be related to Erikson's (1968) theory of generativity that stated as adults pass through life stages, particularly during the ages of 40 to 60, there is a desire to leave a legacy to the next generation. This often takes the form of parenting, teaching, leading, and participating in activities that benefit the community. Third, it is also possible that more recent graduates have enrolled in graduate school, a factor not considered in this survey. Recent graduates who are attending graduate school may not be involved in community service activities due to academic pressures and time constraints.

The number of community service hours per year was a complex variable to describe. Even though the older alumni reported more hours of community service hours per year, the group of alumni that graduated after 1991 still performed significantly above the average for the general population. Lopez (2003) referred to this as episodic volunteering compared to regular volunteering. Group 4, younger alumni with the combination of the 40-hour community service requirement and the service-learning experience, reported an average of 374 hours of service per year to the community, compared to Group 3, alumni with the 40-hour community service requirement, which reported 142 hours per year of community service. The combined service-learning experience and the 40-hour graduation service requirement seemed to have had a stronger impact on postgraduate participation in community activities than the 40-hour community service requirement alone. These findings support Dewey's (1938) vision of higher education as instrumental in developing engaged citizens, specifically in the area of social responsibility. As discussed by Keeter, Andolina, Jenkins, and Zukin (2002), attending a school that arranged service work was one of the factors that led to greater postgraduate civic engagement (p. 13).

Sixth, the results indicate a higher rate of participation in community service activities than what has been found in the general population. The reports for civic engagement vary in the literature, but for the general population the engagement rate was 31.7% of those 15 years old and older who reported on volunteering (Lopez, 2003) or 48% of the population being categorized as disengaged (Andolina et al., 2003). The alumni in this study reported a community service participation rate of 72.6% for all respondents. The younger group reported a 63.5% rate of participation. These results support current research that cites education as a significant predictor in future community service activities.

Seventh, this study found that alumni who engage in a higher number of postgraduate community service hours per year are more likely to accept positions of civic leadership in the community. Using Westheimer and Kahne's (2003) visions of citizenship, most respondents in this study fell into the categories of the personally responsible citizen and the participatory citizen. Few respondents identified activities in the area of the justice-oriented citizen. However, these leadership skills require training and time, something that might be unfair to expect of someone 20 years old. Thus, involving younger students in service-learning experiences may provide a bridge to more mature leadership activities.

The methodology characteristics of this study strengthened the results and conclusions. The responses covered 41 years of postgraduation experiences since the participants graduated between 1961 and 2002. Twenty-one different majors were represented in our sample, with a balance between the number of majors that required or did not require a service-learning experience, allowing for the analysis of four different types of service.

The major limitation of this study was that the results might only be generalizable to small private institutions with a similar commitment to service. As suggested by Kahne, Westheimer, and Rogers (2000), important research questions remain regarding the impact of an institution's size, religious mission, and funding base on its civic mission and service-learning opportunities.

A second methodological limitation was the use of a survey that implied an expected response rate of 15% to 20%. This methodology raises issues about the characteristics of alumni who did not return the surveys. Besides, the self-report format is always subject to response selection bias.

Another limitation is the fact that the students who select service-learning experiences are generally more interested in service-related occupations. Consequently, the direction of the relationship between service-learning experiences and job opportunities is unclear. Due to the correlational nature of the study, the causal effects of service-learning on job selection could not be identified.

The results of this study could significantly be strengthened by additional research that compares the effects of service-learning experiences among institutions of similar size and religious mission. Studies might also consider the type of citizenship skills being developed by specific service-learning experiences.

Another interesting question related to this finding is the effect of the cohort on the results. It is possible that the baby boomers who would comprise the oldest respondents in this study were more likely to engage in community service than the "generation X'ers," who would represent the younger participants in this study. Follow-up studies on the alumni who graduated after 1991 may determine if their level of community involvement increases as a function of age and perhaps generativity. The level of postgraduation service commitment of current college students known as the "Millennials" is yet to be determined.

This study would be further enhanced by a qualitative analysis of the effects of service-learning experiences on career decision making. Consequently, a final recommendation is to utilize methodology that incorporates mix-designs to develop a body of literature on causal effects of undergraduate service-learning programs on postgraduate employment choices, community engagement, and civic leadership.

CONCLUSION

In conclusion, the results of this study offer support for service-learning as an important tool in the development of employment choices and civic leadership. Alumni with a history of high-quality service-learning experiences were more likely to accept employment in service-related fields. In addition, alumni with a history of service-learning did increasingly more volunteer service as they got older. Although these results represent only one small sample of participants in service-learning experiences from a small college with a strong mission to service, they do provide an impetus for further research into this area.

ACKNOWLEDGMENT

This project described in this chapter was supported in part by a grant from Pennsylvania Campus Compact (2003, Spring).

REFERENCES

Alvernia College. (2003). Catalog. Retrieved June 16, 2004, from http://www.alvernia.edu/about/mission.htm

Andolina, M., Keeter, S., Zukin, C., & Jenkins, K. (2003). *A guide to the index of civic and political engagement.* College Park, MD: The Center for Information and Research on Civic Learning and Engagement.

Astin, A. W., Sax, L. J., & Avalos, J. (1999). Long-term effects of volunteerism during the undergraduate years. *The Review of Higher Education. 22,* 187–202.

Astin, A. W., Vogelgesang, L. J., Ikeda, E. K., & Yee, J. A. (2000). *How service-learning affects students: Executive summary.* Los Angeles: University of California Higher Education Research Institute.

Billig, S. H. (2000, May). Research on K–12 school-based service-learning: The evidence builds. *Phi Delta Kappan, 81*(9), 658–665.

Boyte, H. C., & Farr, J. (2000, May). The work of citizenship and the problem of service-learning. *Campus Compact Reader, 1*(1), 1, 4–10. Retrieved June 14, 2004, from http://www.compact.org/publication/Reader/Reader-V1-I1.pdf

Bringle, R. G., & Hatcher, J. A. (1995). A service learning curriculum for faculty. *Michigan Journal of Community Service Learning, 2,* 112–122.

Bringle, R. G., & Hatcher, J. A. (2000, Fall). Meaningful measurement of theory-based service-learning outcomes: Making the case with quantitative research. *Michigan Journal of Community Service Learning,* 68–75.

Dewey, J. (1916). *Democracy and education.* New York: Macmillan.

Dewey, J. (1938). *Experience and education.* New York: MacMillan.

Erikson, E. (1968). *Identity: Youth and crisis.* New York: Norton.

Eyler, J., & Giles, D. E. (1999). *Where's the learning in service-learning?* San Francisco: Jossey Bass.

Eyler, J., Giles, D. E., & Braxton, J. (1997). The impact of service-learning on college students. *Michigan Journal of Community Service Learning, 4,* 5–15.

Eyler, J., Giles, D. E., & Gray, C. (1999). *At a glance: Summary and annotated bibliography of recent service-learning research in higher education.* Minneapolis, MN: Learn and Serve America National Service-Learning Clearinghouse.

Furco, A. (2002). Issues of definition and program diversity in the study of service-learning. In S. H. Billig & A. S. Waterman (Eds.), *Studying service-learning: Innovations in education research methodology* (pp. 13–33). Mahwah, NJ: Lawrence Erlbaum Associates.

Furco, A., & Billig, S. H. (2002). Establishing norms for scientific inquiry in service–learning. In A. Furco & S. H. Billig (Eds.), *Advances in service-learning research: Vol. 2. Service-learning through a multidisciplinary lens* (pp. 13–32). Greenwich, CT: Information Age.

Gray, M. J., Ondaatje, E. H., & Zakaras, L. (1999). *Combining service and learning in higher education: Summary Report.* Santa Monica, CA: RAND.

Kahne, J., Westheimer, J., & Rogers, B. (2000, Fall). Service-learning and citizenship: Directions for research.. *Michigan Journal of Community Service Learning,* 1–19.

Keeter, S., Andolina, M., Jenkins, K., & Zukin, C. (2002, August–September). *Schooling and civic engagement in the U.S.* Presentation at the annual meeting of the American Political Science Association, Boston.

Kirlin, M. K. (2003). *Civic engagement in central Indiana: Youth activities key to future.* Indianapolis: Indiana University-Purdue University Indianapolis. Center for Urban Policy and the Environment. Retrieved June 9, 2004, from http://www.urbancenter.iupui.edu/reports/CivicEngagement.pdf

Kolb, D. A. (1984). *Expanding learning: Experience as a source of learning and development.* Englewood Cliffs, NJ: Prentice Hall.

Korn, J. S. (1999). *Contribution to society among graduates of the University of Washington.* University of Washington OEA: Research & Assessment Reports, 99–10. Retrieved May 23, 2004, from http://www-world.cac.washington.edu/oea/9910.htm

Krumboltz, J. D. (1994). Improving career development theory from a social learning perspective. In M. L. Savickas & R. W. Lent (Eds.), *Convergence in career development theories: Implications for science and practice* (pp. 9–31). Palo Alto, CA: Consulting Psychologist Press.

Krumboltz J. D., Mitchell, A., & Gellat, H. G. (1975). Applications of social learning theory of career development. *Focus on Guidance, 8*(3), 1–16.

Krumboltz, J. D., & Worthington, R. L. (1999). The school to work transition from a learning theory perspective. *The Career Development Quarterly, 47,* 312–325.

Lopez, M. H. (2003, June). *Volunteering among young people.* College Park: University of Maryland, The Center for Information & Research on Civic Learning & Engagement, School of Public Affairs.

Mitchell, L. K., & Krumboltz, J. D. (1984). Social learning approach to career decision making: Krumboltz theory. In D. Brown & L. Brooks (Eds.), *Career choice and development: Applying contemporary theories to practice* (pp. 235–280). San Francisco: Jossey-Bass.

Mitchell, L. K., & Krumboltz, J. D. (1990). Social learning approach to career decision making: Krumboltz theory. In D. Brown & L. Brooks (Eds.), *Career choice and development: Applying contemporary theories to practice* (pp. 145–196). San Francisco: Jossey-Bass.

Patrick, J. J. (1998). *Education for engagement in civic society and government.* (ERIC Document Reproduction Service No. ED423211)

Sax, L. J. (2000). Citizenship development and the American college student. In T. Ehrlich (Ed.). *Civic responsibility and higher education.* Phoenix, AZ: Oryx Press

Toole, J., & Toole, P. (1992). *Key definitions used: Commonly used terms in the youth service field.* St. Paul, MN: National Youth Leadership Council.

Westheimer, J., & Kahne, J. (2003, Winter). What kind of citizen? Political choices and educational goals. *Campus Compact Reader,* 1–13. Retrieved June 14, 2004, from http://www.compact.org/publication/Reader/Winter_2003.pdf

EFFECTS OF INTERCULTURAL SERVICE-LEARNING EXPERIENCES ON INTELLECTUAL DEVELOPMENT AND INTERCULTURAL SENSITIVITY

Peggy Fitch

ABSTRACT

This quasi-experimental study examined effects of service-learning and cultural course content on undergraduates' intellectual development and intercultural sensitivity for four types of courses: (1) cultural content plus intercultural contact/service-learning; (2) service-learning only; (3) cultural content only; and (4) no cultural content or service-learning. Participants ($N = 92$) completed pre- and post-test versions of the *Learning Environment Preferences* (Moore, 1989), the *Intercultural Development Inventory* (Hammer & Bennett, 2001), and the *Modern Racism Scale* (McConahay, 1986). Course group predicted Acceptance/Adaptation in a linear regression. Pre-/post-test differences were not statistically significant, though means were in

New Perspectives in Service-Learning: Research to Advance the Field, pages 107–126

expected directions. Compared with the other groups, a greater percentage of individuals in the cultural content plus intercultural contact/service-learning group both decreased in Denial/Defense and increased in Acceptance/Adaptation. Regression analyses suggest that intercultural sensitivity leads to intellectual development.

INTRODUCTION

Eyler and Giles (1999) proposed that two common goals for service-learning experiences include advancing students' critical thinking skills and increasing their openness to perspectives that differ from their own. This chapter describes models of intellectual development and the development of intercultural sensitivity and discusses the theoretical connections between them. Empirical research on the effects of service-learning on each of these potential student outcomes is included.

INTELLECTUAL DEVELOPMENT

Perry's (1968/1999) scheme of intellectual and ethical development described how college students come to reason more complexly about knowledge, truth, learning, and commitment. Perry's scheme is a developmental model that includes nine positions within four broad stages; as such, higher positions and stages reflect more complex perspectives. In the first stage, Dualism (Positions 1 and 2), students view all knowledge as black and white. Multiplicity is the second stage, during which students begin to see that knowledge includes some "gray" areas and that multiple theories and perspectives about the same issue exist. Early in this stage (Position 3), they assume that these gray areas are things we do not know yet, but will someday. Later in this stage (Position 4), students realize that the gray areas are actually fairly large and include things we might never know. Because there seem to be no right and wrong answers, anyone's opinion is as good as another's. Not until stage three, Contextual Relativism (Positions 5 and 6), do students fully understand that nearly all knowledge is constructed in specific and limited contexts; as such, it is relative to a particular set of conditions and parameters.

Moreover, there are standards for judging the adequacy of opinions and these standards depend upon the specific context. For example, one might use principles of the scientific method to judge the conclusions of a medical research study, whereas judgments about paintings or poems would be based on principles of aesthetics particular to these forms of artistic expression.

Moore (1994) described the transition between Multiplicity and Contextual Relativism as

perhaps the most fundamental shift in one's perspective—from a vision of the world as essentially dualistic, with a growing number of exceptions to the rule in certain specific situations, to the exact opposite vision of a world as essentially relativistic and context-bound with a few right/wrong exceptions. (p. 49)

Stage four, Commitment within Relativism (Positions 7, 8, and 9), is qualitatively different from the three prior stages in that the changes that occur involve ethical and identity development more than cognitive or intellectual development. In this stage individuals are faced with the challenge of making commitments that reflect their identities—to an area of study, a career, a relationship, a value system—within an essentially relativistic world. Moore (1994) noted that although students in Perry's (1968/1999) original sample reflected perspectives found in stage four, most researchers agree that stage four is not typically seen in undergraduate students.

Some researchers have used Perry's (1968/1999) scheme or related theoretical models to analyze service-learning experiences. McEwen (1996) described how students at different stages on Perry's scheme might respond to service-learning experiences. Those in transition between Dualism and Early Multiplicity think simplistically and concretely and do not see themselves or peers as agents in their own learning. By contrast, students in Late Multiplicity see themselves and peers as active makers of meaning, but do not understand why professors ask them for evidence to support their opinions.

The chapter on critical thinking in Eyler and Giles's (1999) report of two national studies of service-learning cogently explored how intellectual development is related to students' understanding of complex social problems. They used King and Kitchener's (1994) reflective judgment model, which is derived from Perry's (1968/1999) scheme, to illustrate the evolutions in students' conceptions of causes and solutions for various social problems such as homelessness and AIDS. Students in lower stages of the model saw social problems as having essentially clear definitions and right answers, if only they could find them. By contrast, students in the upper stages of the model understood that social problems are inherently messy and ill defined, have multiple causes, and that appropriate solutions depended on how one defined the problem. They recognized the importance of seeking alternative perspectives and of making a tentative commitment to a solution, but appreciated that the solution could change with new information about the problem.

Olney and Grande (1995) designed the *Scale of Service Learning Involvement* to measure the development of social responsibility in college students as a function of service-learning experiences. They found moderate correlations between stages in their model and subscales on a questionnaire designed to measure Perry's (1968/1999) scheme that were in the directions they predicted. For example, Dualism was positively correlated with Exploration, the lowest stage of social responsibility, and negatively correlated with Internalization, the highest stage of social responsibility. Conversely, Commitment was negatively correlated with Exploration and positively correlated with Internalization.

INTERCULTURAL SENSITIVITY

Bennett (1993) extended Perry's (1968/1999) scheme to the development of intercultural sensitivity and proposed a six-stage model that describes how an individual interprets and responds to cultural differences. The first three stages of the Developmental Model of Intercultural Sensitivity (DMIS) are ethnocentric (Denial, Defense, Minimization), while the last three are ethnorelative (Acceptance, Adaptation, Integration). In Denial, individuals fail to even acknowledge that legitimate cultural differences exist. Instead they view their experience as reality and tend to dehumanize people from other cultures and rely on the most superficial of stereotypes. Defense is characterized by dualistic thinking brought on by the recognition that cultural differences exist. Typically, the greater the contrast between another culture and one's own, the more negative is the view of the other culture. Occasionally, however, the dualism in this stage can lead to a kind of reversal that manifests itself in denigrating one's own culture. Minimization of differences is the hallmark of the next stage, in which the mantra is "After all, we're all human" or "We're all children of God." The emphasis is on similarities; differences are largely ignored or assimilated into familiar categories.

The transition to the next stage, Acceptance, is characterized by a shift from an ethnocentric to an ethnorelative worldview. Different cultures are recognized as legitimate and are accepted as neither good nor bad, just alternative perspectives. Individuals in this stage begin to recognize cultural contexts, though cultural relativity is still largely the norm. Adaptation involves accommodating one's perspective (i.e., frame shifting) or behavior (i.e., code shifting) to be able to communicate across cultural boundaries. Bennett (1998) noted that this stage is "similar to 'contextual relativism' in Perry's terms" (Appendix A, p. 5) and that empathy is a hallmark. In the final stage, Integration, individuals have internalized a truly bicultural or multicultural identity, though they may vary in how comfortable they are with the sense of marginality brought on by the lack of identification with a particular culture. A hallmark of this stage is the acceptance of one's identity development as dynamic and recursive with respect to one's experience of various cultural frames of reference. Bennett (1993) wrote, "the integrated person understands that his or her identity emerges from the act of defining identity, itself" (p. 40). This process enables one to make ethical choices and actions "in the profoundly relativistic world implied by ethnorelative identity" (p. 40). Integration in Bennett's model is, thus, parallel to Perry's (1968/1999) stage of Commitment within Relativism.

Berry (1990) promoted service-learning as a method to enhance intercultural learning. While more empirical research must be conducted, some evidence can be found in the literature to support this assertion. Frazier (1997) described the effects of a service-learning experience in his English composition course. College students, primarily European American and middle class, read aloud stories with multicultural themes to children from a local public elementary school who were primarily African American and Latino. Frazier summarized the outcome:

> All of my students recognized the emphasis on cultural diversity and justice in the books they read, and, for most, it reinforced the legitimacy of college-level readings and discussions of diversity, injustice, and cultural representation, making real what often remains an uneasy abstraction on many privileged campuses. (pp. 101–102)

More specific empirical support is provided by Myers-Lipton (1996) who used a quasi-experimental nonequivalent control group design to study the effect of a comprehensive service-learning experience on college students' racial attitudes. This panel study compared scores on the *Modern Racism Scale* before, during, and after 2 years of service-learning with scores of two comparable control groups: (1) volunteers who were not involved in service-learning, and (2) a random sample of students from the same institution. Myers-Lipton found moderate to strong positive changes in the attitudes of the service-learning group over and above the effects of background variables such as gender, race, political attitudes, and parents' education.

Fitch (1999) compared the cultural attitudes of European American college students involved in two types of service-learning opportunities offered in a child and adolescent development course. The cultural awareness group had direct contact with people from different ethnic or racial groups (e.g., tutored children in inner-city after-school programs). The community group served at sites that offered no contact with other cultural groups (e.g., provided child care during parenting programs). On all comparisons the cultural awareness group demonstrated greater positive change than did the community group. The usual cautions should be applied, however, when these data are considered. The sample size is small ($N = 25$) and students were not randomly assigned to service-learning project groups. Thus the possibility of selection bias is real: those who are more interested in other cultural groups chose such sites and might have been more open to changing their attitudes. Notable here is the observation that some of the pre-test scores were lower for the cultural awareness group than for the community group. Nevertheless, this pilot study provides initial encouragement that service-learning experiences can be designed specifically to enhance cultural awareness.

Boyle-Baise's (2002) qualitative study of multicultural service-learning with preservice teachers illuminated specifically how students make sense of their service-learning experiences and how this meaning-making may affect outcomes related to intercultural sensitivity. The 24 preservice teachers included two African American women, two Latinas, and 20 white students (13 females and 7 males). They were matched with one of six sites that included churches, community centers, a Head Start program, and Girl Scout troops, all of which afforded students direct contact with children from diverse racial/ethnic and socioeconomic backgrounds. Over the course of their service-learning experiences most of the white preservice teachers shifted their perceptions of the children they worked with from deficit notions about parents and poverty to a focus on commonalties expressed by the perspective that *all kids are just kids.* For the male students, however, this shift was easier for those serving in churches, where they had contact with families, than for those placed at community centers. By contrast, most of the preservice teachers of color as well as two white students who had prior experience living in diverse settings had more sophisticated notions about the children they served. That is, they understood that *kids are kids,* but they had more accurate perceptions of the social and economic circumstances of children's lives and did not gloss over these very real differences.

Purpose of the Study

Students' intellectual development has implications for their awareness, tolerance, and openness to other perspectives. Indeed, a fundamental aspect of growth from Dualism to Multiplicity in Perry's (1968/1999) scheme or from Denial/Defense to Minimization in Bennett's (1993) model depends upon the realization that other worldviews exist, and the transition from Multiplicity to Contextual Relativism or from Minimization to Acceptance/Adaptation requires that the student accept these multiple worldviews as legitimate within their particular contexts. Thus, both intellectual development and intercultural . sensitivity are inherently entwined with students' experiences with others who are demonstrably different from them. One question asked in this research is whether one of these lines of development leads the other.

This study uses a quasi-experimental nonequivalent control group design to examine the effects of service-learning and cultural course content on college students' intellectual development, intercultural sensitivity, and racial attitudes. Students were invited to participate from four types of courses that varied in their use of service-learning and their explicit inclusion of content designed to address learning about other cultures:

1. Cultural awareness content plus intercultural contact/service-learning;

2. Service-learning only (no intercultural contact);

3. Cultural awareness content only; and

4. No cultural awareness content or service-learning (comparison group).

At the beginning and end of the semester students completed the *Learning Environment Preferences* (LEP) (Moore, 1989), the *Intercultural Development Inventory* (IDI) (Hammer & Bennett, 2001), and the *Modern Racism Scale* (McConahay, 1986). Increases were expected in intercultural sensitivity (IDI) and intellectual development (LEP), and decreases were expected in racism for the courses that integrated cultural awareness content with intercultural contact/service-learning compared with the courses that had neither cultural content nor intercultural contact. The patterns of changes for the "service-learning only" and "cultural content only" courses were expected to fall between these two.

METHOD

Participants

Participants were 92 undergraduates (74 females, 18 males) from Central College, a small, co-ed, liberal arts institution located in Pella, Iowa, and affiliated with the Reformed Church in America. Eighty-five percent of the students who attend the institution are from Iowa. All students in the sample were between 18 and 22 years old (modal age = 20). Breakdown by year in school was: 9% freshman; 53% sophomore; 30% junior; 9% senior. The majority of participants identified their ethnic/racial background as European American (76.4%); other identities included 7.6% other (e.g., "American"); 6.7% European; 5.4% European American and American Indian; 2.2% Asian American; and 1.1% Hispanic/Latino/American. Self-reported estimates of parents' income (63% earned between $30,000 and $75,000), mothers' education (20.7% high school; 67.4% some college or college degree), and fathers' education (30.4% high school; 55.4% some college or college degree) reflected a predominately middle- to upper-middle-class socioeconomic status for the sample. Concerning participants' prior experience with service-learning and/or volunteerism, more than half (56.5%) reported having had one or two courses that included service-learning, community service, and/or volunteerism; 21.7% had none) and a little more than 63% had volunteered between once and a few times during the past year; 8.7% had not volunteered at all. Of those who had volunteered, half had spent 1 to 15 hours of their time in service during the past year.

Students were invited to participate from 10 classes. All were volunteers and signed an informed consent agreement that conformed to the American Psychological Association's ethical standards. In four of the 10 classes the professor offered students extra credit for participation. As an incentive and to show appreciation, $40 was offered to each class from which at least half the students participated; five classes received this token of appreciation. In addition, individual students had a chance to win $25 if they completed the pre-test and the post-test; three names were drawn after post-test data were collected.

Measures

A pilot study was conducted during the semester prior to data collection to

1. Compare two different measures of intercultural sensitivity;
2. Check for social desirability; and
3. Refine the phrasing of demographic items.

A sample of 75 undergraduates (59 females, 16 males) in psychology courses completed the LEP (Moore, 1989), Helms and Carter's (1990) *White Racial Identity Attitude Scale* (WRIAS), the *Modern Racism Scale* (McConahay, 1986), and Paulhaus's (1991) *Balanced Inventory of Desirable Responding* (BIDR, Version 6, Form 40A). Scores on the BIDR were within normal range and did not indicate a pattern of socially desirable responding. A comparison of students' responses to the WRIAS and the *Modern Racism Scale* led to the selection of the latter inventory as a more general, valid, and reliable measure of intercultural sensitivity, not the least because the WRIAS assumes the respondent is white.

Intercultural Sensitivity

Two questionnaires were used to measure intercultural sensitivity. The IDI (Hammer & Bennett, 2001) measured the development of an individual's perceptions about, and responses to, people from other cultures and was based on Bennett's (1993) Developmental Model of Intercultural Sensitivity. It comprised six subscales of 10 items each (60 items total). Participants rated their level of agreement with each item on a 7-point scale (1 = strongly disagree to 7 = strongly agree). Ratings were averaged for each subscale, thus scores ranged from 1 to 7. For the purposes of this study the subscales were combined into three broad stages: Denial/Defense, Minimization, and Acceptance/Adaptation (Cognitive and Behavioral). Sample items are shown in Table 6.1.

Table 6.1.   Sample Items From the Learning Environment Preferences (LEP) and Intercultural Development Inventory (IDI)

Learning Environment Preferences (LEP)	
	My ideal learning environment would...
Dualism	... emphasize basic facts and definitions.
Early Multiplicity	... stress the practical applications of the material.
Late Multiplicity	... allow me a chance to think and reason, applying facts to support my opinions.
Contextual Relativism	... emphasize learning simply for the sake of learning or gaining new experience.
Intercultural Development Inventory (IDI)	
Denial	I do not like to be around people who look like they are from other cultures.
Defense	My culture is closer to being perfect than most other cultures in the world.
Minimization	All people are basically the same.
Acceptance	People should not describe culture as superior or inferior.
Cognitive Adaptation	I use different cultural criteria for interpreting and evaluating situations.
Behavioral Adaptation	Although I feel I am a member of my own culture, I am nearly as comfortable in one or more other cultures.

The second measure of intercultural sensitivity was the *Modern Racism Scale* (McConahay, 1986), which was labeled "Social Attitudes Scale" on the questionnaires. Participants rated their level of agreement with seven statements on a 5-point scale where 1 = strongly disagree and 5 = strongly agree (e.g., "Discrimination against blacks is no longer a problem in the United States."); and two statements on a 4-point scale where 1 = none and 4 = many (e.g., "How many black people in Iowa do you think miss out on jobs or promotions because of racial discrimination?"). Scores ranged from 9 to 43. Higher scores indicated more racist attitudes.

Intellectual Development

The LEP (Moore, 1989) was an objective measure of intellectual development per Perry's (1968/1999) scheme. It included five domains of 13 items each, for a total of 65 items:

1. Course Content/View of Learning;
2. Role of Instructor;
3. Role of Student/Peers;
4. Classroom Atmosphere/Activities; and
5. Evaluation Procedures.

One item in each domain was a foil phrased in a sophisticated, but meaningless way intended to identify respondents who answer in a socially desirable fashion. The other 12 items were keyed to Perry's scheme stages of Dualism (Position 2), Early Multiplicity (Position 3), Late Multiplicity (Position 4), and Contextual Relativism (Position 5); Commitment within Relativism was not indexed by the LEP (see Table 6.1 for sample items keyed to each stage). Students rated the significance of each item for their own learning on a 4-point scale where 1 = not at all significant and 4 = very significant. They also ranked the top three items in each domain. These ranked items were scored to obtain four position subscores, which were proportions that ranged from 0 to 1.00, as well as a total Cognitive Complexity Index (CCI) that ranged from 200 to 500.

DESIGN

Students were invited to participate from four types of courses that varied in their emphasis on cultural awareness content and use of intercultural contact in the form of service-learning or experiential learning that met the same criteria, even if it was not explicitly referred to as such. The criteria for service-learning required sustained contact with members of a community or agency usually over the course of the semester plus integration with the course through some kind of written and/or oral assignment, usually in the form of a paper, report, project, or journal. None of the courses simply involved volunteer work that was not integrated into courses. Courses were identified based on their liberal arts core designations and on the researcher's familiarity with faculty who were using service-learning. The researcher obtained syllabi and interviewed the faculty who taught each course to learn specifically what intercultural contact entailed and to confirm whether courses had been assigned to the appropriate groups. All courses were offered at the sophomore (200) or junior (300) level; none were required for all students, though some were required for students in that major. Given that students were not randomly assigned to groups, a quasi-experimental nonequivalent control group design was used and attempts to control for potential selection bias were implemented in the data analysis.

Cultural Awareness Content Plus Intercultural Contact/Service-Learning

All courses in this group included opportunities for intercultural contact that were integrated into cultural course content; as such, they were explicitly designed to meet the liberal arts core requirements of experiential learning and cultural awareness, which requires at least 15 hours of intercultural contact. Students in Ethnic Encounters met weekly to develop relationships with members of a particular ethnic community. Examples included socializing with Bosnian or Sudanese refugees in their homes, interacting with children in a daycare center for Hispanic/Latino families, and participating in group activities for African American young women served by a community service agency. Integration with the course material included a 12-page paper, oral presentation, class discussions, and individual meetings with the professor. Intermediate Spanish students were matched with members of the Hispanic/Latino community to help adults complete immigration paperwork or practice English, or to work with children in a daycare or after-school program. Integration with course material included six papers written in Spanish, as well as an oral proposal conducted in Spanish and delivered to the class members who functioned as a hypothetical council with funds to dispense to the agency or community with whom the student worked. Students in Human Relations led lessons or group activities with children from the Sac and Fox American Indian tribes on the Meskwaki reservation or with African American children in an urban setting. They also hosted the children during a visit to the college. Students kept a weekly journal and turned in their lesson plans. The last course in this group was Managing and Valuing Cultural Diversity. The intercultural contact students selected in this course involved attending biweekly meetings with the organization for gay, lesbian, bisexual, transgender students, and allies. Though this experience did not involve contact with a different ethnic/racial group, it still served to get students outside of their comfort zones as described on their post-test questionnaires. Students reflected on their experiences through journals and class discussion.

Service-Learning Only (No Intercultural Contact)

This group included two courses that integrated service-learning projects that do not explicitly involve contact with other cultural groups.

Students in Psychological Investigations conducted research projects for local agencies, such as a survey of residents' satisfaction with an assisted living facility for older adults, college students' awareness of services offered by Planned Parenthood, and neighbors' perceptions of a transitional living facility in an urban area. Course integration included using research skills and working with agencies to design and implement the projects, writing a group research report, and orally presenting the results to students, faculty, and agency representatives. Adapted Physical Education students participated in two service-learning projects that involved working with individuals that have disabilities: weekly bowling sessions with adults at a local assisted-living facility and organizing a mini-Olympics day for children aged 4 to 8 years. They designed individualized education plans for each group and journaled about their experiences.

Cultural Awareness Content Only

Courses in this group included Intercultural Communication and Cultural Anthropology. Both courses fulfilled the liberal arts core requirement for cultural awareness. Neither integrated intercultural contact as a requirement in the course.

No Cultural Awareness Content or Service-Learning (Comparison Group)

This group served as the control/comparison condition and included Theories of Personality and Introduction to Business Management. Content related to culture comprised less than 10% of either course and no intercultural contact or service-learning opportunities were offered.

PROCEDURE

At the beginning and end of the semester students completed the LEP (Moore, 1989), the IDI (Hammer & Bennett, 2001), the *Modern Racism Scale* (McConahay, 1986), and answered demographic items. These pre-test and post-test sessions were conducted outside of class. Of the 139 students who took the pre-test, 47 (21 males and 26 females, or 35%) were dropped because of missing information on their questionnaires or because they did not complete the post-test. Thus, the final sample size was 92.

RESULTS

Multiple linear regression with backward elimination was used to test hypotheses about the theoretical connections between intellectual development and intercultural sensitivity. Multiple analysis of variance was used to test the hypothesis that courses involving cultural awareness content plus intercultural contact/service-learning would be more effective than service-learning alone, cultural awareness content alone, or the comparison courses. Finally, Pearson correlations were computed between the post-test scores on the LEP, the IDI subscales, and the *Modern Racism Scale,* using an alpha level of .01 after applying Bonferroni's correction (.05/7 tests = .01).

Multiple Regression Analyses

Multiple linear regression analyses with backward elimination were used to determine which variables contributed most to post-test scores on Acceptance/Adaptation, Denial/Defense, intellectual development (LEP:CCI), and racism. Backward elimination was used because there were few if any significant correlations among the predictors. Predictors for each regression always included pre-test scores on the dependent variable, group (i.e., type of course), sex, race, family income, parents' education, age/class, and total volunteer experience (number of service-learning courses + frequency and number of hours volunteered during the past year). In addition, the post-test scores of the other dependent variables were included as predictors (e.g., post-LEP:CCI as a predictor of post-Acceptance/Adaptation, and vice versa). As expected, pre-test scores were the largest significant positive predictors of post-test scores for each dependent variable. In addition, group ($\beta = -.16$, $t = -2.43$, $p = .017$) and total volunteer experience ($\beta = -.14$, $t = -2.01$, $p = .048$) were significant negative predictors of post-Acceptance/Adaptation, $R^2 = .64$, $F(4, 82) = 36.81$, $p < .000$. The negative beta was expected for group and indicates that the highest scores for Acceptance/Adaptation were for the cultural content plus intercultural contact/service-learning group, which was coded 1, and lowest for the comparison group, which was coded 4. However, the negative beta for total volunteer experience was not expected, particularly given that the zero-order correlation between this variable and post-Acceptance/Adaptation as listed in the regression analysis is $r(87) = .042$, $p = .35$. Age/class ($\beta = -.14$, $t = -2.07$, $p = .042$) was a significant negative predictor of post-Denial/Defense, $R^2 = .61$, $F(2, 84) = 66.11$, $p < .000$; post-Acceptance/Adaptation ($\beta = .21$, $t = 2.37$, $p = .02$) was a significant positive predictor of post-intellectual development (LEP:CCI), $R^2 = .35$, $F(3, 82) = 14.47$, $p < .000$; and post-Denial/Defense ($\beta = .28$,

$t = 3.43$, p = .001) was a significant positive predictor of post-racism, R^2 = .65, $F(3, 76)$ = 47.22, $p < .000$.

Analyses of Variance

One-way analyses of variance (ANOVAs) by type of course (4) found no pre-test differences on any measures, thus the groups were equivalent at the beginning of the semester. Multivariate ANOVAs of post-test scores for each dependent variable by type of course (4) using an alpha level of .05 and pre-test scores as covariates were not statistically significant, though means were in expected directions (see Table 6.2). For example, all three experimental groups increased in Acceptance/Adaptation, whereas the comparison group decreased. Similarly, only the group that included both cultural awareness content and intercultural contact decreased in Denial/Defense. Two of the three experimental groups (CA + IC/SL and SL Only) decreased in racism, as did the comparison group. The two experimental groups that included cultural content (CA + IC/SL and CA Only) increased in intellectual development (LEP:CCI).

Descriptive Comparisons

Given that analyses of mean differences can obscure relevant patterns of change, particularly when pre-test scores absorb so much of the variability in post-test scores, comparisons were also made between the percentage of individuals in each group whose scores changed in the directions predicted. As shown in Table 6.3, 35% of individuals in the cultural awareness content plus intercultural contact/service-learning group both decreased in Denial/Defense and increased in Acceptance/Adaptation compared with 19% for the service-learning only and comparison groups and 13% for the cultural awareness only group. The benefit of direct intercultural contact/service-learning appears to come primarily from a decrease in Denial/Defense (53% compared to 25%–39% for the other groups). All three experimental groups had higher percentages of individuals who increased in Acceptance/Adaptation (range = 56%–59%) than did the comparison group (44%).

Correlations

As predicted, Acceptance/Adaptation was positively correlated with intellectual development (LEP:CCI), $r(91)$ = .23, p = .027, and negatively

Table 6.2. Means and (SDs[a]) for Dependent Variables (LEP, IDI, Modern Racism Scale) by Type of Course

DVs	Type of Course				
	CA + IC/SL	SL Only	CA Only	Comparison	All Courses
LEP:CCI[b]					
Pre-test	339.84	345.10	345.79	345.34	344.38
	(32.49)	(47.75)	(45.34)	(45.08)	(42.93)
Post-test	351.75	339.97	357.64	341.30	347.23
	(33.05)	(74.10)	(37.15)	(55.82)	(51.44)
IDI: D/D[c]					
Pre-test	1.91	1.99	2.07	2.35	2.14
	(.59)	(.63)	(.75)	(.78)	(.73)
Post-test	1.87	2.20	2.20	2.44	2.23
	(.65)	(.74)	(.80)	(.83)	(.79)
IDI: Min[d]					
Pre-test	4.28	4.99	4.40	4.48	4.51
	(.99)	(1.02)	(.72)	(.93)	(.92)
Post-test	4.43	4.89	4.57	4.64	4.63
	(1.02)	(.86)	(.74)	(.96)	(.90)
IDI: Ac/Ad[e]					
Pre-test	4.87	4.91	4.91	4.71	4.83
	(.60)	(.55)	(.55)	(.48)	(.55)
Post-test	5.05	4.98	4.97	4.67	4.87
	(.67)	(.68)	(.69)	(.48)	(.62)
Racism					
Pre-test	17.59	17.13	18.00	19.59	18.36
	(4.56)	(4.66)	(4.40)	(6.13)	(5.19)
Post-test	16.56	16.20	18.45	19.19	17.98
	(5.37)	(5.47)	(3.92)	(6.22)	(5.46)

[a] Standard deviations
[b] Learning Environment Preferences: Cognitive Complexity Index
[c] Intercultural Development Inventory: Denial/Defense
[d] Intercultural Development Inventory: Minimization
[e] Intercultural Development Inventory: Acceptance/Adaptation
CA + IC/SL: Cultural Awareness + Intercultural Contact/Service-Learning; SL Only: Service-Learning Only; CA Only: Cultural Awareness Only

Table 6.3.   Percentage of Individuals Whose Scores Changed in Predicted Directions on the Dependent Variables (LEP, IDI, Modern Racism Scale) by Type of Course

DVs	Type of Course			
	CA + IC/SL (n = 17)	SL Only (n = 16)	CA Only (n = 23)	Comparison (n = 36)
Increased Intellectual Development (LEP: CCI[a])	59%	50%	70%	56%
Increased Denial/Defense (IDI: D/D[b])	53%	25%	30%	39%
Increased Acceptance/Adaptation (IDI: Ac/Ad[c])	59%	56%	57%	44%
Both: ↓ IDI: D/D ↑ IDI: Ac/Ad[d]	35%	19%	13%	19%
Decreased Racism	47%	63%	39%	53%

[a] Learning Environment Preferences: Cognitive Complexity Index;
[b] Intercultural Development Inventory: Denial/Defense;
[c] Intercultural Development Inventory: Acceptance/Adaptation
CA + IC/SL: Cultural Awareness + Intercultural Contact/Service-Learning; SL Only: Service-Learning Only; CA Only: Cultural Awareness Only

correlated with racism, $r(90) = -.41$, $p = .000$, whereas Denial/Defense was negatively correlated with intellectual development (LEP:CCI), $r(91) = -.22$, $p = .039$, and positively correlated with racism, $r(90) = .59$, $p = .000$, though the p-values for the LEP did not reach the .01 criterion. Intellectual development (LEP:CCI) was not significantly correlated with racism, $r(89) = -.068$, $p = .53$.

DISCUSSION

A primary question in this research has been to elucidate the direction of the relationship between intellectual development and intercultural sensitivity. The two constructs are both theoretically and empirically related. Indeed, the LEP and IDI both seem to reflect analogous cognitive structures that underlie an individual's construal of meaning about knowledge and truth on the one hand and cultural difference on the other. But can it be determined whether development in one domain leads development in the other? The regression analyses provide a starting point to answer this question. Post-Acceptance/Adaptation scores positively predicted post-intellectual development scores, but the reverse was not found. In fact, post-intellectual development scores were dropped after the first step of the backward regression. Zero-order correlations between pre-tests of one measure and post-tests of the other measure also support the interpretation that the development of intercultural sensitivity may lead intellectual development: Pre-Acceptance/Adaptation is significantly related to post-intellectual development, $r(91) = .27$, $p = .009$, whereas pre-intellectual development is not significantly related to post-Acceptance/Adaptation, $r(91) = .091$, $p = .393$. Thus it appears that being open and willing to adapt one's thinking and behavior to another culture may be a precursor to more sophisticated conceptions of knowledge and truth as context-bound. These findings also imply that intercultural contact through service-learning experiences might be an effective pedagogical tool to promote intellectual development.

Another major research question examined the effects of different types of courses that varied in cultural course content and service-learning, with and without intercultural contact, on intercultural sensitivity, intellectual development, and racism. Type of course (i.e., group) was a significant predictor of the higher stages of intercultural sensitivity (Acceptance/Adaptation), but not of the lower stages (Denial/Defense), intellectual development, or racism. Pre-post changes in intercultural sensitivity and intellectual development as a function of the type of course were in the predicted directions, though several of these differences were not statistically reliable. Given the relatively small and uneven cell sizes (range = 16 to 36), the relatively short time span of one semester, the potential selection bias (students were not randomly assigned to groups), and the conservative use of pre-test scores as covariates to attempt to control for these limitations, the lack of statistically significant results is not surprising. Nevertheless, the trends found suggest that intercultural contact/service-learning integrated into courses that focus on cultural issues may better prepare students to develop intercultural sensitivity and may also promote intellectual development more than courses that have neither of these features. The pattern of means also implies that cultural course content alone and/or service-learning that does not provide intercultural contact may still contribute to intercultural sensitivity, and that cultural content by itself may increase intellectual development. In particular, the decrease in racism found for two of the three experimental groups is consistent with that reported by Myers-Lipton (1996) who used a similar design, though his service-learning experience was longer and more intensive and his study included a randomly selected comparison group.

One finding that is difficult to explain is why total volunteer experience was a negative predictor of Acceptance/Adaptation in the regression analyses. ANOVAs found no differences between the four groups on any of the three items that had been positively correlated and combined for this variable. Moreover, these three items were not significantly correlated with any other demographic variables. Given the institution's church-affiliation and the religious background of a portion of the student body, the author explored the hypothesis that perhaps the finding could be explained by involvement in mission trips, which might be indicated by the item's measuring frequency or number of hours volunteered. This analysis, however, made the pattern even more puzzling. Contrary to what was expected, the number of prior courses that required service-learning accounted for the negative relationship more than did the frequency or number of hours volunteered during the past year. The best explanation for this unexpected finding seems to come from one or more outliers clearly visible in the scatterplot between the number of service-learning courses and Acceptance/Adaptation scores. In any case, the author welcomes any creative interpretation of this counterintuitive finding readers may offer.

Civic engagement in an increasingly diverse society calls for citizens who are intellectually able to consider complex issues as well as being culturally aware and sensitive, minimally, and ideally culturally competent. One contribution of this chapter is the demonstration that intercultural development is likely tied to, and may lead to, intellectual development, and that both might be enhanced through intercultural service-learning experiences that are explicitly connected to cultural course content. O'Grady (2000) noted that, if not done well, such service-learning experiences also have the potential to simply reinforce stereotypes and cultural superiority. Thus, this study raises the following questions for future research:

- How can we best use intercultural service-learning—direct contact and interaction with others who are culturally different from the student and who can present another context for knowing—to facilitate intellectual development and cultural competence?
- What particular advantages and challenges does service-learning present as a type of intercultural experiential learning, and what are the implications of these factors for the design of these experiences?

SUMMARY

This study built on prior empirical research on the effects of service-learning on intellectual development/critical thinking/problem-solving skills (e.g., Eyler & Giles, 1999; Steinke, Fitch, Johnson, & Waldstein, 2002) and on cultural awareness and racial attitudes (e.g., Boyle-Baise, 2002;

Fitch, 1999; Frazier, 1997; Myers-Lipton, 1996). The theoretical basis came from Perry's (1968/1999) scheme of intellectual and ethical development and Bennett's (1993) Developmental Model of Intercultural Sensitivity. Both theories described desirable outcomes of higher education and goals many faculty aspire to achieve with students. Moreover, the results of this study suggested that both outcomes might be enhanced through intercultural service-learning experiences that are integrated into courses that focus explicitly on learning about culture.

ACKNOWLEDGMENTS

The author thanks the Central College Faculty Research and Development Committee for financial support for this project, research assistant Melissa Faber, and the faculty and students involved who gave generously of their time.

REFERENCES

Bennett, M. J. (1993). Towards ethnorelativism: A developmental model of intercultural sensitivity. In R. M. Paige (Ed.), *Education for the intercultural experience* (2nd ed., pp. 21–71). Yarmouth, ME: Intercultural Press.

Bennett, M. J. (1998). Handout: A developmental model of intercultural sensitivity. In M. J. Bennett & M. R. Hammer (Eds.), *The Intercultural Development Inventory (IDI) manual* (Appendix A). Portland, OR: The Intercultural Communication Institute.

Berry, H. A. (1990). Service-learning in international and intercultural settings. In J. C. Kendall & Associates (Eds.), *Combining service and learning: Vol. 1. A resource book for community and public service* (pp. 311–313). Raleigh, NC: National Society for Internships and Experiential Education.

Boyle-Baise, M. (2002). *Multicultural service learning: Educating teachers in diverse communities.* New York: Teachers College Press.

Eyler, J., & Giles, D. E. (1999). *Where's the learning in service-learning?* San Francisco: Jossey-Bass.

Fitch, M. (1999, June). *Specifically designed service-learning experiences promote cultural awareness.* Poster session presented at the annual meeting of the American Psychological Society, Denver, CO.

Frazier, D. (1997, Fall). A multicultural reading and writing experience: Read aloud as service-learning in English class. *Michigan Journal of Community Service Learning,* 98–103.

Hammer, M. R., & Bennett, M. J. (2001). *Intercultural Development Inventory (IDI) Manual.* Portland, OR: Intercultural Communication Institute. (For information about this instrument, contact the institute at 503-297-4622 or ici@intercultural.org)

Helms, J. E., & Carter, R. T. (1990). Development of the White Racial Identity Inventory. In J. E. Helms (Ed.), *Black and white racial identity: Theory, research, and practice* (pp. 67–80). New York: Greenwood Press.

King, P. M., & Kitchener, K. S. (1994). *Developing reflective judgment: Understanding and promoting intellectual growth and critical thinking in adolescents and adults.* San Francisco: Jossey-Bass.

McConahay, J. B. (1986). Modern racism, ambivalence, and the Modern Racism Scale. In J. F. Dovidio & S. L. Gaertner (Eds.), *Prejudice, discrimination and racism* (pp. 91–125). San Diego, CA: Academic Press.

McEwen, M. K. (1996). Enhancing student learning and development through service-learning. In B. Jacoby & Associates (Eds.), *Service-learning in higher education* (pp. 53–91). San Francisco: Jossey-Bass.

Moore, W. S. (1989, November). The Learning Environment Preferences: Exploring the construct validity of an objective measure of the Perry scheme of intellectual and ethical development. *Journal of College Student Development, 30,* 504–514.

Moore, W. S. (1994). Student and faculty epistemology in the college classroom: The Perry scheme of intellectual and ethical development. In K. Prichard & R. M. Sawyer (Eds.), *Handbook of college teaching: Theory and applications* (pp. 45–67). Westport, CT: Greenwood Press.

Myers-Lipton, S. J. (1996, Fall). Effect of a comprehensive service-learning program on college students' level of modern racism. *Michigan Journal of Community Service Learning,* 44–54.

O'Grady, C. R. (2000). *Integrating service-learning and multicultural education in colleges and universities.* Mahwah, NJ: Lawrence Erlbaum Associates.

Olney, C., & Grande, S. (1995). Validation of a scale to measure development of social responsibility. *Michigan Journal of Community Service Learning, 2,* 43–53.

Paulhaus, D. L. (1991). Measurement and control of response bias. In J. P. Robinson, R. P. Shaver, & L. S. Wrightsman (Eds.), *Measures of personality and social psychological attitudes* (pp. 17–59). San Diego, CA: Academic Press.

Perry, W. G. (1999). *Forms of intellectual and ethical development in the college years: A scheme.* New York: Holt, Rinehart and Winston. (Original work published 1968)

Steinke, P., Fitch, P., Johnson, C., & Waldstein, F. (2002). An interdisciplinary study of service-learning predictors and outcomes among college students. In S. H. Billig & A. Furco (Eds.), *Advances in service-learning research: Vol. 2. Service-learning through a multidisciplinary lens* (pp. 171–194). Greenwich, CT: Information Age.

CHAPTER 7

SERVICE-LEARNING TAKEN TO A NEW LEVEL THROUGH COMMUNITY-BASED RESEARCH

A Win–Win for Campus and Community

Brenda Marsteller Kowalewski

ABSTRACT

A community-based research (CBR) project employed as service-learning pedagogy in a research methods course is first described and then evaluated against a well-defined theoretical model. CBR is a form of action research wherein course content is taught and practiced through conducting research for and with a community partner. The perspectives of faculty, students, and community partners are considered in this evaluation. The impact of this service-learning pedagogy on student learning is also assessed using feedback from course evaluations and project evaluations administered to both students and community partners. Findings suggest that the CBR project described in this chapter is a very powerful learning experience for students

New Perspectives in Service-Learning: Research to Advance the Field, pages 127–147
Copyright © 2004 by Information Age Publishing

and produces important outcomes for community partners. This lends support for the assertion that CBR is the penultimate form of service-learning.

Service-learning is a pedagogy that enables students to accomplish course objectives through both classroom and service experiences. Real-world experiences addressing pertinent community issues are at the heart of service-learning. Mintz and Hesser (1996) viewed the fundamental principles of service-learning through what they called lenses of collaboration, reciprocity, and diversity. Through the collaboration lens, Mintz and Hesser suggested that service-learning engages people in responsible and challenging actions for the common good with clearly articulated service and learning goals and opportunities for critical reflection. Through the reciprocity lens, service-learning empowers those with needs to define those needs first and recognizes the needs as dynamic rather than static, thus fostering a genuine, active, and sustained organizational commitment (Mintz & Hesser, 1996). Finally, service-learning through the diversity lens involves participation by and with diverse populations wherein the differences in backgrounds and orientations are viewed as assets (Mintz & Hesser, 1996).

These principles of service-learning are in essence the fundamental principles of community-based research (CBR), a teaching strategy that some have called the "highest stage of service-learning" (Porpora, 1999, p. 121). CBR lends itself to service-learning as it is research that is done *for* and *with* the community, not *on* the community. Students actively engage in providing a service by conducting needed research the community has identified. Simultaneously, students learn and utilize research methodologies and concepts. The many opportunities for collaboration and direct application of course content experienced in CBR have led some to argue that it is the penultimate service-learning pedagogy. Strand, Marullo, Cutforth, Stoecker, and Donohue (2003a, 2003b) proposed three key elements to CBR, which directly mirror the lenses of service-learning described by Mintz and Hesser (1996). The fundamental elements of CBR involve: (1) collaboration; (2) validation of multiple sources of knowledge; and (3) social justice for less empowered populations. These elements are discussed in more detail below. It is important to establish that CBR can be a form of service-learning pedagogy. Consequently, CBR interfaces nicely with service-learning in an introductory research methods course. This approach allows students to learn and apply research methodologies and concepts while providing indirect service in the community.

This chapter describes a CBR project, employed as a pedagogical tool in an upper division research methods course in sociology. This chapter also (a) evaluates the use of CBR in the research methods course against a clearly delineated CBR model proposed by Strand and colleagues (2003a, 2003b); and (b) explores the impact of this CBR project on student learning.

A brief review of CBR and its impact on student learning is discussed. Then the central components of the CBR model are outlined (Strand et al., 2003a). A description of the CBR project employed in the research methods course follows. The methods and results of the evaluation of the CBR project and its impact on student learning are presented. Finally, conclusions about CBR and its relationship to service-learning are drawn.

REVIEW OF COMMUNITY-BASED RESEARCH

Community-based research (CBR) is a form of action-oriented research that can be used as a pedagogical tool. In many regards, CBR is just one of many labels for action-oriented research used today. Historically, Lewin (1948) coined the term *action research* to describe an approach to research that combined theory and practice. In more recent years, a number of different models have been proposed for doing action oriented research (Green et al., 1997; Murphy, Scammell, & Sclove, 1997; Nyden & Wiewel, 1992; Porpora, 1999; Small, 1995; Stoecker, 1999, 2003; Strand, 2000; Strand et al., 2003a; Stringer, 1999). Although each model has its own unique qualities, Stringer (1999) noted the similarities in these models. These include:

- Collaboration with community members;
- Engaging a co-learning process;
- Taking a systemic perspective;
- Capacity building for community groups;
- Challenging existing canons of disciplinary research and pedagogical practice; and
- Striking a balance between research and action (p. 5).

Couto (2003) suggested action research has reached an important developmental point as a field. Many researchers and practitioners have written about action research models and how to employ them (Murphy et al., 1997; Nyden et al., 1997; Porpora, 1999; Stoecker, 1999, 2003; Strand, 2000; Strand, et al., 2003a; Stringer, 1999). However, few researchers have assessed their use of CBR with any specific criteria of these models.

It is important for researchers and practitioners to understand and test the theoretical underpinnings of the action research models (Stoecker, 2003) and assess the challenges employing such models (Ferman & Shlay, 1997; Hite, 1997; McNicoll, 1999). However, it is also important to evaluate the application of the models from the perspectives of all partners involved in the research.

Many action researchers have published their personal reflections on their specific action-oriented research project (Chapdelaine & Chapman,

1999; Gedicks, 1996; Willis, Peresie, Waldref, & Stockmann, 2003). Some have reflected on the challenges employing this pedagogy as well as on the outcomes for students (Chapdelaine & Chapman, 1999; Willis et al., 2003). Much of this research does not focus on the student or community partner experience. However, two studies include the students' perspectives. Chapdelaine and Chapman (1999) used student evaluations with faculty reflections to evaluate a CBR project employed in their class. Willis and colleagues (2003) presented insights from four undergraduates with extensive experience in CBR.

IMPACT OF CBR ON STUDENTS

Reports of the impact of the CBR on students is limited. Ferrari and Jason (1996) investigated the impact of CBR projects on students' attitudes after engaging in projects that were independent research projects. Students reported the CBR project resulted in personal growth, enriched their education, and influenced their career goals. Ferman and Shlay (1997) reported the quality of their students' writing was bolstered by a CBR project. Hite (1997), looking more specifically at student learning, provided limited qualitative evidence from student journals that the CBR employed in her course contributed to accomplishing course objectives. Chapdelaine and Chapman (1999) found evidence that a CBR project positively impacted students learning specific course content and meeting particular course objectives. Willis and colleagues (2003) reported that CBR:

- Enriched traditional academic coursework;
- Provided a sense of empowerment;
- Provided greater understanding of social problems; and
- Integrated academics and service.

Although these studies investigated the impact of CBR on students, they were written mostly from a faculty perspective without considering very much data from the students themselves.

Strand and colleagues (2003b) argued that CBR fundamentally involves critical pedagogy that helps students think critically, become effective agents of change, and realize that their skills and knowledge can be used to help others. Eyler and Giles (1999) provided some evidence that service-learning experiences involving intense reflection and deliberate connections to course content result in more critical thinking among students. If CBR is employed according to the theoretical model, then one would expect similar outcomes to those described by Eyler and Giles; however, this has yet to be explored.

THEORETICAL MODEL OF CBR

Strand and colleagues (2003a) defined CBR as "a partnership of student, faculty, and community members who collaboratively engage in research with the purpose of solving a pressing community problem or effecting social change" (p. 3). Given this definition, Strand and colleagues created a model based on three general principles that differentiates CBR from other traditional academic research.

1. CBR is a collaborative enterprise between researchers (professors and/or students) and community members.
2. CBR validates multiple sources of knowledge and promotes the use of multiple methods of discovery and dissemination of the knowledge produced.
3. CBR has as its goal social action and social change for the purpose of achieving social justice (p. 8).

Collaboration is the element of the CBR model that underscores the fact that CBR is research *with* and *for* the community. Ideally, Strand and colleagues (2003a) suggested that community partners should be working with students and professors at every stage in the research process. The second element of the CBR model has been referred to as democratization of knowledge (Strand et al., 2003b) or new approaches to knowledge (Strand et al., 2003a). Strand and colleagues (2003a) listed four key components to the democratization of knowledge:

1. Knowledge brought to the project by all partners involved is equally valued.
2. Multiple research methods are used.
3. User-friendly approaches to the dissemination of knowledge are provided.
4. Conventional assumptions about knowledge itself are challenged (pp. 11–13).

The last principle of CBR, social action and social change, points to the central purpose for engaging in CBR: to produce information that can be used to bring about needed change. The findings of the research or the process itself might contribute to social change (Strand et al., 2003a).

IMPACT OF CBR AS CRITICAL PEDAGOGY

Using the three principles described earlier, Strand and colleagues (2003b), argued that CBR fundamentally employs critical pedagogy. They suggested critical pedagogy has three goals:

1. A focus on collective or collaborative learning that deemphasizes hierarchy.
2. A demystification of conventional knowledge.
3. Teaching for social change (p. 11).

Accordingly, CBR will help students develop "the capacity to think critically and analytically about existing structures of oppression and injustice, skills that prepare them to operate as effective change agents in the public sphere, a commitment to values of social justice and human dignity, and a belief in their own and others' ability to apply their knowledge and skills to bring about improvement in people's lives" (p. 12).

FAMILY SELF-SUFFICIENCY PROJECT DESIGN AND IMPLEMENTATION

Thirty students enrolled in an upper division Social Research Methods course were involved in a CBR project for two local housing authorities in neighboring cities. Two program administrators in each agency were identified as community partners in the project.

Selection and Design of Project

The partnership between the university and the two housing authority agencies began approximately 3 months before the start of the semester. The coordinator for the city Neighborhood Development project suggested to a group of faculty engaging in service-learning activities that many community agencies, including the city housing authority, were in need of evaluation research. In a follow-up conversation the coordinator offered to act as a "matchmaker" between the faculty member and the administrators of the local housing authority. A meeting was scheduled and the match was made.

The first step taken was the identification of the agency's needs. Three possible projects were outlined and discussed. One project, the evaluation of the Family Self-Sufficiency (FSS) program, was determined to be the most important to the agency and the best project for facilitating the course objectives in an upper division sociology course on research methods. The

FSS program is a federally funded program through the Department of Housing and Urban Development designed to move participants from dependence on welfare assistance to self-sufficiency. Clients have five years to meet their program goals. The FSS program targets lower socioeconomic families who are eligible for public housing assistance. The majority of the FSS clients are single, female heads of households with three or fewer children; have a high school diploma, a GED, or less education; and have an annual household income of less than $20,000 a year. The majority of the clients are Caucasian; however, the Hispanic or Latino(a) populations are disproportionately overrepresented in both cities' programs.

At the outset, a partnership with only one housing authority was being pursued to evaluate the FSS program run within their agency. However, another FSS program operated by a housing authority in a neighboring city was added at the request of the original housing authority partner.

In early discussions, the community partners and faculty member determined that a longitudinal 5-year study involving newly enrolled participants was most appropriate. A cross-sectional study of current FSS participants would also be conducted to produce more immediate results for the agency. All decisions regarding the project and research questions were determined by the community partners and faculty member prior to the start of the semester.

Role of Students

Thirty upper division undergraduate students worked in four groups on the evaluation of the FSS program in both cities. A basic outline of the research design had already been determined by the faculty member and community partners prior to the semester. Students carried out the design and made suggestions for improving it as the project unfolded. All data collection instruments were developed by students with frequent feedback from the instructor. Students then administered those data collection instruments. Compilation and analysis of the data were also completed by students. The instructor created the code books for surveys and students entered the data in a statistical software package commonly used in the social sciences. The qualitative data collected through interviews were transcribed and analyzed by students with some guidance from the instructor to ensure that all community-driven questions were answered. Students and faculty initially interpreted the results of the study. Students then prepared and presented a PowerPoint report for the staff and administrators of the FSS programs in class. It was at this point that the community partners participated in the interpretations of the findings. Each of the four groups of students wrote a summary of their individual portion of the project, which were then compiled into two reports by an undergraduate teaching assistant and the faculty member.

Use of Class Time

Approximately 65% of the class time was devoted to the project. The class met twice a week for 75 minutes. Most weeks would involve one day of lecture to understand course material explained in the text and the other day was spent on the project. The lectures were structured in such a way that the "project day" following the "lecture day" was a direct application of the material discussed in lecture. Students spent much of the last 8 weeks of the course directly applying the course material in the CBR project. Every day was devoted to the project when the data were being compiled and analyzed and during the 2-week period of constructing the data collection instruments. The last 2 weeks of the semester were spent preparing the oral presentations to the community partners for the last day of class.

Data Collection and Analysis

The FSS project required students to employ at least one research method addressed in the course. Most groups of student researchers employed only one research method in depth. The overall project involved four different methods:

1. Content analysis;
2. Nonparticipant observation;
3. Face-to-face interviews; and
4. Survey research.

Given the nature of the research questions the housing authorities wanted addressed, the research developed into two distinct studies: employing a longitudinal study and a cross-sectional study.

Longitudinal study. The longitudinal study utilized a quasi-experimental design using an experimental and control group for program evaluation of the FSS program in one housing authority over a 5-year period of time. The experimental group consisted of the new clients in the FSS program while the control group consisted of Section 8 Housing Choice Voucher clients who did not participate in the FSS program. These groups were asked to complete a survey at three separate points in time: at the time they were accepted into the FSS program; during the third year in the FSS program; and again at the end of the 5-year program. Student researchers collected and analyzed data from the initial phase. Survey instruments were administered to all new FSS participants at their one-on-one introductory meeting with their FSS caseworker.

Cross-sectional study. The cross-sectional study involved four different modes of data collection:

1. Content analysis;
2. Observation of staff-client interaction;
3. Interviews; and
4. Survey research.

Three student groups were responsible for the cross-sectional study. One group was responsible for a content analysis of all printed documents used by both housing authorities as well as nonparticipant observations of FSS administrators interacting with FSS participants in one agency on 10 separate occasions. Another group conducted face-to-face interviews with FSS staff members in each housing authority. A total of six interviews with all FSS staff members, three interviews in each housing authority, were audiotaped and then transcribed from tape for analysis. The last group of student researchers was responsible for the cross-sectional survey administered in each city to current FSS clients and a control group consisting of a random sample of Section 8 Housing Choice Voucher participants.

PROJECT REPORTS AND DISSEMINATION OF RESEARCH RESULTS

Each group of student researchers was required to write a report describing the FSS project. Various sections of the report were turned in throughout the course of the semester for feedback and revisions before turning in the final draft at the end of the semester. Each of these reports were components to the larger overall evaluation of the FSS programs. The faculty member and a teaching assistant collaboratively synthesized the four reports into two reports. One described the longitudinal study and one described the cross-sectional study. These reports were given to both housing authorities.

Findings of the research were also orally presented on two separate occasions. First, each group of student researchers presented their research findings at an annual department research conference held on campus. Second, FSS staff and administrators from both housing authorities were invited to campus for an oral presentation of the research findings. Each student group presented their particular piece of the overall project.

PROJECT FINDINGS

Students conducting this study assessed four areas in each FSS program:

1. The structure of the FSS program;
2. How well the programs promoted self-sufficiency to its clients;
3. The self-sufficiency of program clients compared to a control group of Section 8 housing clients; and
4. The clients' perceptions of the program's effectiveness.

In terms of the structure of the FSS programs in both cities, the student researchers observed that each program functioned under a different structure. In one city, the staff members were responsible for administering more than just the FSS program to clients. In the other city, the staff members were responsible for administering the FSS program only. Although both structures seemed to work, there was a higher level of staff satisfaction among those responsible for administering the FSS program only.

Students also conducted a content analysis of all documents produced to promote the FSS program to clients. The analysis revealed that three out of five dimensions of self-sufficiency were inadequately addressed in both cities. The home ownership, health, and transportation dimensions were neither adequately described nor promoted in program description pamphlets. This finding prompted each program to consider developing new documents that describe and promote their programs.

Another group of student researchers examined the differences between FSS clients and a control group of Section 8 housing clients on five dimensions of self-sufficiency:

1. Financial;
2. Personal development;
3. Home ownership;
4. Health; and
5. Transportation

As expected, the first phase of data collection for the longitudinal study showed that new FSS clients did not differ from the control group on these dimensions of self-sufficiency. It is only with participation in the program that the levels of self-sufficiency are expected to increase. The cross-sectional study, comparing current FSS clients in both cities with the control groups in both cities, revealed that the FSS programs in both cities seem to be positively affecting their clients and helping them to become more self-sufficient. FSS clients in both cities are more likely than Section 8 housing clients to:

- Be employed full time;
- Have an income of at least $10,000 a year;
- Have a higher credit rating;
- Have higher self-esteem;
- Be saving money to purchase a home; and
- Access more forms of assistance.

Generally, the findings suggest the FSS programs in both cities are most effective in the financial, personal development, and home ownership dimensions of self-sufficiency. Both programs were least effective in the transportation dimension. Improving the clients' access to transportation may increase the effectiveness of the program even more.

Lastly, the FSS clients' perceptions of the FSS programs in both cities were explored. Overall, the clients in both programs were very satisfied with the program and the role it played in their progress toward self-sufficiency. Both housing authorities have used these findings to help them secure funding to sustain and improve their programs.

ASSESSING THE IMPACT OF CBR AS A TEACHING TOOL

The project was assessed by applying theoretical principles proposed by Strand and colleagues (2003a). Data were collected from 30 participating students and 4 community partners to evaluate the FSS project. Reflections from the faculty member served as a qualitative evaluation measure.

Data Collection

Data collection from students occurred at two different time periods using two different instruments: a course evaluation and a project evaluation. The course evaluation was administered with the final exam. All 30 students completed the form. The project evaluation was administered via mail 2 months after the course was completed. Of the 30 evaluations mailed, 13 were returned representing a 43.3% response rate.

The four key individuals at the participating agencies received a short evaluation form at the same time students received theirs. Three of the four key partners completed and returned the evaluation forms. Evaluation forms were sent to agencies after the final written report had been submitted to both agencies.

Faculty reflections on the CBR project were used for the evaluation of the project. Most of these insights evaluate the overall project with respect to the ideal type CBR model discussed in the theory section of this chapter.

Given the collaborative nature of CBR, the faculty member is as much of an integral player in the partnership as students and community agencies. Hence, the inclusion of these data is relevant for the study.

RESULTS

The results of this assessment are organized around the two research objectives. First, the FSS project was evaluated using the criterion of the theoretical CBR model described by Strand and colleagues (2003a). Relevant data from faculty, student, and community partner evaluations were used in this analysis. Second, the impact of the FSS project on student learning as it relates to course objectives and critical thinking was assessed.

Theoretical CBR Model Evaluation Criteria

The theoretical CBR model proposed by Strand and colleagues (2003a) includes:

- Collaboration between faculty, students, and community partners;
- The democratization of knowledge; and
- Social change as the basic elements in any CBR model.

The presence of each of these criterion in the FSS project is evaluated from the perspectives of all partners involved.

Collaboration

Faculty perspective. The research design of the FSS project was deliberately constructed to be collaborative in nature. Strand and colleagues (2003a) suggested that collaboration should take place in every stage of the research process. Table 7.1 shows which partners were involved in which stages of the research process. The only stage in which all three partners were collectively involved was during the interpretation of the results.

The problem and research questions were identified solely by the community partner. The community partner also played a central role again in the later part of the process wherein initiatives are implemented. Consequently, the FSS project was moderately collaborative in nature.

Student perspective. Students were asked to rate the degree of collaboration with peers, faculty, and community partners on a 5-point scale. Students' responses suggest the FSS project facilitated collaboration with all three groups (see Table 7.2). The mean scores for each collaboration measure is above the average score of 3 on the 5-point scale, and the percentage of students agreeing or strongly agreeing with the

Table 7.1.   Partners' Involvement Throughout the Research Process

Research Process	Faculty	Students	Community Partners
Identifying the issue or problem			✓
Constructing research questions	✓		✓
Developing research instruments	✓	✓	
Collecting and analyzing data	✓	✓	
Interpreting results	✓	✓	✓
Writing final report	✓	✓	
Issuing recommendations	✓	✓	
Implementing initiatives			✓

Table 7.2.   Mean Scores and Percentages of Students Responding to Collaboration Measures (*n* = 13)

Collaboration Measure	Mean Score	SD*	Percent Responding Agree or Strongly Agree
The FSS project afforded me the opportunity to:			
a. Work collaboratively with peers.	4.25	0.97	83.3%
b. Work collaboratively with faculty.	4.38	0.77	84.6%
c. Work directly with community workers.	3.92	1.04	61.6%

* Standard deviation

statements is above average. However, a higher percentage of students agreed and strongly agreed that the peer and faculty collaboration opportunities were more readily available than collaboration with community partners. This finding may be explained by the research design. In fact, not all groups of student researchers had as much direct contact with community partners as did others. The students involved in face-to-face interviews and nonparticipant observations constituted approximately half the class (14 out of 30 students) and these students had the most opportunity for collaboration.

Community partner perspective. The community partners were to evaluate collaboration and communication between their agency and faculty and students as well as their overall satisfaction of the role their agency played in the project. Overall, the evaluation of collaboration was very positive. All community partners responded that they were satisfied or very satisfied with all areas of collaboration measured.

Interestingly, faculty and students rated the collaboration with community partners as lower than collaboration with each other. These ratings represent a minimal level of collaboration as defined by the theoretical model expecting collaboration at each stage of the research process (Strand et al., 2003a). However, community partners were satisfied or very satisfied with this level of collaboration. The community partners' responses call into question the theoretical level of acceptance. Perhaps in practice, collaboration in every step of the research process may not be attainable or desirable on the part of community partners. Participating in a CBR project, although beneficial to the agency, is time consuming and a potential drain on already scarce resources.

Democratization of Knowledge

Theoretically, CBR involves the democratization of knowledge that includes four key components:

1. Knowledge brought to the project by all partners involved is equally valued.
2. Multiple research methods are recognized and incorporated into the project.
3. User-friendly approaches to the dissemination of knowledge.
4. Conventional assumptions about knowledge itself are challenged.

Faculty reflections were used to measure the first three elements of this principle. Student data were used to evaluate the last element regarding conventional assumptions being challenged. Community partner data were used to evaluate the approaches to disseminating research findings.

Faculty perspective. Overall the democratization of knowledge appears to be present in the FSS project. All partners involved in the FSS project contributed new knowledge. Community partners defined the problem and brought knowledge about housing in general and about the program specifically to the project. Students also contributed knowledge regarding the program and some of its outcomes after conducting a brief review of the literature on self-sufficiency. The faculty member provided knowledge regarding the research process and research methods.

Multiple research methods, such as content analysis, nonparticipant observation, face-to-face interviews, and survey research, were used. Additionally, the oral presentations given by students were very user-friendly, straightforward, easy to understand, and logically organized. The two final reports, however, were written in a standard academic structure describing objectives, literature review, concepts, methods, results, and conclusions. This format was less familiar to interpretation by community representatives and therefore less user friendly than the oral presentations.

Community partner perspective. Community partners were asked to evaluate the approaches to disseminating data. All of the community partners responded that they were very satisfied with the oral presentations of the research findings. One partner even wrote, "Student presentations were very well done. It was obvious [that] the students were learning through the process of gathering information on an actual program."

Student perspective. Only the aspect of challenging conventional assumptions about knowledge itself was assessed by students. The conventional knowledge of students, before taking the class, was that research is scientific and therefore objective. The way our society uses research results to "prove" positions on issues has led to the construction of this conventional knowledge. Theoretically, CBR should help challenge that conventional wisdom. Students were asked to agree or disagree on a 5-point scale if the FSS project afforded them the opportunity to realize that doing social research is not always objective. An overwhelming majority of students (92.3%, $n = 13$) agreed or strongly agreed with this statement. It appears the students perceived the CBR project as successful in helping them to view the research process as an art as much as a science.

All partners rated the application of the democratization of knowledge criteria very favorably. These criteria of the CBR model seem both theoretically and practically important and desirable from the perspective of all partners involved.

Social Change and Social Justice

Social change is a salient feature of CBR. Faculty and students' reflections of the project, and information about how the community partners are using the findings of the research, have been used to determine to what extent the social change principle of the CBR model was realized.

Faculty perspective. One of the main goals of the project from the outset was the production of an outcome that was useful to the community partner. In this way, bringing about social change through CBR was really left in the hands of the community agency. This is evident in the previous discussion of collaboration wherein community partners were left to implement recommended changes without further input from academic partners.

Student perspective. Students also recognized the application of social change. For example, when asked what they liked best about the FSS project, one student articulated how social change was apparent to them: "There was a positive outcome. It wasn't just a mock assignment. We actually produced research that is going to help people (hopefully) in the future." Although students recognized the social change element in the FSS project, most saw their contribution no further than to the end of the semester.

Community partner perspective. Community partners were asked how the findings of the research were going to be used. They responded with general comments about how the findings have helped them determine what is working for current FSS clients and what is not. The findings are helping them to reinforce the positive aspects of the program and improve what is not working. One community partner wrote: "The information that came out of the survey backed up many conclusions that support the thoughts of staff. We were able to use this information to back up our requests for more grant funding!"

While these are small steps for social change, the FSS project did indeed produce a product that is being used to create social change minimally. Of the three key principles of CBR, the FSS project seems to satisfy the social change principle the least. All partners involved recognized the importance of social change in the project. Although not satisfied completely in the FSS project, the social change criteria seems theoretically important to all partners, even if not practically implemented.

IMPACT OF CBR ON STUDENT LEARNING

Student feedback on the FSS project was analyzed to evaluate the impact of the project on meeting course objectives and promoting critical thinking.

Course Objectives

The FSS community-based research project, the text, and course lectures were used to provide students with knowledge and application of research methods, the fundamental course objectives. Course evaluation data suggest these objectives were accomplished. Of the 30 students enrolled in the course, 86.7% reported that classroom activities were supportive of the course objective—a rating of 4 or 5 on a 5-point scale.

Course evaluation data also suggest that 73.3% of the 30 students enrolled in the course rated the outside-of-class assignment as above average (a 4 or 5 on a 5-point scale with 5 being the highest) in terms of its contribution to their understanding of research methods. An analysis of responses on the FSS evaluation form lend additional support for the positive impact of the CBR project on student learning. Students were asked to rate the effectiveness of the FSS project in the four knowledge/skill areas listed in Table 7.3. Students rated the FSS project well above average in its effectiveness on each indicator. An overwhelming majority of

Table 7.3. Mean Scores and Percentages of Students Responding to CBR Effectiveness Measures

Course Outcome Measure Knowledge/Skill Areas	FSS Project			Textbook			Difference of Means
	FSS Mean Score	SD[1]	Percent Responding 4 or 5 (n = 13)	Text Mean Score	SD	Percent Responding 4 or 5 (n = 13)	FSS Project-Text
1. Providing you with knowledge of a research method.	4.62	0.65	92.3%	3.54	0.97	53.9%	1.08**
2. Providing you an opportunity to practice research methods.	4.69	0.63	92.3%	2.92	1.12	30.8%	1.77**
3. Helping you retain your knowledge of research methods.	4.15	0.90	84.7%	3.08	1.04	46.2%	1.08**
4. Teaching you the process of doing research.	4.46	0.66	92.3%	3.46	0.88	61.5%	1.00*
Overall FSS project effectiveness rating on these four indicators	4.48	0.53	84.7%	3.25	0.85	23.1%	1.23*

[1] Standard deviation; * level of significance = .05; ** level of significance = .01

students (92.3%) rated the project as especially effective in providing them with knowledge regarding research methods, giving them an opportunity to practice their research skills, and teaching them the process of doing research. The overall mean (4.48) suggests a very positive reaction on the part of the students to the FSS project and how it contributed to their knowledge of research methods overall.

The effectiveness of the FSS project was compared with the effectiveness of the textbook in contributing to students learning course outcomes. The percentage of students rating the effectiveness of the project on any one of the course outcomes is much higher than the percent of students rating the text as especially effective on any outcome. A test of means was calculated to determine if the students' rating of the FSS project was significantly more effective than the text book in producing the course outcomes. The last column in Table 7.3 indicates the difference in means on each of the four course outcomes. On each course outcome, students rated the FSS project as significantly more effective than the textbook.

Students were also asked to respond to open-ended questions regarding the most important thing they learned from the FSS project. Many of these comments made reference to the application of skills and knowledge related to the course material. One student responded: "I learned how to conduct research through different techniques (surveys, interviews, etc.), and more importantly, I learned how to interpret and analyze the research I gathered." Most students reported they learned that research is more time consuming than they thought. Others pointed out the importance of working together in a research process to get the work done. Students also made comparisons between what they learned from the project versus what they learned from the text. The majority of responses indicated a preference for the CBR project rather than the text for learning research methods: "...there are many considerations that come to light when actually doing field research. While the text may highlight and explain research, it does not do so as effectively as actual field application."

Although the CBR project was the favored teaching tool, students recognized the text as an important reference. Many students noted the importance of learning about different research methods presented in the text, even if they were not employing them in the CBR project. Others wrote how the text was useful for helping them to outline the research project from beginning to end: "It was useful to refer to [the text] when writing the survey. It helped us know what categories to put questions in to and how to arrange the actual survey."

Overall, the qualitative responses to open-ended questions regarding the most important material learned from the CBR project and text supports the quantitative findings reported above. The CBR project appears to have had a profound impact on students learning the course material, even more so than just reading the textbook, as done in traditional research methods courses.

Critical Thinking from Critical Pedagogy

Critical thinking is embedded in CBR, almost by default. Strand and colleagues (2003b) proposed that students involved in CBR develop the capacity to think critically, become effective change agents, and come to believe in their skills to help others. The only element of critical thinking measured in this study was students' recognition of their abilities and the belief in those skills to help others.

Students reported they liked "the feeling of doing something for the community" and that they enjoyed the project because "it was real and in our own community." Very often students appeared to be empowered by their ability to use their skills to influence social change or to help someone. For example, one student wrote: "I learned that it is not just useless knowledge that is never used in life. We used what we learned. There was a sense of satisfaction at the end of the semester." Another wrote: "I liked how involved the class was. The instructor allowed us to take over certain areas and it allowed us to dig deep and use the skills we have learned." These student responses provide fairly strong evidence in the ability of CBR, and this project in particular, to produce students who believe in their abilities to impact someone's life for the better.

DISCUSSION AND CONCLUSIONS

Outcomes of this course evaluation suggest that the FSS community-based research project employed in a sociology research methods course generally meets the criteria for the CBR model described by Strand and colleagues (2003a). All partners involved in the project agreed that the three main principles of collaboration, democratization of knowledge, and social change were met on some level by the FSS project. Although collaboration was rated the lowest from the perspective of faculty and students, community partners were satisfied with the level of collaboration in the project. This discrepancy may call into question the theoretical expectation for complete collaboration throughout the research process. Second, student feedback suggested that using service-learning to conduct CBR was a very good pedagogical tool that appears to have positively impacted students' learning and, to some degree, critical thinking. These findings demonstrate the potential of service-learning coupled with CBR as a pedagogical tool. The FSS project met all three criteria for CBR, from a minimal to moderate degree.

The evaluative data used are based on course and project evaluations. These instruments were designed for course and project assessment and feedback rather than as part of a research design involving a carefully controlled experimental study. As such, future research employing a comparison group is needed. Even so, the findings reported here support the notion that CBR coupled with service-learning has potential as a teaching and learning tool. Service-learning is enhanced through CBR in that it offers opportunities for collaboration, direct application of course content, and potential for social change. Additionally, CBR changes the focus and process of research. CBR moves research away from the traditional research model (Strand et al., 2003a), which distinctly changes the nature and quality of research. The quality of the research being conducted in an academic setting is fundamentally changed by CBR because the purpose of that research is not just for the sake of adding to our knowledge of a particular subject. CBR is a pedagogical tool that fundamentally changes the nature and quality of service-learning and research in universities and communities.

REFERENCES

Chapdelaine, A., & Chapman, B. L. (1999). Using community-based research projects to teach research methods. *Teaching Psychology, 26,* 101–105.

Couto, R. A. (2003). Community-based research: Celebration and concern. *Michigan Journal of Community Service Learning, 9,* 69–74.

Eyler, J., & Giles, D. E. (1999). *Where's the learning in service-learning?* San Francisco: Jossey Bass.

Ferman, B., & Shlay, A. B. (1997). The Academy hits the streets: teaching community-based research. In P. Nyden, A. Figert, M. Shibley, & D. Burrows (Eds.), *Building community: Social science in action* (pp.129–133). Thousand Oaks, CA: Pine Forge.

Ferrari, J. R., & Jason, L. A. (1996). Integrating research and community service: Incorporating research skills into service-learning experiences. *College Student Journal, 30,* 444–451.

Gedicks, A. (1996). Activist sociology: personal reflections. *Sociological Imagination, 33* [Special Issue: Sociology and Social Action, Part I], 55–72.

Green, L. W., George, M. A., Daniel, M., Frankish, C. J., Herbert, C. P., Bowie, W. R., & O'Neil, M. (1997). Background on participatory research. In D. Murphy, M. Scammell, & R. Sclove (Eds.), *Doing community-based research: A reader* (pp. 53–66). Amherst, MA: Loka Institute.

Hite, L. M. (1997). An action learning project on diversity: Pitfalls and possibilities. *Journal on Excellence in College Teaching, 8,* 49–67.

Lewin, K. (1948). *Resolving social conflicts.* New York: HarperCollins.

McNicoll, P. (1999). Issues in teaching participatory action research. *Journal of Social Work Education, 35,* 51–63.

Mintz, S., & Hesser, G. (1996). Principles of good practice in service-learning. In B. Jacoby (Ed.), *Service-learning in higher education* (pp. 26–52). San Francisco: Jossey-Bass.

Murphy, D., Scammell, M., & Sclove, R. (Eds.). (1997). *Doing community-based research: A reader.* Amherst, MA: Loka Institute.

Nyden, P., Figert, A., Shibley, M., & Burrows, D. (1997). University-community collaborative research: Adding chairs at the research table. In P. Nyden, A. Figert, M. Shibley, & D. Burrows (Eds.), *Building community: Social science in action* (pp.3–13). Thousand Oaks, CA: Pine Forge.

Nyden, P., & Wiewel, W. (1992). Collaborative research: Harnessing the tensions between research and practitioner. *American Sociologist, 23,* 43–55.

Porpora, D. (1999). Action research: The highest stage of service-learning? In J. Ostrow, G. Hesser, & S. Enos (Eds.), *Cultivating the sociological imagination: Concepts and models for service-learning* (pp. 121–133). Washington DC: American Association for Higher Education.

Small, S. (1995). Action-oriented research: Models and methods. *Journal of Marriage and the Family, 57,* 941–956.

Stoecker, R. (1999). Making connections: Community organizing, empowerment planning, and participatory research in participatory evaluation. *Sociological Practice, 1,* 209–232.

Stoecker, R. (2003). Community-based research: From practice to theory and back again. *Michigan Journal of Community Service Learning, 9,* 35–46.

Strand, K. J. (2000). Community-based research as pedagogy. *Michigan Journal of Community Service Learning, 7,* 89–96.

Strand, K., Marullo, S., Cutforth, N., Stoecker, R., & Donohue, P. (2003a). *Community-based research and higher education: Principles and practices.* San Francisco: Jossey-Bass.

Strand, K., Marullo, S., Cutforth, N., Stoecker, R., & Donohue, P. (2003b). Principles of best practice for community-based research. *Michigan Journal of Community Service Learning, 9,* 5–15.

Stringer, E. T. (1999). *Action research* (2nd ed.). Thousand Oaks, CA: Sage.

Willis, J., Peresie, J., Waldref, V., & Stockmann, D. (2003). The undergraduate perspective on community-based research. *Michigan Journal of Community Service Learning, 9,* 36–43.

PART III

INSTITUTIONALIZATION OF SERVICE-LEARNING

CHAPTER 8

TEACHER PERCEPTIONS ON IMPLEMENTING SCHOOLWIDE SERVICE-LEARNING

Patricia J. Mintz and A. J. Abramovitz

ABSTRACT

This research examines the overarching hypothesis that specific teacher attitudes are present in a successful implementation of schoolwide service-learning and that these attitudes exist as a byproduct of conscious choices made by teachers. The research explored classroom teacher participation in service-learning projects as related to the tendency to collaborate, service-learning recruitment, professional responsibility, and perceived support for service-learning.

One hundred sixty-nine teachers in five schools in Ohio, recognized for schoolwide service-learning implementation, completed an anonymous survey. It is a finding of this chapter that a teacher's discretionary choice to implement service-learning projects has a strong relationship with the elements of how teachers were recruited into the service-learning sphere. The positive relationship to personal recruitment of individual teachers suggests that school leadership, seeking to establish schoolwide service-learning, needs to make an

New Perspectives in Service-Learning: Research to Advance the Field, pages 151–167
Copyright © 2004 by Information Age Publishing

investment in resources and organizational development that supports collegial relationships among teachers.

INTRODUCTION

Background and Purpose

Service-learning is a contemporary initiative that promotes educators reaching out into the community to add relevancy to existing curriculum and to connect students with real life experiences. Service-learning is defined as "a teaching and learning approach that integrates community service with academic study to enrich learning, teach civic responsibility, and strengthen communities" (National Commission on Service-Learning [NCSL], 2001). Many teachers and administrators advocate this applied approach to learning because it gives students tangible applications of the curriculum within the context of a community service experience.

The purpose of this research is to examine schoolwide implementation of service-learning projects from the teachers' perspective. The scale development and data collection examine the related reasons and perceptions teachers possess that contribute to their discretionary choice to engage in service-learning. This research proceeds under the assumption that service-learning is a valuable and useful method for achieving curriculum objectives through an applied and active learning approach as stated in the NCSL report (2001).

Each service-learning project requires a reflective exercise to evaluate and discuss the service experience and its application to the learning objectives. This requires extensive teacher planning. Consequently, implementation of service-learning projects is a discretionary choice teachers must make.

Research Question and Method

The primary research question for this inquiry is: "What attitudes and perceptions do teachers identify to make the discretionary choice to implement service-learning projects not mandated by their job description?" Posing this overall question allows the researchers to examine some of the pertinent motivating factors that buttress schoolwide implementation of service-learning from a group of respondents that teaches in schools with currently active service-learning initiatives.

The survey instrument designed by the researchers allows respondents to reply anonymously without pressure. Five different schools within and outside the Cleveland, Ohio, area that were recognized for the implementation of service-learning participated. All of the teachers in the studied schools had the opportunity to respond whether they had or had not implemented service-learning projects in their own classrooms.

Effort and Scope

This research is focused on discovering why teachers go beyond their job description requirements in the school environment to affect service-learning. Aspects of service and volunteerism have been a part of the American experience since before the 1830s when Americans routinely gathered to accomplish work and needed tasks in voluntary associations (Hammack, 1998). The contemporary use of service-learning in K–12 classrooms is an effort to provide the next generation of American students with learning experiences that engage them in contributing to the life of their communities, and to show them that genuine and valuable learning can occur in places other than the conventional classroom.

REVIEW OF PERSPECTIVES ON TEACHER CHOICE AND VOLUNTEERISM LITERATURE

Service-learning has its roots in the concepts of experiential learning. In the essay, "The School and Society," Dewey (1964) argued that the range of the work of a school needs broadening beyond the individual student, their relationship to the teacher, and their individual academic progress (p. 295). Although individual student accomplishments are an important measure of the school experience, introducing forms of *active occupation* renews the vitality of the entire school and provides a location for a student to learn through *directed living* (Dewey, 1964). Learning through community service projects becomes the vehicle for students to engage in and reflect upon their understanding of academic concepts and skills in an applied community setting.

Within the theories of intrinsic motivation, the theory of self-determination stands out, supporting the notion that a teacher makes a conscious choice to participate in service-learning activities, as opposed to other discretionary activities. "When people are self-determining, they make choices and have the opportunity to become more fully involved with the activity itself" (Deci & Ryan, 1985, p. 57) captures the essence of the decision making that challenges teachers daily. The teacher identifies his or her own personal capacity, flexibility, and interest in trying a new approach to complete a required curriculum objective, additionally providing a way for students and teachers to give back to their own community (Ammon, 2002).

In addition, the school's administration espouses and demonstrates the ability to implement the organizational citizenship behaviors of altruism and conscientiousness (Organ, 1988) in the environment of the classroom. By engaging in service-learning that is not mandatory, a teacher demonstrates the ability to go beyond what is professionally required for the role of a teacher. Service-learning projects expect a level of altruism that requires the assistance of a specific person with an organizationally relevant task. The implementation of schoolwide service-learning demonstrates a conscientiousness that goes beyond the requirements of the teaching position when the decision to participate is discretionary.

The scale development work of Toole (2001) described the characteristics of sustainability that assess an individual teacher's perception of leadership support. The survey instrument provides statements that allow a respondent to reflect upon the value of their service-learning projects and the support that school leadership provides for their efforts.

Additionally, in a study of 10 New Hampshire schools, Billig (2002b) demonstrated that choosing and maintaining participation in service-learning caused an integration of service-learning into the culture of the school. This integration was consistent with the educational values and teaching beliefs of the teachers involved. This study also indicated that strong leadership is needed to engage teachers in the vision of service-learning and the sense of the community that is established from participation.

The institutionalization of service-learning appears bolstered by the development of a professional learning community that creates more extensive agreement about a shared purpose that develops greater teacher participation and willingness to engage in change (Toole, 2002).

Billig (2002a) indicated in the Kellogg Retrospective report that adoption and implementation of service-learning occurs more readily when support exists throughout the school. This support again grows out of the commonly held teaching beliefs and practices among the teachers in a particular school.

In summary, the work of Dewey (1964), Deci and Ryan (1985), Organ (1988), Billig (2002a), and Toole (2002), combine the theoretical constructs that support and enhance the idea of a discretionary choice for implementing service-learning projects within an individual teacher's classroom. The aggregate action of individual teachers meeting their own needs and the contribution to the schoolwide effort constitutes the organizational change that results in schoolwide service-learning.

PROCESS OF VOLUNTEERISM IN SCHOOL AS RELATED TO SERVICE-LEARNING

The conceptual model for this research includes four independent constructs:

1. Tendency among teachers to collaborate with one another.
2. Recruitment of teachers for service-learning projects.
3. Attitudes of teachers concerning aspects of professional responsibility.
4. Perception of support for service-learning efforts.

A mediating construct, volunteerism in the school, defines behaviors that demonstrate an individual teacher's willingness to engage in helping actions in school. There are three dependent constructs at work that determine the participation level of a respondent:

1. Implementation of service-learning;
2. School activity participation; and
3. Community activity participation.

Figure 8.1 provides the diagram of the proposed relationships among the constructs in the model.

Independent Constructs

The tendency for teachers to collaborate within the school work environment reflects the opportunity to work with new projects and seek interactions with colleagues to fulfill professional job requirements. Not

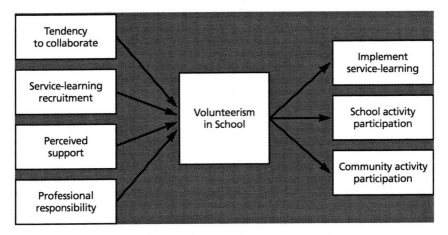

Figure 8.1. **Volunteerism in school as related to service-learning.**

specific to service-learning, this construct seeks to capture the attitude about collaboration in the school work environment. A professional community supports and encourages collective efforts that minimize the isolation of individual teachers (Senge et al., 2000). This construct measures the sense of association among teachers.

Service-learning recruitment defines the act of asking a teacher directly to be involved in service-learning (Pearce, 1993). Determining who asks a teacher to participate may be related to the actual participation of a teacher within the realm of service-learning.

Perceived support is the support of school administration and the coordination work of colleagues to ensure the sustainability of service-learning projects. This construct addresses concerns of institutionalization of service-learning (Billig, 2002a; Toole, 2001).

Professional responsibility explores the teacher's ability to have and make choices in their teaching role rather than being pressured to do so by outside forces. Grounded in the theory of self-determination (Deci & Ryan, 1985), this construct defines the issues of personal capacity, flexibility, freedom, and accomplishment in teacher's daily classroom work.

Dependent Constructs

The three dependent constructs examine the tension between discretionary choices and personal time devoted to service-learning. Service-learning implementation is the primary dependent construct, but school activity participation and community activity participation are also part of the concept of unpaid volunteerism. The focus of these constructs is not on compensation, but rather a choice of how time is spent.

These three categories contain a common theme of selecting time to give teachers for other personal and professional interests both inside and outside of the classroom. Teachers are often pressed for time throughout the school day. Nothing in the job description requires a teacher to move learning from the classroom to the community, give time to other school activities, or give time to community activities. These three constructs provide a partial description of a respondent's commitments with their personal discretionary time.

Mediating Construct

The researchers posit that the teachers' decision to participate is mediated by volunteerism in school. This construct is defined to address specific individual actions that reflect the concepts of altruism and conscientiousness in organizational citizenship behavior (Organ, 1988). It is characterized by an individual's willingness to go beyond what is required of his or her job to help other colleagues and employees in their workplace. With respect to service-learning, this construct defines altruism in school in response to the needs of an individual colleague. It captures the idea of an individual teacher's willingness to support a colleague in response to a personal request to help with service-learning.

MEASUREMENT DEVELOPMENT

The development of the survey instrument used with K–12 teachers began with a review of existing scales for their applicability to each of the previously defined constructs. In addition, the researchers proposed original items and modified items from existing scales that placed some of the items in the context of service-learning implementation.

Six expert education and/or service-learning practitioners reviewed the draft instrument and provided suggestions and edits to better reflect the desired variable measurements. The final constructs emerged through exploratory factor analysis from the 56 items that were included on the original survey.

DATA COLLECTION

Setting and Participants

Not all of the teachers in each school were engaged in service-learning. All, however, were aware of service-learning endeavors within their respective schools. In each school, the implementation of service-learning projects was not required.

Data Collection Procedures

In January 2003, the researchers distributed 305 individual survey packets in the participating schools as shown in Table 8.1.

Table 8.1.   Summary of Distribution and Response Rate

School	Surveys Distributed	Surveys Returned	Percent of Total	Response Rate
A	100	60	35.5	60.0%
B	50	28	16.6	56.0%
C	65	36	21.3	55.4%
D	45	27	16.0	60.0%
E	45	18	10.7	40.0%
Total	305	169	100.0	56.7%

Responses showed that 123 of teachers in the sample population teach 6th-grade through 8th-grade students of which 127 were women and 42 were men. Respondents averaged 10 years of teaching experience in their current school. The educational completion levels of the teachers in the population ranged from the bachelor's degree through doctoral degree. There were 86 teachers that implemented service-learning projects and 128 teachers that assisted with service-learning in their school.

Data Preparation

Missing individual responses were scattered throughout the returned surveys. Missing values were replaced with the mean of the individual respondent's completed reply for each specific construct in the survey (Cool, 2000).

The mean and the histograms for each survey item on a 5-point Likert scale were shifted toward the positive or agree end of the scale. This was expected, because the selection of school sites was not random, but rather focused on schools recognized for a high level of service-learning implementation.

An exploratory factor analysis of the original list of 29 survey items showed 16 converged to generate four factors:

1. Tendency to collaborate;
2. Service-learning recruitment;
3. Perceived support; and
4. Professional responsibility.

An additional exploratory factor analysis tested all the items related to volunteerism in school, implementing service-learning, school activity participation, and community activity participation. The final construct items are listed with associated reliability alphas in Table 8.2 below, which provides a detailed continuous view of the stronger reliability of the independent constructs, as well as the reduced effect of the dependent constructs.

Table 8.2. Constructs and Reliability Alphas

Independent Constructs

Tendency to Collaborate   Alpha = .75

- I look for ways to interact with my colleagues during the school day.
- I enjoy working on a team to complete a new school project.
- If the school develops any new project, I find a way to be involved.
- I make innovative suggestions to improve my school.

Table 8.2.   Constructs and Reliability Alphas (Cont.)

Service-Learning Recruitment   Alpha = .76

- If the school develops a new service-learning project, the project coordinator asks teachers to participate.
- I have been asked to participate in training sessions for service-learning.
- One of my colleagues asked me to participate in a service-learning project.

Professional Responsibility   Alpha = .80

- I have the freedom to develop the way that my classroom teaching is done.
- Most days I feel a sense of accomplishment for my work as a teacher.
- I make an extra effort to welcome colleagues to a new work group.
- I accept responsibility to support other teachers in my school.
- I am able to achieve new skills in my teaching role.
- I am satisfied with the amount of personal growth that I experience in my job.

Perceived Support   Alpha = .68

- The school district policies support a teacher's interest to use service-learning.
- Most teachers in my school are not familiar with service-learning concepts. (reverse)
- Service-learning would disappear from this school if a few key people left. (reverse)

Mediating Construct

Volunteerism in School   Alpha = .58

- I enjoy the opportunity to help my colleagues while at my school.
- I volunteer to mentor new teachers in my school.
- If I develop a service-learning project, my colleagues would assist me if asked.

Dependent Constructs

Implement Service-Learning   Alpha = .64

- Attended a training session for service-learning.
- Implemented a service-learning project in my classroom.
- Assisted a colleague with a service-learning project.
- Lead a schoolwide project in service-learning.
- May consider implementing a service-learning project in the future.

School Activity Participation   Alpha = .43

- Serve as a coach of a student team.
- Serve as an advisor to a student club.
- Participate in recreational athletic teams.

Community Activity Participation   Alpha = .38

- Participate in clubs and/or groups for my personal satisfaction.
- Participate in religious organizations.
- Other community-based volunteer activities.

The results of the Pearson rho correlations, as defined by Porkess (1991, p. 53), indicated that the reliability alphas were stronger in the independent variables as compared to the dependent constructs. The correlations that are significant confirm that the variables are distinct. Correction for the influence of outliers (items outside of three standard deviations in subsequent regressions) caused the deletion of three respondents because of their adverse affect on the regression results from the independent variables to volunteerism in school. Because of the deletion of outliers, the number of analyzed responses reduced to $n = 166$. There were no other cases of individual items outside of three standard deviations in subsequent regressions.

Multiple regressions, using the Baron and Kenny (1986) model, tested mediation relationships between and among the variables, and the Sobel Formula (Holmbeck, 1997) was used to test their significance.

RESULTS

A review of the univariate statistics for volunteerism in school for respondents with an average of 10 years of teaching experience revealed several significant tendencies. As a group, more than 92% of the teachers indicated that they enjoyed the opportunity to help a colleague while at school. About 50% of the teachers agreed that they would volunteer to mentor a new teacher, and approximately 80% indicated a willingness to assist a colleague with a service-learning project. The willingness to be involved would seem innately to be self-evident, but it does not necessarily happen until factoring in service-learning recruitment.

Using the path relationships in the conceptual model, 13 linear regressions were completed. Figure 8.2 provides the full summary of the significant beta results. Coefficients significant at the 0.01 level (**) indicate a strong relationship between the constructs, while coefficients significant at the 0.10 level (*) indicate a tendency toward a relationship.

Within 166 respondents, there is a highly significant relationship ($\beta = .51$) between being asked to participate in a service-learning project by a colleague, and actually implementing or assisting with a service-learning project. Among these teachers, 50.9% have actually implemented a service-learning project, and 75.7% of the respondents have assisted a colleague with a service-learning project; yet only 42.6% of the teachers have actually attended a training session for service-learning.

The results of the regression between the independent variables and school activity participation provide two significant paths to service-learning recruitment and perceived support. The negative sign on the beta value ($\beta = -.19$) of perceived support may be related to the fact that the

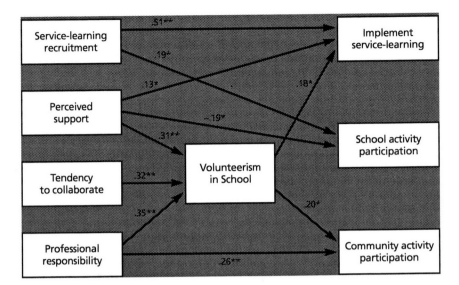

Figure 8.2. **Volunteerism in school as related to service-learning.**
* Coefficient significance at 0.10 level; **Coefficient significance at 0.01 level

items are focused on service-learning. In contrast, school activity participation means all other school-based activity outside of service-learning implementation. If a teacher is involved in other school activities, a negative relationship with service-learning would not be unexpected.

The relationship between professional responsibility and community activity provides the only significant result in the third regression analysis, in terms of community activity participation (β = .26).

In the third and final set of linear regressions, each of the dependent variables is regressed on the independent variables and the mediating variable, volunteerism in school. The beta value of .50 represents the incremental effect of service-learning recruitment after accounting for volunteerism in school. This is consistent with the result of the direct relationship of β = .51 between service-learning recruitment and implementing service-learning. The effect of service-learning recruitment is more than two times the effect of volunteerism in school.

Allowing for the consideration of results at the 0.10 level of significance due to reduced power, volunteerism in school does have a mediating effect on the implementation of service-learning. The 0.10 level is more often recognized as a trend that might develop into more significant results in a larger study.

In the next regression of this final set, the incremental effect of service-learning recruitment is 0.16, after accounting for volunteerism in school. This result is consistent with the direct effect of 0.19 between service-learning recruitment and school activity participation. The effect of service-learning recruitment is four times the effect of volunteerism in school. This result indicates that there is a significant relationship between colleagues asking teachers to participate in service-learning and the actual implementation of service-learning projects. The collegial aspects of the interaction seem to be the most important contribution to successful implementation.

However, school activity participation, which includes many other activities outside the classroom at school, had no significant mediating effect from volunteerism in school. From the surveys, it becomes clear that respondents that participated in these activities did not view them as volunteer work. Additionally, the incremental effect of perceived support ($\beta = -.20$) after accounting for volunteerism in school is consistent with the direct relationship between perceived support and school activity participation ($\beta = -.19$).

This counterintuitive negative result makes sense because items that were listed for response for school activity participation included coaching teams and club advising, which teachers often perform with an additional contract and compensation. In retrospect, it might have been better to consider only school activities that were volunteer and were not monetarily compensated. However, by including coaching and advising, how teachers allocated their time was considered in the responses. The following relationships are positively related:

- Service-learning recruitment to implement service-learning;
- Service-learning recruitment to school activity participation;
- Perceived support to implement service-learning; and
- Professional responsibility to community activity participation.

There is a mediating effect of volunteerism in school on implementing service-learning and on community activity participation. However, there is no mediating effect of volunteerism in school on school activity participation.

DISCUSSION

The main research question focused on five possible motivators that might affect a teachers' choice to implement or participate in service-learning projects when not mandated as part of ongoing job duties. The results of this research indicate that a strong relationship between service-learning recruitment and actual project implementation exists ($\beta = .51$); a mediating effect from volunteerism in school was also extant. The most important points are embedded in the actual phrasing of the items in the variable, service-learning recruitment. Each item is stated to measure the strength of agreement as to whether a teacher has been asked to participate in training, collaboration, or implementation of a service-learning project through a colleague's initiative.

Inherent in these findings is the need for teachers to recognize his/her colleagues as the driving force for implementation of service-learning projects. This becomes a decision made through a teacher's choice to participate in service-learning and thus participate in the changing school culture. Service-learning in the school environment is not a form of recreation, but rather a manifestation of work (Schindler-Rainman & Lipitt, 1975). The professional aspects of service-learning focus on the accomplishment of learning goals through service. The driving force for the decision to implement or participate in a service-learning project seems to be tethered to one colleague performing recruitment and a mentoring role for another colleague, to further the expansion of service-learning. In several of the schools in this research study, teachers are organized in teaching teams by grade level. There is an expectation that collaboration and cooperation will occur for academic subject areas. This organizational structure might also contribute to the sustainability of the service-learning implementation because there are established collegial relationships for other purposes.

Deci and Ryan (1985) stated that self-determination requires one to have the capacity to be able to recognize that there are choices available and then be able to make those choices. Teachers consider choices every day, but there seems to be an extrinsic factor as to how teachers make their choices. In the case of service-learning, teachers are more likely to make the choice to be responsive to a collegial request to get involved in a service-learning endeavor. After taking the initial step, many teachers make the choice to stay with service-learning.

This finding is important to educational practitioners who embrace this newest iteration of experiential learning. To illustrate, one can look at the population for this study. This group of 166 valid respondents has a strong connection to successful collegial support, which implies that educators hoping to implement schoolwide service-learning projects need to make an investment of time and effort to build the collegial relationships needed to make the project salable. The notion of collegial relationship-building has implications for administrative decision making and the way schools are managed as organizations.

This connection to collegial support is also reflected in the significant direct relationship between service-learning recruitment and a teacher's participation rate in school activities. Similarly, the school-based team activities that represent a high level of teacher involvement are related to the variables that quantify the level of collegial asking that occurs. Teacher involvement in other school events is a natural extension of the school-based activities that provides for learning experiences in and out of the classroom. This significant relationship confirms that this group of respondents is committed to their professional life in the school, whether inside or outside of the classroom.

For the service-learning advocate, there is always a challenge to identify those teachers interested in sustaining a continuing service-learning effort. It is important to understand that perceived support through school policies is important to service-learning implementation, but the actual collegial aspects of the process seem to be the more significant relationship to this research.

Initially the negative relationship between perceived support and school activity participation seems counterintuitive ($\beta = -.19$). However, the individual items in perceived support specifically describe support and collegial understanding of service-learning. If a teacher strongly participates in other school activities and has minimal contact with service-learning, it implies that the result of a negative relationship with perceived support is plausible.

Although a teacher is part of a school staff and perhaps a grade-level team of teachers, there are still a myriad of individual decisions each day when developing teaching and learning strategies. If a teacher views the use of service-learning as a way to complete the curriculum work that is required, then encouragement from a colleague that is already involved with service-learning will probably facilitate more commitment to service-learning projects.

The mediating variable of teacher volunteerism in school particularly addresses volunteerism as part of the work to support colleagues on a daily basis and in service-learning projects if asked. The mixture of these two ideas may have reduced the mediating effect of this motivating factor in the theoretical model. In addition, this group of respondents could make a distinction between general helpful behavior and participation in service-learning as all teachers in each school were invited to respond to the survey.

The dependent variable, community activity participation, represents a particular maturity and confidence in the teacher's individual professional framework of understanding and reference. Decisions made to participate in community activity appear to be separate from the implement service-learning and school activity participation variables. Respondents have not relayed their personal community participation and connections to their community to their interest and involvement in service-learning within their work environment. This is an important message to those who advocate for service-learning as pedagogy. It says to the practitioner that a teacher may have personal volunteer interests in his/her own life, but there needs to be a solid connection to the learning objectives before service-learning will be considered as an approach to achieving learning mastery in the classroom.

The theory to support this research used an intrinsic approach to consider how teachers decide to be involved in service-learning. However, the data results indicate that there are extrinsic factors that are important to service-learning implementation. There seems to be a factor of initial contact and then a factor of continuing support from a colleague that is needed for a teacher to continue his/her involvement in service-learning. Practitioners seeking successful schoolwide implementations will need to work with administrators and teachers to build the collegial relationships needed to sustain service-learning initiatives as the call for national implementation gains more momentum (NCSL, 2001).

Limitations

This research study faced the challenges of accessibility and time constraints in order to gather responses from classroom teachers who had tremendous day-to-day responsibilities for classroom preparation. Additionally, the schedule and stress of preparation for Ohio Proficiency Testing added an extra demand in the context of gathering data. Therefore, data collection was limited to one 6-week period of time.

Although the sample size was less than 200 respondents, the mix of respondents from different schools and different geographical locations increased the variety of the responses in this research effort. The identity and location of the five schools were not shared. In the future, in order to build larger research studies, it would be useful to commonly share school locations to encourage broader participation in research efforts.

Future Directions

Since this research combines a variety of scales and theoretical ideas, more extensive research efforts will be needed in the future. Future research needs to pursue greater details in describing teacher motivation for the discretionary choice in how teachers spend their noninstructional professional time, and how they spend their personal time. Extrinsic factors will need to be considered in future efforts to define the motivational factors for schoolwide service-learning implementation. Additionally, the role of administration needs to be researched to enhance an understanding of schoolwide implementation of service-learning.

The mediating variable, volunteerism in school, has demonstrated some effect on implementing service-learning and community activity participation. However, even though a teacher's participation might be slightly influenced by his or her tendency to volunteer, it is more likely to be a decision influenced by a colleague that seeks their involvement in a service-learning project. Before service to community becomes a factor, the decision to implement the pedagogy of service-learning is a work-related decision that must be supported by the teacher and the administration of the school.

Future efforts should also find a way to link teacher motivation to be involved with service-learning with its observable effects on student behavior and performance. With continued emphasis on real-world applications for the K–12 classroom, service-learning projects provide teachers with ways to combine learning objectives with civic engagements. The final reward for the teacher comes from the students' experience that enhances their learning and performance.

The publication of *Learning In Deed: The Power of Service-Learning for American Schools* (NCSL, 2001) closely followed the September 11 attack on the World Trade Center in New York City. The expansive volunteer efforts throughout the country in support of people affected by this tragic event raised national awareness of the impact of volunteer efforts. The power and impact of service-learning gained new meaning for the national discussion on the recommendation to implement the use of service-learning in every K–12 classroom in the United States. With sustained commitment from teachers already engaged in service-learning, the opportunities for growth and creativity will be available to any teacher.

REFERENCES

Ammon, M. S. (2002). Probing and promoting teachers' thinking about service-learning. In S. H. Billig & A. Furco (Eds.), *Advances in service-learning research: Vol. 2. Service-learning through a multidisciplinary lens* (pp. 33–54). Greenwich, CT: Information Age.

Baron, R. M., & Kenny, D. A. (1986). The moderator–mediator variable distinction in social psychology research: Conceptual, strategic, and statistical considerations. *Journal of Personality and Social Psychology, 51,* 1173–1182.

Billig, S. H. (2002a). Adoption, implementation, and sustainability of K–12 service-learning. In A. Furco & S. H. Billig (Eds.), *Advances in service-learning research: Vol. 1. Service-learning: The essence of the pedagogy* (pp. 245–267). Greenwich, CT: Information Age.

Billig, S. H. (2002b). *Retrospective evaluation of K–12 service-learning projects, 1990–2000.* Denver, CO: RMC Research Corporation.

Cool, A. (2000, January). *A review of methods for dealing with missing data.* Paper presented at the annual meeting of the Southwest Educational Research Association, Houston, TX.

Deci, E. L., & Ryan, R. M. (1985). *Intrinsic motivation and self-determination in human behavior.* New York: Plenum Press.

Dewey, J. (1899). The school and society. In R. D. Archambault (Ed.), *John Dewey on education: Selected writings*. Chicago: University of Chicago Press.

Hammack, D. C. (Ed.). (1998). *The making of the nonprofit sector in the United States*. Bloomington: Indiana University Press.

Holmbeck, G. N. (1997). Toward terminological, conceptual, and statistical clarity in the study of mediators and moderators: Examples from the child-clinical and pediatric psychology literatures. *Journal of Consulting and Clinical Psychology, 25*(4), 599–610.

National Commission on Service-Learning. (2001). *Learning In Deed: The power of service-learning for American schools*. A report from the National Commission on Service Learning (NCSL). Retrieved June 9, 2004, from http://www.learningindeed.org/slcommission/report.html

Organ, D. W. (1988). *Organizational citizenship behavior: The good soldier syndrome*. Lexington, MA: Lexington Books.

Pearce, J. L. (1993). *Volunteers: The organizational behavior of unpaid workers*. New York: Routledge.

Porkess, R. (1991). *HarperCollins Dictionary of Statistics*. New York: HarperCollins.

Schindler-Rainman, E., & Lipitt, R. (1975). *The voluntary community: Creative use of human resources*. San Diego, CA: University Associates, Inc.

Senge, P., Cambron-McCabe, N., Lucas, T., Smith, B., Dutton, J., & Kleiner, A. (2000). *Schools that learn*. New York: Doubleday.

Toole, J. C. (2001). *Construction of scales: Service-learning institutionalization (school-level)*. Scale provided by Toole with permission to use in this author's work.

Toole, J. C. (2002). *Mental models, professional learning community, and the deep structure of school improvement: Case studies in service-learning*. St. Paul: University of Minnesota.

CHAPTER 9

FACULTY ENGAGEMENT IN SERVICE-LEARNING

Individual and Organizational Factors at Distinct Institutional Types

Meaghan E. Mundy

ABSTRACT

The purpose of this survey research was to determine the institutional and individual factors that affect faculty participation in service-learning and to examine their impact on faculty teaching perceptions and behavior. Faculty responses from more than 300 surveys completed at 15 institutions of higher education were analyzed by institutional type, academic discipline, faculty rank, tenure status, gender, age, ethnicity, political affiliation, number of years teaching, and number of publications. In addition, scale variables measured individual behaviors and perceptions in relation to teaching beliefs and philosophy, graduate school socialization, perceived campus support for service-learning, and personal perceptions of service-learning.

Though some important differences were found between faculty who participate in service-learning as compared to those who do not participate, this study's most significant finding concerned faculty perceptions of service-

New Perspectives in Service-Learning: Research to Advance the Field, pages 169–193

learning; that is, faculty with awareness and positive perceptions of service-learning were much more likely to participate in service-learning than those without knowledge and positive perceptions. Based on the findings, directions for future research and practice are described as well as strategies for increasing faculty knowledge and awareness of service-learning as a valuable educational philosophy, instructional pedagogy, and institutional program.

INTRODUCTION

Over the past 10 years, the examination of faculty and service-learning has been identified as one of the key research agenda items in the field of service-learning (Driscoll, 2000; Giles & Eyler, 1998; Giles, Porter Honnet, & Migliore, 1991). Specifically, there has been a call for research that examines the factors that explain faculty involvement in service-learning and how participants are affected by their involvement (Giles & Eyler, 1998). Moreover, Holland (2000) asserted that many of the questions and issues raised about faculty roles, expectations, motivations, and concerns often are linked, in some way, to institutional and organizational issues.

Consequently, current research agendas are also identifying the necessity for studies that examine institutional contexts and service-learning. For example, identifying the characteristics of campus environments that are conducive to service-learning would be of great utility to the field's understanding of service-learning and its institutionalization on campuses across the nation (Giles & Eyler, 1998). Wade, Berk, and Siddens (2000) echoed this sentiment and affirmed that a better understanding of the personal and organizational factors would be helpful as well as research that focuses on the complexity and interaction of these factors and their impact on the longevity of service-learning. Astin (2000) offered a model that encourages service-learning research to examine both individual and collective/organizational/structural influences because each set of factors influences the other. Finally, Giles and Eyler (1998) proposed that questions about faculty and institutional involvement be framed around the issue of higher education reform.

As a curricular innovation, service-learning faces certain hurdles at institutions of higher education (Austin, 1996; Boyer, 1990; Clark, 1987, 1991; Cohen & March, 1986) and many stakeholder groups need to be considered in terms of their power to affect change as well as their motivation to promote and implement change (Holland, 2000; Rogers, 1983; Ward, 1998). Key service-learning stakeholder groups include students, faculty, community, and administrators, each with differing needs and agendas that affect institutionalization efforts (Bringle & Hatcher, 1996, 2000; Holland, 2000; Ward, 1998). However, faculty are a particularly influential stakeholder group when considering curricular innovations like service-learning since generally they have autonomy in how they choose to structure a course and in the types of instructional methodologies used (Bowen & Schuster, 1986).

Although faculty support and involvement is essential to service-learning institutionalization efforts, the nature of faculty work and faculty reward structures makes garnering their support a major challenge (Bess, 1997; Blackburn & Lawrence, 1995; Fairweather, 1996). In addition, variables such as individual characteristics (gender, ethnicity, age), institutional type, institutional mission and policies, disciplinary culture, and perceptions of teaching and learning all play major roles in faculty members' curricular decisions and teaching role performance (Braxton, 1995; Braxton & Hargens, 1996; Braxton, Olsen, & Simmons, 1998; Einarson, 1999; Furco, 2002; Gelmon, Holland, Shinnamon, & Morris, 1998). Given these many factors that affect faculty behavior, particularly in regard to service-learning, this study addressed both individual and institutional determinants of faculty teaching behavior so that service-learning's potential on campuses might be realized.

Literature on the institutionalization of service-learning describes various factors that affect the integration of service-learning on campuses across the nation (Bringle & Hatcher, 1996, 2000; Holland, 1997; Serow, Calleson, Parker, & Morgan, 1996; Ward, 1996, 1998; Zlotkowski, 1996). One of the key variables representing a constant thread in the literature on institutionalization involves faculty. Therefore, as Abes, Jackson, and Jones (2002) and Driscoll (2000) demonstrated, given that relatively few studies have examined how faculty perceive service-learning and what individual and institutional factors motivate or deter faculty from service-learning engagement, the author's study addressed the following research question: *What individual and institutional factors influence faculty engagement in service-learning?*

This study's main purpose was to develop an enhanced understanding of the institutional and individual factors that encourage or inhibit faculty service-learning participation in specific types of higher education institutions across the nation. Consequently, in conjunction with the Abes and colleagues (2002) study, this analysis contributes to the literature as a foundational study that examines key factors for service-learning institutionalization in regard to faculty. In addition to enhancing the growing body of literature exploring factors that affect faculty participation in service-learning, groundwork is laid for future studies that can delve more deeply into this area. Moreover, this study provides policymakers and administrators with information to assist in service-learning institutionalization strategies appropriate to various types of higher education institutions, thereby impacting both future research and practice.

RESEARCH DESIGN AND METHODOLOGY

Variables

The independent variables (see Table 9.1) for this study fell within two main groupings: (1) Institutional Characteristics and (2) Individual Characteristics. Within these two umbrella groupings, six broad categories existed. The category of Institutional/Organizational Factors came under Institutional Characteristics. The other five broad categories related to Individual Factors included:

1. Sociodemographic characteristics;
2. Academic background;
3. Scholarly productivity;
4. Disciplinary affiliation; and
5. Employment status.

In addition, eight scale variables addressed individual behaviors and perceptions in relation to:

- Teaching beliefs and philosophy
  1. *student-centered*
  2. *community-oriented*
- Graduate school socialization
  3. *socialization to teaching*
- Perceived campus support for service-learning
  4. *administrative support*
  5. *promotion/tenure*
  6. *course development/assistance*
  7. *campus resources/support*
- Personal perceptions of service-learning
  8. *service-learning perceptions*

Research Questions

Research foci were categorized based on individual faculty characteristics, academic/disciplinary characteristics, and institutional/organizational characteristics. These questions are based on the conceptual framework and literature review since few previous research studies existed in relation to faculty and service-learning.

Table 9.1.   Independent Variables and Measures

Independent Variable	Measures
Institutional Characteristics	*Type/Carnegie Classification*
	Doctoral/Research
	Masters/Comprehensive
	Baccalaureate/Liberal Arts
Individual Characteristics	*Gender*
Sociodemographic Characteristics	Male
	Female
	Age
	Under 30
	31–40
	41–50
	51–60
	60+
	Race/Ethnicity
	African American
	American Indian
	Asian American/Asian
	Asian Indian
	Mexican American/Chicano
	Puerto Rican American
	White/Caucasian
	Other
	Political Orientation
	Liberal
	Middle of the Road
	Conservative
Academic Background	Number of Years Teaching
	Less than 1
	1–5
	6–10
	11–15
	15+
Scholarly Productivity	Number of Publications
	None
	1–3
	4–6
	7–10
	10+
Disciplinary Affiliation	Principal Teaching Discipline
	Low/Applied
	High/Applied
	Low/Pure
	High/Pure

Table 9.1.   Independent Variables and Measures (Cont.)

Independent Variable	Measures
Employment Status	*Full-Time/Part-Time Rank* Full Professor Associate Professor Assistant Professor Lecturer/Instructor *Tenure Status* Nontenured Tenure-track Tenured
Scale Variables	*Student-Centered; Community-Oriented; Administrative Support; Promotion/Tenure; Course Development/ Assistance; Campus Resources/Support; Socialization to Teaching; Service-Learning Perceptions*

The following questions are adapted from Antonio, Astin, and Cress (2000).

Personal/Individual Characteristics

- Are student-centered and/or community-oriented faculty more likely to participate in service-learning than other faculty members?
- Are women of color and/or lower-ranking faculty more likely to participate in service-learning than other faculty members?
- Are high-ranking, older, and/or stronger "intellectual orientation" faculty less likely to participate in service-learning than other faculty members?
- Are faculty with a liberal political affiliation more likely to participate in service-learning than those faculty with more conservative beliefs?

Academic Background/Disciplinary Differences

- Are faculty in low-consensus disciplines (e.g., education, history) more likely to participate in service-learning than faculty in high-consensus disciplines (e.g., biology, math)? (Biglan, 1973; Braxton, 1995; Braxton et al., 1998)
- Are faculty who are socialized to their teaching role in graduate school more likely to participate in service-learning than those who were not socialized to their teaching role? (Austin, 2002; Nyquist et al., 1999)

Institutional/Organizational Characteristics

- Are faculty at research-oriented institutions less likely to participate in service-learning than faculty at other types of institutions? Conversely, are faculty at teaching-oriented institutions more likely to participate in service-learning than faculty at research-oriented institutions? (Einarson, 1999; Ward, 2002)
- Are non-tenure-track and tenured faculty more likely to participate in service-learning than tenure-track faculty? (Morton & Troppe, 1996; Stanton, 1994; Ward, 1998)
- Are faculty with campus resources and support for service-learning more likely to participate than those without similar resources? (Abes et al., 2002)

Sampling Procedures and Subjects

Campus Compact, an organization that assists colleges and universities with service-learning initiatives at state and national levels, provided a list of member states and schools from which the random institutional sample was selected. The decision to utilize Campus Compact–affiliated states (and their respective institutional members) afforded appropriate and representative numbers of faculty that participate in service-learning as well as those that do not participate.

From the 30 Campus Compact state organizations, a purposive sample comprised of 15 institutions was selected: five institutions from each of three Carnegie-classification institutional types (see Basinger, 2000).

1. Doctoral/research universities-extensive;
2. Master's (comprehensive) colleges and universities I; and
3. Baccalaureate colleges-liberal arts.

These institutional types were selected because their missions and culture represent a continuum of research-oriented to teaching-oriented, going from Doctoral/Research to Master's/Comprehensive to Baccalaureate/Liberal Arts. By randomly selecting five institutions of each type from all of the Campus Compact state organizations' member schools, a national sample was provided to address issues of generalizability and to strengthen this study's external validity.

A systematic, random sample of all of the full-time undergraduate faculty within each of the 15 colleges and universities was selected. To be considered a full-time undergraduate faculty member, participants had to have a faculty appointment in an undergraduate college/school within his or her respective institution and carry full-time status.

Data Collection

In February 2003, the *Faculty Teaching Behaviors* survey was sent to select study participants at each designated institution. Additionally, a Web site address was available so respondents could complete the survey online. A program called SurveySuite was utilized. Three forms of the *same* survey allowed for coding of institutional type. Items on all surveys were the same. Mailed hard copies were coded for institutional type by color as well as title. One week after the initial mailing, a follow-up postcard was sent. A third and final contact was made one week after the postcard via e-mail to again thank the faculty sample for their participation and to remind them once more to complete and return the survey (either by snail mail or e-mail).

Of the 1,004 surveys mailed to potential faculty respondents, 13 were undeliverable. Of the 981 remaining mailed surveys, 364 surveys were returned for an overall response rate of 37.1%. Of the 364 returned surveys, nine respondents returned blank surveys as an indication that they were unwilling to participate in the study. Additionally, 33 were not included in data analyses because the respondents were either not full time or were retired. This resulted in a total of 322 useable surveys for data analysis.

Instrument

The *Faculty Teaching Behaviors Survey* was designed to gather baseline data about the characteristics of faculty and the individual and organizational influences on their behavior toward service-learning. Because there was no other survey in existence specifically examining the individual and institutional factors affecting faculty engagement in service-learning, the instrument utilized the literature, concepts, and items from four other faculty surveys conducted in recent years (Blackburn & Lawrence, 1995; Einarson, 1999; Hammond, 1994b; Higher Education Research Institute, 1998). In addition, two focus groups of faculty and service-learning practitioners helped conceptualize and critique various drafts of the survey. An initial group of colleagues participated in a roundtable discussion at the First International Service-Learning Research Conference, and the second group, comprised of faculty involved in a year-long service-learning seminar, offered suggestions on the final draft of the survey.

Because this study sought to describe the given institutional contexts of service-learning, the term "service-learning" was *not* defined in the survey for participants. This decision was intentional and given much consideration though it was apparent that for those who did not know what service-learning was, they might be much less likely to participate in the study. However, since this study's focus was also on the institutional factors that promoted the use of or deterred faculty from utilizing service-learning on their respective campuses, allowing service-learning to be defined by survey respondents provided each individual an opportunity to identify his or her understanding and definition of service-learning *within his or her institution*.

The following survey item attempted to examine faculty members' definitions and understanding of service-learning activities.

At my institution service-learning includes the following types of activities (check all that apply):

a. _____ Community or volunteer service unrelated to a course
b. _____ A one-credit service option connected to an academic course
c. _____ Reflection activities that help integrate classroom theory and community service experiences
d. _____ Mandatory service requirement for graduation
e. _____ Academic activities that are enhanced by a planned service activity that meets a community need
f. _____ Don't know
g. _____ Other

Table 9.2 displays responses to this question.

Table 9.2. Understanding/Defining Service-Learning Activities

Responses	N	Percent
a. Community or volunteer service unrelated to a course	186	59.8
b. A one-credit service option connected to an academic course	65	21.0
c. Reflection activities that integrate classroom theory and community service experiences	139	44.7
d. Mandatory service requirement for graduation	27	8.7
e. Academic activities enhanced by a planned service activity that meets community needs	160	51.4
f. Don't know	85	27.3
g. Other	21	8.9

These data show that over half of the respondents (59.8%) considered service-learning a community or volunteer service unrelated to a course, although the definition used most often in the field of service-learning currently is more aligned with Bringle and Hatcher's (1995) definition of service-learning:

A course-based, credit-bearing educational experience that links academic study with community service wherein students: (a) participate in an organized service activity that meets identified community needs, and (b) reflect on the service activity as a means of gaining a deeper understanding of course content, a broader appreciation of the discipline, and/or an enhanced sense of civic responsibility. (p. 113)

Responses for 'c' and 'e' (see Table 9.2) are aligned with the definition above and received the second and third highest response rates (44.7% and 51.4%, respectively). Twenty-one percent described service-learning on their campuses as a one-credit service option connected to an academic course (b). These responses indicate a working knowledge of service-learning for approximately half or fewer of the respondents.

However, in analyzing the data regarding understanding/defining service-learning activities more closely, it was discerned that the majority of respondents that marked *community service or volunteer work not related to an academic course* also marked the other responses that more aptly define service-learning (reflection activities that integrate classroom theory and community service experiences and academic activities enhanced by a planned service activity that meets community needs). This might be a logical thought process for faculty who view community service or volunteer work as a building block toward service-learning and the eventual integration of such activities into academic coursework.

More than one fourth, or 27.3%, of the sample reported not knowing what types of activities comprised service-learning activities on their campuses. Coupled with the most significant response of service-learning as a volunteer or community service activity unrelated to a course (59.8%), these findings support what recent research has demonstrated (Abes et al., 2002): There are a significant number of faculty who do not know what service-learning is, what activities it includes, or how it relates to academic goals and curriculum.

Eight scale variables were also included in the survey:

1. Student-centered is a scale that measures a faculty member's teaching focus and goals for teaching and his or her students, particularly in relation to students' psychosocial development and citizenship behaviors;

2. Community-oriented relates to the role of both service and outreach and its interaction with faculty members' personal values and beliefs;

3. Administrative and collegial support concerns perceived support for service-learning from colleagues and administrators;

4. Promotion and tenure represents a variable relating to whether or not a faculty member's institution rewarded service-learning within tenure and promotion decisions;

5. Course development/assistance focuses on whether or not a faculty member perceived tangible support (release time, reduced teaching

load, graduate assistantships) from his or her institution to develop and implement service-learning courses;

6. Campus resources and support regards the institutional resources and support available to faculty to assist in creating and implementing a service-learning course;

7. Socialization to teaching concerns the graduate school socialization a faculty member received regarding teaching methodologies, philosophy, and personal style; and

8. Service-learning perceptions deals with how service-learning is viewed as a teaching methodology.

Defining the Dependent Variable

The dependent variable, service-learning participation, was measured by assessing faculty members' experiences with service and service-learning. Table 9.3 details the items related to faculty participation in community service and service-learning.

Table 9.3. Community Service/Service-Learning Participation (N = 322)

Item		N^*/Yes	Percent	N^*/No	Percent
c5.	I have taught at least 1 SL course in my teaching career.	79	26.6	218	73.4
c9.	I have never offered a SL course.	169	58.5	120	41.5
c3.	I am currently engaged in community service.	181	58.2	130	41.8
c4.	I currently teach a SL course.	33	11.1	264	88.9
c7.	I did SL once and do not plan to do it again.	16	5.8	262	94.2
c8.	I have no plans to engage in SL.	83	29.5	198	70.5
c10.	I would consider offering a SL course.	219	78.6	56	20.3

* Total number of *yes* and *no* answers

The data demonstrate that 26.6% ($n = 79$) of the faculty respondents indicated having taught at least one service-learning course in their teaching careers, while 58.2% ($n = 181$) indicated engagement in community service. Thirty-three or 11.1% of the faculty in the study currently teach a service-learning course, whereas 29.5% ($n = 83$) have no intention of engaging in service-learning. A small percentage (5.8%) had engaged in service-learning once and did not plan to do it again; and in contrast, a vast majority of the respondents, 78.6% ($n = 219$), indicated that they would consider offering a service-learning course.

RESULTS

Chi square tests, *t* tests, and binomial logistic regression were statistical analyses utilized in this study to determine: (a) whether or not differences existed for faculty who participate in service-learning versus those who do not participate, and (b) whether or not any of the variables in this study could predict faculty engagement in service-learning. The chi square analysis did not demonstrate any significant differences for those faculty who participate in service-learning versus those who do not for any of the categorical independent variables. The *t* tests did demonstrate significant differences with regard to six of the eight scale variables:

1. Student-centered;
2. Community-oriented;
3. Promotion and tenure;
4. Administrative and collegial support;
5. Campus resources and support; and
6. Service-learning perceptions.

However, it is important to keep in mind that these were zero order findings for which other variables were not controlled. The two scale variables that did not demonstrate significance included support for course development and socialization to teaching.

Logistic regression was used to determine if any of the independent variables could be utilized to predict service-learning participation. Because the final logistic regression model controlled for the largest number of items, and due to the fact that no items in preliminary models lost significance in the final model, the major statistically significant finding is presented based on this analysis (see Table 9.4). Interestingly, only one factor, the scale variable related to service-learning perceptions, demonstrated significance in the final model. Thus, the key finding is that faculty with positive perceptions of service-learning were three and a half times as likely (Exp.B = 3.54) to participate in service-learning.

Discussion

No significant differences were discerned based on institutional type, disciplinary affiliation, rank, tenure status, age, gender, ethnicity, political beliefs, years teaching, or number of publications. Six of the eight scale variables demonstrated zero order significant differences for faculty who participate in service-learning (vs. those who do not participate in service-

**Table 9.4. Final Logistic Regression Model
(All Control Variables and Scales)**

	B	Exp.B	SE
Institutional Type			
Research	*Ref.*	—	—
Masters	.610	1.84	.71
Liberal Arts	.188	1.21	.76
Disciplinary Affiliation			
Low/Pure	*Ref.*	—	—
High/Pure	−.140	.869	.59
High/Applied	−.020	1.021	.781
Low/Applied	−.310	.733	.561
Rank			
Full Professor	*Ref.*	—	—
Asst. Professor	1.553	4.725	.826
Lecturer/Instructor	−2.099	.123	1.68
Tenure Status			
Tenured	*Ref.*	—	—
Tenure-Track	−.594	.552	.672
Nontenured	2.656	14.233	1.538
Gender			
Female	*Ref.*	—	—
Male	.107	1.113	.483
Ethnicity			
White	*Ref.*	—	—
Nonwhite	−.209	.811	.75
Age	.084	1.088	.278
Political Values			
Conservative	*Ref.*	—	—
Middle of Road	.44	1.55	.673
Liberal	−.287	.75	.69
Years Teaching	.405	1.500	.352
Publications	−.074	.929	.210
Scales			
Student-Centered	.029	1.030	.396
Community-Oriented	−.130	.878	.320
Administrative Support	.425	1.53	.358
Promotion/Tenure	−.041	.959	.257
Course Development	.150	1.162	.299
Campus Resources/Support	.230	1.258	.259
Socialization to Teaching	.144	1.155	.208
Service-Learning Perceptions	1.265*	3.542	.437
Overall R^2		.30	

* $p <$ or $= .01$

learning). These findings indicated that faculty who participate in service-learning generally:

- Are more concerned with student learning and development—both in regard to course content and in terms of broader outcomes related to social, community, and personal values;
- Are more community or service oriented wherein community service and/or values related to community are evidenced;
- Perceive greater support for service-learning work from campus administrators and colleagues;
- Perceive less support from their institution in relation to service-learning participation and promotion and tenure policies and decisions;
- Perceive greater campus resources and support available to assist in service-learning endeavors (workshops, funding, release time, center/staff); and
- Perceive service-learning as an effective teaching methodology.

However, in the final logistic regression analysis, which controlled for the largest number of items, only one scale remained statistically significant: service-learning perceptions. Meanwhile, the categorical variables (institutional type, discipline, rank, tenure, status, gender, age, ethnicity, political affiliation, years teaching, and number of publications) continued to demonstrate no significance, as evidenced previously in the chi-square analysis.

What these somewhat surprising outcomes indicate is that an individual faculty member's *perceptions of service-learning* are the greatest indicators of his or her support for or participation in service-learning. And, for the respondents in this study, aspects of faculty life, such as tenure status, rank, disciplinary affiliation, number of years teaching, or number of publications, do not make a difference with regard to faculty participation in service-learning. Furthermore, this study demonstrated that personal characteristics, such as gender, age, ethnicity, and political beliefs, also do not make a difference in relation to faculty service-learning participation.

Lastly, in the final analysis, given the 10 research questions this study was designed to address, none of the questions were answered in the affirmative. Questions related to student-centeredness and community-orientedness, institutional type, gender, ethnicity, rank, political leaning, disciplinary affiliation, tenure status, campus resources and support, and graduate school socialization were all rejected as plausible influences on faculty participation in service-learning.

And although Abes and colleagues (2002) found very few differences in light of the various factors they analyzed, they noted one important difference in regard to academic discipline. They found non-service-learning faculty in high-consensus disciplines, such as math and science, perceived service-learning as lacking relevance and rigor within their disciplines. This finding, however, was not substantiated in this study.

Other studies that have examined faculty and service-learning in the past 10 years have demonstrated that:

- Student learning outcomes and curricular concerns are key motivators for faculty participation in service-learning (Abes et al., 2002; Hammond, 1994a);
- Faculty participation in service-learning is more likely if it is a faculty-led initiative (Morton & Troppe, 1996);
- Faculty are more likely to engage in service-learning when they see respected colleagues participate (Gelmon et al., 1998);
- Community members and students are strong motivators to faculty participation in service-learning (Abes et al., 2002);
- Colleagues and department chairs are an important impetus to service-learning use (Abes et al., 2002); and
- Deterrents include logistical concerns, evidence of improved academic outcomes, and service-learning "how to" for effective integration into courses (Abes et al., 2002).

Findings from these other studies over the past 10 years are in contrast with the current study's main conclusion that faculty perceptions of service-learning *are the most significant factor* affecting faculty participation in service-learning. In the current study, it was not logistical or curricular concerns or institutional type, disciplinary affiliation, or campus resources that proved to be of utmost importance to faculty participation in service-learning. It was simply whether or not faculty had knowledge and positive perceptions of service-learning. Therefore, this study's findings propose that lack of faculty participation in service-learning may have more to do with lack of knowledge about service-learning (its philosophy and teaching strategies), its positive outcomes, or how it might be implemented into a course. And although some service-learning practitioners and researchers might argue that faculty do not participate in service-learning *simply because they do not like it,* the current study suggests other plausible rationale.

When considering strategies for institutionalizing service-learning, these findings have a significant impact. While many of the other studies have advocacy strategies to get faculty *involved* in service-learning, this study's findings stress the importance of simply getting the word out by disseminating information about service-learning and helping faculty understand what service-learning is and how it works. Thoroughly and effectively educating faculty and campuses about service-learning is critical to increasing knowledge and hence, positive perceptions of service-learning, so that more faculty will become engaged.

Limitations

Though the findings from this study account for approximately 30% of the variation in faculty participation in service-learning, limitations must be noted. First, a response rate of 37% was reached for this study. Though the 37% response rate is below the acceptable minimum of 50% noted in social science research literature (Babbie, 1999), this response rate is aligned with other similar studies on faculty and service-learning. For example, Abes and colleagues (2002) had a 39% response rate on their study of faculty and service-learning, while also having a gatekeeper at each institution helping to gather data. Additionally, since the Higher Education Research Institute's (see Sax, Astin, Korn, & Gilmartin, 1999) national faculty norms survey had a response rate of 43%, and the National Campus Compact (1999) faculty survey resulted in a 21% response rate, the 37.1% response rate procured for the current study was deemed within an acceptable range.

Second, there may be additional individual and organizational characteristics that influence faculty participation in service-learning that were not included in this study. For example, institutional control (public vs. private) would be another important variable to consider in regard to organizational characteristics. As well, examining the personal beliefs that affect faculty members' teaching styles and methodologies might shed additional light on why faculty members choose certain pedagogies over others. Moreover, an in-depth focus on the role of discipline beyond the high, low, pure, and applied dimensions might also facilitate a greater understanding of faculty engagement in service-learning. Departmental culture and the department as socializing agent could also benefit service-learning research by examining the departmental role in regard to faculty service-learning participation.

Finally, lack of a clear definition of service-learning in the survey may have been problematic, particularly for faculty who had never heard of service-learning (27% of respondents) or who were unclear about its definition. The lack of a definition may have also been a deterrent for others who either did not fill out and return the survey or who may have begun to fill it out and then, realizing they did not know what service-learning was, declined to complete and return the survey. A small number of faculty did e-mail to obtain clarification about the definition of service-learning. Though determining faculty members' knowledge and understanding of service-learning *for their institution* was one of the aims of this study, perhaps providing a working definition within the survey would have been be useful. Given that qualitative inquiries also demonstrated differences in terminology and definitions for service-learning within and among participating institutions, the need for consistent and coherent language and definitions was substantiated.

Implications for Practice

To illustrate some of the inherent tensions that exist around knowledge and perceptions of service-learning, the following is an example from a mathematics faculty member who e-mailed comments regarding this study.

> I tried to be a good academic citizen and fill out your survey but I stopped in the middle because I had no idea what your questions meant—you use constantly a jargon term "service-learning," which in 37 years in a major research university I have never heard, so I couldn't give any reasonable answers to your questions. This is why there is so seldom any communication between educational researchers and other faculty—if you are going to ask us questions, you have to do it in language that makes sense outside of education schools. The data from your project will be useless because most real faculty will simply discard the survey as incomprehensible.

To these comments, a response was sent thanking this faculty member for his feedback, explaining what service-learning is, and sharing that his institution has one of the top service-learning programs in the nation along with other nationally recognized activities. The math professor sent a final e-mail that said:

> I suspect that familiarity with these programs is very strongly correlated with field. I would be very surprised if any mathematics faculty knew anything about this or would be interested. I think community service is fine, but it isn't what should be going on in a university classroom. There are much more important intellectual tasks to be done there . . .

This example sharply illuminates this study's major finding: knowledge and positive perceptions of service-learning are critical for service-learning's widespread acceptance and institutionalization. The fact that a faculty member of 37 years at an institution with one of the best service-learning programs in the nation had never even heard of service-learning speaks to the need for greater and improved dissemination of information about service-learning. But this example also carries with it an important reminder: not all faculty members in all disciplines can be expected to be service-learning proponents. Nevertheless, in sharing information about service-learning with as many faculty members as possible, an opportunity can be provided to offer students a broader and deeper education, not only regarding content knowledge, but also about themselves and their communities. At a minimum, all faculty members should have knowledge about alternative teaching methodologies, such as service-learning, so that they might have the option to choose *how* they teach their subject matter. In turn, this might afford their students and themselves education that extends beyond the classroom's four walls.

In thinking about how service-learning knowledge and perceptions can be impacted systemically, three critical areas include:

1. Graduate training and socialization;
2. Teacher education; and
3. Campus specialization.

Graduate Training and Socialization

Graduate training and socialization provide a foundation for future faculty members' careers in academia (Austin, 2002); however, an emphasis on teaching has often been usurped by a primary focus on research (Bringle, Games, & Malloy, 1999; Cuban, 1999). For service-learning to become more embedded in institutions of higher education, graduate students need to be trained to be effective teachers with some focus on pedagogy. In addition, they need to be exposed to the role of service in the life of academia (Ward, 2002).

One way to incorporate this service-learning initiative into campus service-learning programs is to offer graduate student service-learning seminars. Similar to faculty service-learning seminars that teach faculty how to incorporate service-learning into their courses while also providing its historical and philosophical background (Jones, 2001; Stanton, 1994), graduate seminars can be offered to provide graduate students with information on how service-learning works and the benefits accrued. Graduate students might develop a project that incorporates a service-learning component into a course for which they assist, create a service-learning syllabus for a course they would like to teach in the future, or even create "brown bag" lunches to inform their department about service-learning and possible options within their field. This effort would align with the work of many campuses that are currently undertaking programs to better train and prepare future faculty members (Austin, 2002; Gaff, Pruitt-Logan, & Weibl, 2000; Nyquist et al., 1999).

Teacher Education

   Teacher education programs are another ripe area upon which service-learning initiatives can build. Since teacher education programs straddle both the higher education and K–12 worlds by providing graduate students with advanced training in content and pedagogy for teaching at the primary and secondary levels, infusing service-learning into these types of programs would provide a strong foundation for service-learning. This foundation would be especially beneficial because it would provide a strong infrastructure for service-learning within schools of education in academia as well as training a cadre of K–12 teachers in service-learning pedagogy as well. This would provide service-learning opportunities for students across all educational levels and would create an expectation for service-learning as graduating high school students enter their respective higher education institutions.

Campus Specialization

   Campus specialization refers to a third area where policymakers and administrators might focus their efforts to bring more attention to service-learning. By looking at one's own institution and its culture—its strengths, weaknesses, opportunities, and threats—*strategic institutionalization* can be implemented. For example, at some institutions the visibility of an *academic* post (as compared to a student services post) can be very influential in raising the status of service-learning. Furthermore, thinking about where service-learning best fits within the curriculum at both the school and department level is also beneficial. Some schools have begun the work of thinking about how service-learning can be implemented within each school or department so that every student has at least one opportunity in their college career to engage in service-learning. Other ideas include building interdisciplinary clusters of faculty around a single issue and creating a service-learning experience in collaboration around said issue. Grants can often be procured for such interdisciplinary work, providing additional resources and support for the project, not to mention credibility and visibility to service-learning efforts.

   Lastly, for faculty and administrators who are working to institutionalize service-learning, building community within the campus is as important for effective service-learning programs as the cultivation of community outside the campus borders. Networks of faculty and administrators that work together, whether through centers (i.e., center for teaching) or between departments, committees, or through learning communities (i.e., residential colleges), can have an enormous impact on the visibility and perceptions of service-learning at a particular campus. The voices of those noted individual faculty members who are involved in and supportive of service-learning are also needed as well as platforms from which their voices can be heard. Students can also be involved in this intracampus network (i.e., residential colleges), since their voices and energy often provide additional motivation and visibility to a worthy cause. It is only through such a multifaceted approach that service-learning knowledge and understanding can be widely and effectively disseminated and hence, increase service-learning participation at campuses nationwide.

DIRECTIONS FOR FUTURE RESEARCH

This study provides fertile ground for further research in the area of faculty and service-learning participation. Though a couple of quantitative studies have focused on motivators and deterrents to faculty use of service-learning, qualitative studies that provide more depth around the issues of individual and institutional factors affecting faculty engagement in service-learning would be useful. This study employed brief interviews with administrators on each campus where faculty were surveyed to obtain a better understanding of the culture of service-learning at each respective campus. In-depth interviews with faculty members are considered to be imperative to developing a comprehensive understanding of the motivators and deterrents to faculty engagement in service-learning.

Being able to hear directly from faculty who are involved in service-learning, those who are not, and those who might consider it about their perceptions and behaviors in regard to service-learning participation would be beneficial. Furthermore, it would be interesting to compare and contrast a qualitative study's findings to the outcomes of quantitative studies completed thus far. In addition, delving more deeply into the intrinsic motivators for individual faculty members seems to be a key question requiring further study. Indeed, this inquiry would align with the finding of Abes and colleagues (2002) that internal motivation rather than external rewards drives faculty service-learning use.

Because this study only examined faculty at three institutional types— Research Extensive, Master's/Comprehensive, and Liberal Arts/ Baccalaureate—it would be interesting to conduct this study at either other institutional types (i.e., tribal colleges, historically black colleges and universities, associate or community colleges) or by institutional control (i.e., public land-grant institutions vs. private institutions). Since institutional type and control strongly affects the values and culture of a college or university, and its faculty members as well, the results of such a study would be beneficial to the field of service-learning. In addition, an assessment of the impact of the department as a key component of an institution might accentuate the role of institutional effects at the departmental level for faculty participation in service-learning.

Moreover, the area of graduate school socialization and faculty socialization in general appears to be an area in the service-learning literature that has not been widely examined. Because the socialization process clearly impacts the teaching methodologies one adopts (Austin, 2002; Sorcinelli, 1999; Tierney & Rhoads, 1994), a study focusing on this aspect of a faculty member's professional development could lead to insights about how this process might be structured to enhance service-learning participation.

A study that solely focuses on graduate students, many of whom will become faculty members in the future, would be of benefit to the field. Assessing graduate students' knowledge, beliefs, and perceptions about service-learning as a pedagogy would provide a baseline for understanding future faculty members' service-learning knowledge, behavior, and perceptions. Since graduate schools train future faculty members, harnessing their enthusiasm, intellect, and skills to integrate service-learning into the mainstream on many campuses seems instrumental to the institutionalization of service-learning at higher education institutions across the nation.

Lastly, Boyer (1990) outlined four areas of scholarship to better address the roles and work of faculty. Although service-learning is often categorized within the scholarship of application, which is associated with engagement and strives to address the responsible application of knowledge to social problems (Boyer, 1990; Braxton, Luckey, & Helland, 2002), examining service-learning's role across all the different types of scholarship would appear worthwhile (Ward, 2002). Since service-learning has the potential to incorporate into its work the three key aspects of most higher education institutions' missions—teaching, research, and service— a study focusing on service-learning as scholarship could prove beneficial. Ward (2002) and Holland (1999) initiate this basis in their work on faculty service roles and the scholarship of engagement (see also Boyer, 1996). This type of study might not only increase faculty members' positive perceptions of service-learning, but might also enhance its image as an increasingly valid and credible pedagogy.

In conclusion, by further determining and examining the relationships between the individual and institutional factors that affect faculty engagement in service-learning, the foundation initiated by Abes and colleagues (2002) was strengthened and the potential to inform future studies on faculty and service-learning was presented. Although the current study included a random national sample, whereas the Abes and colleagues study focused solely on one state, this study demonstrated no differences for faculty who participate in service-learning versus those who do not participate in service-learning. Even though there is much left to explain as to whether faculty will participate in service-learning or not, the variables selected in this study account for approximately 30% of the variation in faculty participation in service-learning.

This study not only contributes to the foundation upon which future studies on faculty and service-learning can build, but also illuminates the fact that for service-learning to become institutionalized on campuses across the nation, proponents and policymakers need to do a better job of promoting service-learning to diverse constituencies and by appropriate means for particular audiences. Campuses need to more widely disseminate their service-learning programs and resources *to increase knowledge and perceptions of service-learning* as an effective pedagogy. Only then will service-learning truly have the opportunity to become deeply embedded as an educational philosophy, curricular pedagogy, and institutional program within the culture of colleges and universities nationwide.

REFERENCES

Abes, E., Jackson, G., & Jones, S. (2002, Fall). Factors that motivate and deter faculty use of service-learning. *Michigan Journal of Community Service Learning*, 5–17.

Antonio, A., Astin, H., & Cress, C. (2000). Community service in higher education: A look at the nation's faculty. *Review of Higher Education, 23*(4), 373–397.

Astin, A. (2000, Fall). Conceptualizing service-learning research using Ken Wilber's integral framework. *Michigan Journal of Community Service Learning* [Special Issue], 98–104.

Austin, A. (1996). Institutional and departmental cultures: The relationship between teaching and research. In *New Directions for Institutional Research* (Vol. 90, pp. 57–66). San Francisco: Jossey-Bass.

Austin, A. (2002). Preparing the next generation of faculty: Graduate school as socialization to the academic career. *Journal of Higher Education, 73*(1), 94–122.

Babbie, E. (1999). *The basics of social research.* Belmont, CA: Wadsworth.

Basinger, J. (2000). A new way of classifying colleges elates some and perturbs others. *Chronicle of Higher Education, XLVI*(49), A31–A42.

Bess, J. (1997). *Teaching well and liking it.* Baltimore: Johns Hopkins University Press.

Biglan, A. (1973). Relationships between subject matter characteristics and the structure and output of university departments. *Journal of Applied Psychology, 57*(3), 204–213.

Blackburn, R., & Lawrence, J. (1995). *Faculty at work: Motivation, expectation, and satisfaction.* Baltimore: Johns Hopkins University Press.

Bowen, H., & Schuster, J. (1986). *American professors: A national resource imperiled.* New York: Oxford University Press.

Boyer, E. (1990). *Scholarship reconsidered: Priorities of the professoriate.* Princeton, NJ: Carnegie Foundation for the Advancement of Teaching.

Boyer, E. (1996). The scholarship of engagement. *Journal of Public Service and Outreach, 1*(1), 11–20.

Braxton, J. (1995). Disciplines with an affinity for the improvement of undergraduate education. In N. Hativa & M. Marincovich (Eds.), *Disciplinary differences in teaching and learning: Implications for practice* (pp. 59–64). San Francisco: Jossey-Bass.

Braxton, J., & Hargens, L. (1996).Variation among academic disciplines. Analytical frameworks and research. *Higher Education: Handbook of Theory and Research, XI,* 1–45.

Braxton, J. M., Luckey, W., & Helland, P. (2002). Institutionalizing a broader view of scholarship through Boyer's four domains. *ASHE-ERIC Higher Education Report, 29*(2). (ERIC Document Reproduction Service No. ED469447)

Braxton, J., Olsen, D., & Simmons, A. (1998). Affinity disciplines and the use of principles of good practice for undergraduate education. *Research in Higher Education, 39*(3), 299–318.

Bringle, R., Games, R., & Malloy E. (1999). *Colleges and universities as citizens.* Needham Heights, MA: Allyn & Bacon.

Bringle, R., & Hatcher, J. (1995). A service-learning curriculum for faculty. *Michigan Journal of Community Service Learning, 2,* 112–122.

Bringle, R., & Hatcher, J. (1996). Implementing service learning in higher education. *Journal of Higher Education, 67*(2), 221–239.

Bringle, R. & Hatcher, J. (2000). Institutionalizing service-learning in higher education. *Journal of Higher Education, 71*(3), 273–290.

Clark, B. (1987). *The academic life: Small worlds, different worlds.* Princeton, NJ: Carnegie Foundation for the Advancement of Teaching.

Clark, B. (1991). The organizational saga in higher education. In M. Peterson, E. Chaffee, & T. White (Eds.), *Organization and governance in higher education* (pp. 46–52). Needham Heights, MA: Pearson.

Cohen, M., & March, J. (1986). *Leadership and ambiguity.* Boston: Harvard University Press.

Cuban, L. (1999). *How scholars trumped teachers: Change without reform in university curriculum, teaching, and research, 1890–1990.* New York: Teachers College Press.

Driscoll, A. (2000, Fall). Studying faculty and service-learning: Directions for inquiry and development. *Michigan Journal of Community Service Learning* [Special Issue], 35–41.

Einarson, M. (1999, November). *Influences on undergraduate teaching methods: Conceptual framework and comparison of personal, disciplinary and organizational contexts across types of postsecondary institutions.* Paper presented at the annual meeting of the Association for the Study of Higher Education (ASHE), Sacramento, CA.

Fairweather, J. (1996). *Faculty work and public trust: Restoring the value of teaching and public service in American academic life.* Needham Heights, MA: Allyn & Bacon.

Furco, A. (2002). *Self-assessment rubric for the institutionalization of service-learning in higher education.* Providence, RI: Brown University.

Gaff, J., Pruitt-Logan, A., & Weibl, R. (2000). *Building the faculty we need: Colleges and universities working together.* Washington, DC: American Association of Colleges and Universities and the Council of Graduate Schools.

Gelmon, S., Holland, B., Shinnamon, A., & Morris, B. (1998). Community-based education and service: The HPSISN experience. *Journal of Interprofessional Care, 12*(3), 257–272.

Giles, D., & Eyler, J. (1998). A service-learning research agenda for the next five years. In R. A. Rhoads & J. P. F. Howard (Eds.), *Academic service learning: A pedagogy of action and reflection: New Directions for Teaching and Learning 73* (pp. 65–72). San Francisco: Jossey-Bass.

Giles, D., Porter Honnet, E., & Migliore, S. (1991). *Research agenda for combining service and learning in the 1990s.* Arlington, VA: National Society for Experiential Education.

Hammond, C. (1994a). Faculty motivation and satisfaction in Michigan higher education. *Michigan Journal of Community Service Learning, 1*(1), 42–49.

Hammond, C. (1994b). *Integrating service and academic study: Service-learning and faculty motivation in Michigan higher education.* Unpublished doctoral dissertation, Michigan State University, East Lansing.

Higher Education Research Institute. (1998). *Faculty survey.* Los Angeles: University of California at Los Angeles.

Holland, B. (1997). Analyzing institutional commitment to service: A model of key organizational factors. *Michigan Journal of Community Service Learning,* 30–41.

Holland, B. (1999). From murky to meaningful: The role of mission in institutional change. In R. Bringle, R. Games, & E. Malloy (Eds.), *Colleges and universities as citizens* (pp. 48–73). Needham Heights, MA: Allyn & Bacon.

Holland, B. (2000, Fall). Institutional impacts and organizational issues related to service-learning. *Michigan Journal of Community Service Learning* [Special Issue], 52–60.

Jones, S. (2001). The service-learning scholars roundtable: A model for engaging faculty in service-learning theory and practice. In J. B. Anderson, K. J. Swick, & J. Yff (Eds.), *Service-learning in teacher education* (pp. 220–233). Washington, DC: AACTE Publications.

Morton, K., & Troppe, M. (1996). From margin to the mainstream: Campus Compact's project to integrate service with academic study. *Journal of Business Ethics, 15*, 21–32.

National Campus Compact. (1999). *1999 National Campus Compact faculty survey.* Providence, RI: Author.

Nyquist, J., Manning, L., Wulff, D., Austin, A., Sprague, J., Fraser, P., Calcagno, C., & Woodford, B. (1999, May/June). On the road to becoming a professor. *Change,* 18–27.

Rogers, E. (1983). *Diffusion of innovations.* New York: Free Press.

Sax, L., Astin, W., Korn, W., & Gilmartin, S. (1999). *The American college teacher: National norms for the 1998–1999 HERI faculty survey.* Los Angeles: Higher Education Research Institute. (ERIC Document Reproduction Service No. ED435272)

Serow, R., Calleson, D., Parker, L., & Morgan, L. (1996). Institutional support for service-learning. *Journal of Research & Development in Education, 29*(4), 220–225.

Sorcinelli, M. (1999). *Principles of good practice: Supporting early-career faculty.* New Pathways II Project Forum on Faculty Roles and Rewards. Washington, DC: American Association of Higher Education.

Stanton, T. (1994). The experience of faculty participants in an instructional development seminar on service-learning. *Michigan Journal of Community Service Learning, 1,* 7–20.

Tierney, W., & Rhoads, R. (1994). Faculty socialization as a cultural process: A mirror of institutional commitment. *ASHE-ERIC Higher Education Report, 93*(6). (ERIC Document Reproduction Service No. ED368321)

Wade, R., Berk, E., & Siddens, S. (2000). Issues involved in faculty implementation of community service-learning in teacher education. *NSEE Quarterly, 26*(2), 1–15.

Ward, K. (1996). Service-learning & student volunteerism: Reflections on institutional commitment. *Michigan Journal of Community Service Learning, 3,* 55–65.

Ward, K. (1998). Addressing academic culture: Service learning, organizations, and faculty work. In R. A. Rhoads & J. P. F. Howard (Eds.), *Academic service-learning: A pedagogy of action and reflection: New Directions for Teaching and Learning, 73* (pp. 73–80). San Francisco: Jossey-Bass.

Ward, K. (2002, November). Faculty service roles and the scholarship of engagement. *ASHE-ERIC Higher Education Report (Jossey-Bass Higher and Adult Education Series), 29*(5). (ERIC Document Reproduction Service No. ED476222)

Zlotkowski, E. (1996). A new voice at the table? Linking service-learning and the academy. *Change, 28*(1), 20–26.

CHAPTER 10

INSTITUTIONALIZING SERVICE-LEARNING ACROSS THE UNIVERSITY

International Comparisons

Sherril Gelmon, Ann Sherman, Marla Gaudet, Carol Mitchell, and Kirsten Trotter

ABSTRACT

As institutions develop service-learning activities and programs, there is increasing interest in understanding the extent of institutionalization of service-learning. The "Furco Rubric" (Furco, 2003), an assessment tool designed to assist institutions both in self-assessing their progress in institutionalization of service-learning *and* as the basis for strategic planning and implementation of enhanced service-learning and related activities, was used for institutional assessments and comparisons at three institutions. All of these institutions are considered leaders in their commitment to service-learning: the University of Natal–Pietermaritzburg in South Africa, St. Francis Xavier University in Canada, and Portland State University in the United States.

New Perspectives in Service-Learning: Research to Advance the Field, pages 195–217

The use of the rubric is illustrated here as a valuable tool for providing a basis for comparisons across institutions with different contexts and missions. This initial set of international comparisons suggests the high potential for a more comprehensive comparative study that could track the progress of institutions over time, and offer opportunities for mutual learning to further advance our knowledge of how service-learning and civic engagement can be promoted and sustained at institutions of higher education.

INTRODUCTION

As institutions develop service-learning activities and programs, there is increasing interest to understand the extent of institutionalization of service-learning. Holland (2000) described institutionalization as "those issues related to the exploration, implementation, expansion and sustainability of service-learning as a programmatic endeavor" (p. 53). Furco (2002) further elaborated this definition to emphasize not only the development of core elements, but also the strategic coordination across elements in a synergistic fashion.

Assessment of institutionalization has posed a challenge because of the multiple forces involved in establishing service-learning as a priority on a campus. Some approaches have focused on assessment of individual components, such as student learning or faculty involvement (Bringle, Phillips, & Hudson, 2004; Gelmon, Holland, Driscoll, Spring, & Kerrigan, 2001). Others have taken a broader view of institutionalization, proposing frameworks for assessment that take into account the multiple forces and factors that drive institutional policy (Furco, 2003; Holland, 1997).

Some of these approaches appear to focus primarily on the United States context. As interest in service-learning grows around the world, opportunities arise to use frameworks for international comparisons—both to better understand the contexts in other countries and to increase understanding of U.S. experiences by comparing them with those elsewhere. In this chapter, the authors use a common approach to describe the institutionalization of service-learning at two institutions in other countries where efforts are well developed: (1) the University of Natal–Pietermaritzburg (UNP) in South Africa and (2) St. Francis Xavier University (StFX) in Canada. They are then compared with Portland State University (PSU), a U.S. institution that is well known for its commitment to service-learning and its initiatives to institutionalize this work. Throughout this chapter, the authors rely upon the *Self-Assessment Rubric for the Institutionalization of Service-Learning in Higher Education* (Furco, 2003; hereafter referred to as the "Furco Rubric").

Comparing different experiences of institutionalization can provide insights into how service-learning occurs in different sociocultural, political, and organizational contexts. For South African institutions, many of which have practiced something like service-learning for years without actually identifying it as such, the post-apartheid climate of transformation within higher education has provided an ideal situation in which to study the extent to which such practices have been institutionalized. For many Canadian institutions, the academic–community collaboration and interchange of ideas and energy is a long-standing tradition through initiatives such as rural development and cooperative education. Thus, as with the South African institutions, an increased level of interest in community-based learning strategies, because of social policy and Canadian government initiatives, provides an opportune time to study how some of these practices have been transformed and consolidated through pedagogies such as service-learning. Comparisons to the U.S. context, where the emphasis on service-learning is highly dependent upon availability of external funding, cohesion or fragmentation of political agendas, and state or local commitments to community development, can offer useful insights across international borders.

ASSESSMENT OF INSTITUTIONALIZATION

The "Furco Rubric" (Furco, 2003) is an assessment tool designed to assist institutions both in self-assessing their progress in institutionalization of service-learning *and* as the basis for strategic planning and implementation of enhanced service-learning and related activities. It builds upon earlier work initiated by Kecskes and Muyllaert (1997) with the Washington State Campus Compact and draws upon lessons learned through an early research study conducted through the Western Region Campus Compact Consortium (Furco, 2002).

The framework of the rubric consists of three stages of institutionalization and five dimensions (Furco, 2002, 2003). The three stages are:

- Stage 1: Critical mass building;
- Stage 2: Quality building; and
- Stage 3: Sustained institutionalization.

The five dimensions are:

1. Philosophy and mission of service-learning, including definition of service-learning, strategic planning, alignment with institutional mission, and alignment with educational reform efforts;
2. Student support for and involvement in service-learning, including student awareness, opportunities, leadership, and incentives and rewards;

3. Faculty support for and involvement in service-learning, including faculty knowledge and awareness, involvement and support, leadership, and incentives and rewards;

4. Community participation and partnerships, including community partner awareness, mutual understanding, and community partner voice and leadership; and

5. Institutional support for service-learning, including coordinating entity, policymaking entity, staffing, funding, administrative support, departmental support, and evaluation and assessment.

The self-assessment involves institutional teams considering each of the five dimensions and assessing their current position, considering multiple components. The teams rely upon their collective knowledge, as well as any relevant documentation (institutional reports, data summaries, community partnership inventories, etc.) that helps them to better determine where the institution is positioned for each element of the rubric. Collective discussion and debate often is the most useful strategy for agreeing upon the level of institutionalization, as the rubric does not have rigidly defined metrics for placement in one level or another. This discussion and reflection process enables the institution to identify opportunities for further effort, and to consider all of these opportunities in the context of other strategic institutional priorities. Table 10.1 illustrates the rubric, and presents the results of the self-assessments conducted by the teams at the three universities described in this chapter.

This study set out to answer one primary question: "How can a standardized assessment tool be used to assess institutionalization of service-learning to determine common factors that transcend international boundaries?" The three institutions were selected based upon the lead author's knowledge and working relationships with them, having identified that each had some common characteristics related to institutional commitment to service-learning, while following somewhat different paths to institutionalization. At UNP and StFX, a team of individuals who are closely involved with service-learning (faculty, service-learning coordinator, senior administrators) conducted the analysis, following the process described above, and documented the results of the assessment. They drew upon a variety of data sources, including survey results, findings from focus groups and other reflective activities (with students, faculty, and community partners), review of relevant documents, results of external reviews, and/or their own personal immersion in the programs and their resultant expert opinions. The PSU assessment draws upon a variety of self-assessments, as well as further examination with comparable institutional representatives.

Table 10.1.   Summary of Institutionalization at Three Institutions

	Stage One	Stage Two	Stage Three
	Critical Mass Building	*Quality Building*	*Sustained Institutionalization*
Philosophy and mission of service-learning (definition of service-learning, strategic planning, alignment with institutional mission, alignment with educational reform efforts)	UNP StFX ▰▰▰	▰▰▰ StFX	PSU
Student support for and involvement in service-learning (student awareness, student opportunities, student leadership, student incentives and rewards)	UNP	StFX ▰▰▰	▰▰▰ StFX PSU
Faculty support for and involvement in service-learning (faculty knowledge and awareness, faculty involvement and support, faculty leadership, faculty incentives and rewards)	UNP	StFX	PSU
Community participation and partnerships (community partner awareness, mutual understanding, community partner voice and leadership)	UNP		StFX PSU
Institutional support for service-learning (coordinating entity, policymaking entity, staffing, funding, administrative support, departmental support, evaluation and assessment)	UNP ▰▰▰ StFX ▰▰▰	▰▰▰ UNP ▰▰▰ StFX PSU ▰▰▰	▰▰▰ PSU

UNP, University of Natal–Pietermaritzburg; StFX, St. Francis Xavier University; PSU, Portland State University

In each case, there is the potential limitation of bias from the view of the assessors being too intimately connected with the various institutional programs; yet this is counteracted by the expert knowledge the assessors had of the interplay among various factors, and therefore their ability to draw upon a wide range of information in conducting the assessment.

In the discussion that follows, the discussion begins with an overview of institutional context for each institution, and then discusses each of the five dimensions of the Furco Rubric.

UNIVERSITY OF NATAL–PIETERMARITZBURG

Context

The University of Natal–Pietermaritzburg is a comprehensive university with a student population of 7,620, offering undergraduate and graduate degrees in a variety of disciplines. It is located in the moderate-sized city of Pietermaritzburg, in the province of KwaZulu-Natal. The reality of life in South Africa after apartheid requires higher education institutions to play a major role in the reconstruction of the social, cultural, and economic fabric of South African society. The university's vision statement, revised prior to the first South African democratic election in 1994, states:

> the University aims to be a socially responsive university, reacting ethically and intellectually to the many problems of South Africa and the rest of the world...The strategic challenge for the University is to integrate development activities into the curricula so that our students are able to learn the lessons they need to play a meaningful role in the reconstruction of our society. (University of Natal, 2000, pp. 2, 4)

Many different disciplines at UNP have been involved in service-learning in a variety of different forms, resulting in a diversity of approaches to this pedagogy on campus. This diversity has been valued and encouraged over time—it is not the intention to have political science practicing service-learning in the same way as soil science—but raises challenges in program coordination. Motivation for involvement in service-learning also varies, and there are differences between why a particular discipline is involved and why "the University" construes it as a positive endeavor.

Philosophy and Mission

The self-assessment at UNP revealed varied levels of institutionalization with respect to philosophy and mission. Although service-learning is cited in the UNP Strategic Initiatives document and other policy documents, it does not appear to be "part of the primary concern of the institution" (Furco, 2003) and is unlikely to become an institutional priority. Strategic priorities echo national education reforms: "...in the context of a history of educational backlog and disadvantaged learners, increased access has become the cornerstone of government policy for the higher education sector" (du Pre, 2003, p. 11).

The institution is divided into two distinct groups when attempting to identify how faculty define service-learning. The majority of faculty fall into

Stage 1 (critical mass building) where there "is no campus-wide definition for service-learning" (Furco, 2003). Many do not know about service-learning and those who practice some form of engagement use a variety of terms for this purpose. However, a small minority are in Stage 2 (quality building).

There is some variation and inconsistency in the application of the term but this is not necessarily problematic as the core concepts are applied differently across disciplinary perspectives. Arriving at a single term for service-learning practice has been difficult in a South African context. There is still a lack of agreement over core terms, such as *community*.

In 1999 a strategic plan for service-learning was drafted and approved at UNP. Although elements of this plan were implemented and initial progress was impressive, on the whole it has not been realized over time. The lack of progress toward achieving these goals appears to be mainly due to the fact that service-learning efforts have been ad hoc and fragmented, and there has been no coordinated institutional effort. Additional changes in leadership, which may be precipitated by the merger of UNP into the new University of KwaZulu-Natal, make the priorities of the new leadership uncertain. This is of concern, as Schneider (1998) noted: "Support from high levels of the administration and guidance by the president are key components for service-learning..." (p. 2).

At the level of national education policy, all higher education institutions in South Africa are being required to focus on the quality of their academic programs. The national framework for institutional assessment identifies service-learning as one of the priority areas for national attention. As this priority is implemented, there may be increased motivation for individual institutions to embrace service-learning more enthusiastically. The overall assessment of UNP in terms of this dimension tends to rest in Stage 1.

Student Support/Involvement

Service-learning courses are not identified in the university calendar. Individual disciplines do, however, make a concerted effort to place information about service-learning on notice boards as a means of informing potential students about these opportunities. Service-learning options, in which service is integrated into core academic courses, are limited to certain groups of students. This varies across disciplines; for example, theology has centralized this pedagogy across its program, whereas political science offers service-learning in one third-year elective. Thus in terms of awareness and opportunities, UNP demonstrates many elements of Stage 2.

The campus has neither formal nor informal mechanisms to encourage students to participate in service-learning. However, there are occasional opportunities (e.g., faculty newsletters) for students to gain recognition for their service-learning efforts. Most importantly for students, though, obtaining letters of reference from their internships is a powerful motivating factor for participating in service-learning, particularly in the current South African climate of intense competition for employment. Overall, UNP demonstrates a Stage 1 level of institutionalization, with some initial movement to Stage 2.

Faculty Support/Involvement

A 2003 update of a UNP 1999 Institutional Audit of service-learning activities revealed a finding that emulates Furco's (2003) statement that "very few members know what service-learning is or understand how service-learning is different from community service, internships, or other experiential learning activities" (p. 2). Only 16 disciplines, approximately 22%, were identified as performing some kind of off-campus engagement. However, while actual faculty numbers may be limited, it is important to note that those who *are* active cover a wide range of disciplines, including chemistry, political science, information studies, and adult education. This is an important factor to recognize, as it appears there is potential for this pedagogy to grow across the entire campus, instead of in a few selected and obvious disciplines.

UNP has suffered in its development of a service-learning critical mass through changes in leadership. A number of "service-learning champions" have left the institution for appointments elsewhere. Fortunately, the new academic leader realizes the importance of off-campus engagement and has resolved to address the need for leadership support at the executive level. However, competing priorities, such as institutional reorganization and the policy emphases alluded to earlier, mean that service-learning has become simply one in a long list of equally important priorities. Thus, as an institution, UNP appears to be located in the quality building stage where "there are only one or two influential faculty members who provide leadership to the campus' service-learning effort" (Furco, 2003, p. 2).

Although criteria apparently exist at UNP for the promotion of staff on the basis of community service–type activities, it appears there is no institutional record of promotion based on this criterion, similar to that noted by some authors (see, e.g., Schneider, 1998). The team's conclusion was that UNP is at Stage 1 with respect to faculty.

Community Participation

In his recent analysis of change in South Africa, du Pre (2003) noted, "community participation has become part of higher education planning. Many higher education institutions have established departments to develop links with the community" (p. 11). There is no center for community partnerships at UNP, although there have been debates about whether a center or a decentralized model is preferable to maintain links with communities. It appears that while UNP is at Stage 1 where few community agencies are partnering with the university, those disciplines that *are* involved in service-learning have well-established and successful relationships with off-campus partners.

To a certain extent at UNP "there is little or no understanding between the campus and community representatives" (Furco, 2003, p. 4). While community organizations may come to view the university as a resource, the needs of the community may be quite different (i.e., jobs for unemployed youth, building of a road) from what the university can facilitate through academically based service-learning, such as library enhancements, tutoring, or environmental assessments. Again, UNP places itself at Stage 1 with respect to community participation and partnerships.

Institutional Support

While there is an informal committee that meets to discuss and promote service-learning at UNP, as mentioned above, there is no campus-wide coordinating entity that is devoted to assisting in the implementation, advancement, and institutionalization of service-learning.

Although an institutional policy document was drafted in 2000, the process of ratification was never completed. Further policy development is not possible given the current institutional merger process. However, a draft senate resolution was tabled, and the issue of service-learning at the University of Natal is officially on "the agenda."

At UNP, there are no staff or faculty whose primary responsibility is to institutionalize service-learning; but certain disciplines have faculty whose appointments have been made on the understanding that they will attempt to promote the development of service-learning within their discipline (e.g., politics and psychology). In other disciplines, such as community resource management, faculty have been appointed on soft money for service-learning activities. Beyond this, there are permanent faculty who are committed to off-campus engagement and the epistemology it offers.

Service-learning at UNP was given increased impetus as a result of an external grant from 1999 to 2002 (Community Higher Education Service

Partnerships [CHESP]). Concurrently and subsequently, the university has provided some funding to support service-learning activities. A wide scope of disciplines offer formal service-learning courses and have committed funds to support this work. The question remains as to whether service-learning will be a priority in the merged institution, and whether funding will be made available for a central office/coordinating body. This is currently being negotiated with the university leadership. There is a new focus on quality assurance at a national level (comparable to the emphasis on institutional accreditation in the United States). As a result of this, UNP is participating in a program to assess the quality of service-learning at a number of levels within the institution. These various activities suggest that UNP remains at Stage 1 with respect to some aspects of institutional support, yet is moving into Stage 2 on other institutional dimensions.

Overall Assessment

Across most of the dimensions, UNP is still in capacity building (Stage 1). However, there are mechanisms in place, such as the emphasis in the Strategic Initiatives document, to suggest the potential for progress beyond this stage. There will be a need for much more support from the institution itself to make substantial progress in institutionalization.

At this point in time, however, university priorities are focused on the impending merger, and further developments in service-learning are on hold until the merger is complete. The merger will result in an institution with a combined student population of over 32,000, approximately four times that of the current UNP population. The implications for development and impact of service-learning will be far greater with a student body of that size. At that point, in order for service-learning to become institutionalized, a central office headed by an academic may be key in order to support, facilitate, and advocate for service-learning at the new university. It will also be important to gain support from the new academic/administrative leadership. The use of the rubric highlights some of the areas where further effort could be invested in order to move UNP forward in its commitment to service-learning.

ST. FRANCIS XAVIER UNIVERSITY

Context

St. Francis Xavier University (StFX) is a liberal arts university located in Antigonish, Nova Scotia, Canada, a small, rural town with a population of approximately 7,000. The university brings together 3,800 students from across Canada and around the world primarily for undergraduate programs in arts, science, business, education, and other applied programs. StFX is widely recognized as one of the top postsecondary institutions in Canada and has been ranked first among primarily undergraduate universities in Canada for the past 2 years in the annual *Macleans* magazine university rankings (Johnson, 2003). These rankings have referenced the university's reputation as a leader in service-learning.

From its beginnings in the mid-1990s, the StFX service-learning program has been founded on the belief that today's undergraduates benefit from a rich university experience that promotes academic excellence, global awareness, and social responsibility. Initially the program was organized by a single faculty member and was limited in its ability to involve faculty, students, and community organizations in the development of alternative service-learning options both at the course-based (local) and immersion (international experience) level. Five years of program development funding was received in 1999 from the J.W. McConnell Family Foundation, making it possible to hire 2.5 FTE staff in positions working directly on creating service-learning opportunities, with a faculty member as program coordinator. With a well-defined staff structure and increased faculty support, service-learning has become recognized as an alternative model for teaching and learning across campus.

With this increase in program size has come an increase in assessment strategies for the service-learning program. Multiple surveys about service-learning experiences are administered to students and community partners for course-based and immersion service-learning experiences. In addition, two external program evaluations have taken place during the 5 years of McConnell funding. These assessments provided the primary data for completion of the Furco Rubric, as well as other statistical evidence that is collected annually. The rubric provides a scale for comparison and helps sets targets for growth and planning.

Philosophy and Mission

StFX aspires to empower its students to effect change in their own sphere of influence, and to teach them how to build communities. The university aims to prepare its graduates to be aware, to understand, to reason, and to act. Although this mission does not speak explicitly to service-learning, the overall orientation of the institution is consistent with and supportive of a service-learning program.

The StFx Service-Learning Vision Statement (2000) included the following perspectives on service-learning:

- Enables students to enhance academic pursuits through community involvement;
- Engages students in active learning that highlights the relationship between academic studies and society; and
- Focuses student awareness on current societal issues as they relate to academic areas of interest.

This approach to service-learning supports the following outcomes, among others:

- Deeper student learning through experiences that encourage critical thinking and the application of academic knowledge;
- Students value community involvement and have a deeper commitment to social justice issues;
- Students feel an increased sense of caring and responsibility toward local and global communities;
- Community investment—augmenting community resources and assisting individuals or groups in need of community-based services; and
- Increased community awareness about the resources and expertise at the university.

Based on these documents the overall orientation of the institution places it at Stage 1 to Stage 2 on the rubric.

Student Support/Involvement

StFX scores well on the Furco Rubric when examining student awareness, opportunities, and leadership. Student involvement in service-learning has increased over the past several years; recent figures show a 21% participation rate (approximately 800 students) per year in course-based opportunities with an additional 55 students per year participating in the immersion service-learning experiences in one of five international locations. The university is very close to its goal of having most students experience service-learning at least once during their 4-year degrees. Formal awards for students are not offered, though student travel bursaries are available based on financial need.

Student demand for courses offering service-learning has increased each year, and more professors are becoming involved in the program. In some interest areas, student demand exceeds the local community's ability to support them. Another indicator of student interest has been the creation by students of a Service-Learning Student Society. It is supported by the Student Union of the university; is open to all students; and focuses on noncredit, short-term group activities that serve the local community. The Student Union also provides funding annually for two student interns to work with the service-learning program thereby providing them the opportunity to assume leadership roles within the program. The Student Union Vice President Academic is also a member of the Service-Learning Advisory Committee.

Overall, StFX rates at Stages 2 to 3 in the area of student support and involvement.

Faculty Support/Involvement

Faculty involvement has grown from one professor in 1995 to the current level where service-learning is offered in 50% of the disciplines. Faculty commitment ranges from providing optional experiences to ones where a major portion of a student grade is assigned to a mandatory service-learning course component. Faculty have also begun to participate in professional development opportunities that focus on service-learning. There is generally more support from within the Faculty of Arts and applied programs within the Faculty of Science than in other academic units. Currently, five faculty serve on the Service-Learning Advisory Committee and five to seven faculty lead immersion trips abroad each year. Faculty knowledge and awareness continues to grow with each year of the program.

One barrier to greater participation is the size and nature of the local community. There have been occasions where faculty and students have been interested in participating in service-learning with a very defined community population (e.g., nutrition work with senior citizens), but an opportunity could not be provided due to limitations related to geographical restrictions, transportation, or the small number and variety of community organizations available. In general, faculty are supportive, but StFX has a history of being quite traditional in its teaching approaches. It has taken a great deal of support and education to get faculty to the level of participation currently enjoyed.

Slowly, faculty are starting to include service-learning work in their rank and tenure applications, under both "service" and "teaching" categories, but service-learning itself is not yet formally recognized as a category in the promotion process. Based on experience of service-learning staff with faculty and the external evaluations, the faculty support was rated at Stage 2.

Community Participation

Next to students, the greatest support is from the community. Support from community partners has enabled the provision of rich learning experiences to students and new services to the community. Many of the partnerships and projects are multiyear, and a few are multidisciplinary. A formal Community Support Committee, consisting of representatives from local businesses and organizations, provides support and direction for the course-based component of the program. A semi-annual community newsletter is published that generates new ideas for community–university partnerships while at the same time thanking the community for its generous support.

In recent years, more than 60 community partners have participated per year, with the community as a whole receiving over 17,000 service hours annually from students. Strong relationships have been developed between the community and the university with clear mutual benefit in most of the university–community partnerships. Community members have commented that the centralized office and availability of staff dedicated to service-learning have made the program more easily accessible to the community.

Using the Furco Rubric, community participation is rated at Stage 2.

Institutional Support

Institutional support is adequate but not yet at a level where financial commitments have been made. Service-learning is identified in all materials sent out by the university and is praised as an initiative of note; however, budgetary restrictions keep it from becoming a true priority of the university. The senior administration is well versed on all aspects of service-learning and the Academic Vice President and Provost serves as the Chair of the Service-Learning Advisory Committee on campus. The university president has also offered personal support for the program, but the program still depends largely on outside financial grants. Institutional support on the Furco Rubric is somewhere between Stages 1 and 2.

Overall Assessment

At this time, StFX is one of only a handful of Canadian universities that offers a comprehensive service-learning program. There is currently no government support, direction, or funding for the program at either a national or provincial level. There is also no umbrella organization to promote the program, similar to Campus Compact in the United States, though initial discussions for such an organization are now underway among university representatives across the country. Additionally, the concept and terminology of service-learning are new on the Canadian academic scene, and as such are not regularly discussed at Canadian academic conferences or in Canadian academic publications. Canadian universities and those promoting the programs at universities do not benefit from the critical mass or widespread recognition of service-learning programs in the United States.

Despite these barriers, the program at StFX continues to grow. Overall, StFX is scoring at Stage 2 on the Furco Rubric when examined for how institutionalized service-learning has become within the university. Areas needing more growth, and places where additional energy can be directed, have been more accurately identified using the Furco Rubric.

COMPARISONS AND THEMES

These two narrative descriptions of individual institutional experiences set the basis for a comparison—both between these two institutions and with other institutions where service-learning is well embedded within curricula and institutional processes. For ease of comparison, one U.S. university will be used as a comparator: Portland State University, which is well known for its commitment to service-learning and other civic engagement activities, and which would likely be considered by many observers as having achieved sustained institutionalization (Stage 3) using the Furco Rubric. The summative comparisons were previously presented in Table 10.1. Each of the five dimensions of the rubric will be discussed and experiences compared and contrasted.

Philosophy and Mission

UNP overall demonstrates that it is at Stage 1 of critical mass building. The embedding of service-learning in the university's strategic plan is a major commitment to promote further institutionalization; however, the current merger activity and the formation of the new University of KwaZulu-Natal means that there is an administrative focus on the merger activities and an inability for academic leadership to continue to maintain their commitment to service-learning. The merger may either facilitate or compromise the commitment to service-learning, especially since anticipated changes in academic leadership will occur and former administrative and academic champions have left the institution. This leaves UNP in a rather tenuous position with respect to philosophy and mission regarding service-learning.

In contrast, service-learning *fits* within the mission of StFX, which sees itself as being at Stage 1 to 2 of quality building; yet service-learning is not a primary concern of academic or administrative leaders. There is strong potential given the institution's history as a faith-based institution and one where service in the context of community development (both internationally and domestically) is an integral part of StFX's mission and activities.

Portland State University, in contrast, can be assessed as being at Stage 3 and demonstrating sustained institutionalization. The motto of PSU is *Let Knowledge Serve the City*, which has guided consistent and sustained activities for a number of years at the university. The substantial revision of the undergraduate general education program into the "University Studies" curriculum with designated community-based learning experiences has provided a considerable basis for this work. This program now ensures that all PSU undergraduates experience service-learning and has enabled the spread of service-learning into other undergraduate and graduate programs. Thus service-learning is well defined and integrated, with a commitment that has withstood changes in academic and administrative leadership.

Student Support/Involvement

UNP demonstrates Stage 1 of critical mass building, with few opportunities to date for student leadership. With less institutional and faculty involvement, opportunities for student leadership have declined, but can be anticipated as a future area of emphasis once faculty and leadership re-engage in a service-learning commitment.

At StFX, the campus-wide coordination by the grant-supported staff facilitates student engagement, such that on this dimension StFX can be rated at Stage 3 of sustained institutionalization. The small size of the campus is a considerable asset, as there can be rapid diffusion of student enthusiasm and leadership, and it is much easier to have a "snowball" effect of engaging students than would be evident at a larger campus.

These two examples offer an interesting contrast with PSU. PSU would generally be at Stage 3 in terms of information available to students and leadership opportunities, in large part due to the established roles for students within the University Studies program as peer mentors, and through other roles such as Student Ambassadors. These roles help to fulfill the institution's commitment to engagement with its communities. However, if focused at the individual department level, a lower level of student engagement might be evident due to disciplinary emphasis and to the extent that service-learning is integrated into major programs of study.

Thus the unit of analysis can lead to a different assessment result, offering the basis for focused future planning to further engage students within the less involved departments.

Faculty Support/Involvement

The emerging research on faculty roles and rewards offers strong evidence of the factors that motivate faculty support for, and involvement in, service-learning. As demonstrated at UNP, only a small number of faculty are involved but they have provided considerable leadership. However, UNP offers few incentives and limited faculty development. When there was a strong and politically astute senior faculty member providing leadership at UNP, there was more potential to interest new faculty. At present, the faculty leaders are junior faculty and they lack the history and connections to be able to motivate other faculty in the same way as a senior leader can, let alone convince academic leadership to consider ways to reward and recognize faculty for service-learning. Thus UNP can be placed at Stage 1 with respect to faculty support/involvement in service-learning.

At StFX, the numbers of faculty are increasing to the extent that there is now a critical mass of engaged faculty, many of whom could be called service-learning champions, thus providing evidence of Stage 2 of institutionalization. Yet at StFX as well there are few incentives, and only modest faculty development. The factor preventing further progress to Stage 3 likely relates to the creation of institutional incentives and rewards for faculty involvement in service-learning.

PSU offers a significant contrast, demonstrating Stage 3 through the integration of recognition for service-learning and civic engagement teaching, research, and service in its 1996 promotion and tenure criteria. The creation of this recognition occurred in a synergistic way with the creation of new curricula emphasizing service-learning (Gelmon & Agre-Kippenhan, 2002). Faculty work in and with the community is recognized and rewarded, and there are considerable faculty development offerings to assist both new and established faculty with expanding their scope of activities to integrate service-learning. Institutional commitment and recognition is clearly a necessary factor in advancing faculty support for service-learning.

Community Participation

Community partnerships exist at UNP, but they are very specific to individual courses and instructors and are not campus-wide. Thus, UNP is at Stage 1 of institutionalization and may not be able to make much progress on this dimension until there is greater institutional support and commitment.

In contrast, StFX is at Stage 3 with well-developed and extensive partnerships, supported and encouraged by a formal Community Support Committee. The presence of full-time staff in coordinating roles also enhances StFX's ability to build partnerships, as there is a common contact point through which community partners can connect with the university. The presence of both staff coordination and the support committee contribute to giving voice to the community agencies and to furthering mutual understanding of needs and assets.

PSU has had similar experiences to those of StFX through formal administrative and community structures that have enabled it to move to Stage 3 of institutionalization. However, while the expression of community voice is generally well established at the institutional level, there continues to be variation across departments and among the schools/colleges, with some "push and pull" between the central university office and the individual academic units. In recent years, the emphasis of the central office has shifted from a focus on community–university partnerships to one on faculty development to establish partnerships. This has left some community members feeling somewhat disconnected from the university because they no longer have a primary university contact point, yet this shift has enabled the staff to devote their efforts to assisting faculty to develop the skills to better work with the community. Clearly there are advantages to both approaches, and the assessment derived from the rubric does not necessarily point in one direction or the other—both are needed to achieve institutionalization.

Institutional Support

This category has been referred to somewhat in the preceding discussion. UNP categorizes itself somewhere bridging Stages 1 and 2, given that there is some institutional recognition, but no clear coordination or administrative support at present. StFX has clear support and dedicated staff, placing it at Stage 2, but this is soft-money dependent and it is unclear what the long-term administrative commitment is to continue support. PSU could be placed bridging Stages 2 and 3. Like StFX it has visible support but also similarly is soft-money dependent for a considerable portion of the support, and the hard money funds are vulnerable sources when there are institution-wide budget cuts. At any of the campuses, institutional support needs to keep pace as interest in service-learning grows among faculty, students, and community members. Without support, it is impossible to sustain growth in interest and participation.

Context

Finally, it is worth considering several contextual variables in attempting to understand the process of institutionalization. Both UNP and StFX have strong rural missions, serving communities in need. PSU, in contrast, is an urban institution; while it can attend to rural issues, most community partners are conveniently located within an urban region well served by public transportation, facilitating movement of students and faculty to community sites.

Environmental forces can play a strong role. In the case of UNP, the post-apartheid climate is one promoting the role of higher education in the creation of a democratic society. In the case of StFX, the university plays a central role in economic development in local, rural communities. In both cases, development is part of what the university does, and political forces that support this have served to promote the role of service-learning. Access to grant funds has also been key to development, but this can only be successful with key faculty champions who are willing to take on the initiative and provide strong and visible leadership. Dependence on external funding is a challenge that must be overcome, but often can only be resolved through a lasting institutional commitment.

Several barriers and challenges have emerged in these institutions' stories as well as those of many other institutions. Perhaps most significant is the matching of community and institution; community need is always greater than the resources the university can offer, and there is a constant tension between community priorities for development and academic priorities for learning and scholarship. These potential areas of conflict must be attended to and addressed in order for all participating in the service-learning activities to achieve their intended goals.

Use of the Furco Rubric for International Comparisons

The process of institutionalization of service-learning is clearly context-specific as these individual narratives illustrate, yet the rubric can transcend international boundaries and offer a useful common assessment tool regardless of the part of the world where it is used. Leadership, essential to guide and sustain the process of institutionalization, can come from the faculty; but without commitment from senior academic and administrative leaders, the sustained commitment may not be feasible. This does not appear to be country dependent; rather, it is dependent upon support from national organizations, policies, or other processes that support and encourage service-learning.

Funding is vital—a situation well known in the United States—and is evident from these stories from Canada and South Africa. Soft funding (i.e., grants or special initiatives) may provide the impetus to initiate a program whether independently (as in the case of StFX) or as part of a national demonstration program (as in the case of UNP); but the very nature of soft funding is that it will end. Thus institutionalization requires a commitment of hard, permanent resources at some point, both to support the programs and activities and as a clear indication of institutional belief in the merits of the service-learning program(s).

The rubric assists in providing a point-in-time "snapshot" rather than a "motion picture" perspective. Over time one would hope and expect to see movement across the dimensions, although not necessarily in a positive direction. Over the last year at UNP critical mass building definitely slowed, and in some places retreated instead of advanced. There are fewer faculty involved at a coordinating level than a year ago, in large part due to the end of the external grant. While a backward movement is evident, UNP's status one year ago may have been a false reading of the state of service-learning because it was driven by external forces (a grant and reporting responsibilities) rather than the institution itself. If the institution did not own the process, then the question of sustainability arises. Would the gains made in institutionalizing service-learning during the grant period have been sustained in the longer term if leadership or funding had continued? What are the implications of this for StFX as it nears the end of its 5 years of private foundation funding? The UNP experience offers a practical reality for any institution currently dependent on soft funding for sustaining its service-learning initiatives.

Some experiences transcend international borders and are the same: the challenges of creating and maintaining partnerships; recognizing and rewarding faculty; and engaging students and interesting them in the experience of serving and learning simultaneously. These similarities provide a basis for international exchanges and reciprocal learning, and offer excellent opportunities for learning from each other in order to advance local and international practice.

Potential Enhancements of the Furco Rubric

The rubric is clearly a useful tool for determining the extent to which service-learning has been institutionalized in any one institution. It addresses areas that are important factors in the success of service-learning programs and institutional commitment to these programs. It reminds institutions to evaluate and measure their progress in each of the essential areas, and provides the framework for subsequent planning to address gaps or areas for improvement. It is particularly useful in framing the components of a successful campus-wide or campus-encompassing service-learning commitment.

However, during this research process, a number of areas emerged as having the potential to deepen the rubric for future use. For instance, when applying the category of "philosophy and mission," the rubric does not address the issue of competing institutional or programmatic priorities. An institution such as UNP may espouse community responsiveness in its mission statement, but other aspects of the mission may in fact result in competing priorities, such that at any one time an institution may be placing more or less emphasis on an element of the mission statement. This is difficult to operationalize, but has a profound impact on the support for institutionalization of service-learning.

The role of resources and their importance in institutionalizing service-learning could also be more fully explored through the rubric. Institutions may possess the will to institutionalize service-learning but resources simply prevent this will from becoming reality. For example, a shortage of faculty may affect the institution's ability to transform curricula or offer existing service-learning courses. The impact of availability (or lack) of resources should not be underestimated.

The research process also revealed the need to identify the nature of the student population. For example, the student population could be largely "mature students" who are combining employment and higher education or they might be students who have entered higher education directly from high school. This has a definite impact on the nature of activity the student is prepared to engage in, as well as their ability to participate in service-learning activities.

The "stages" provided by the rubric may not account for less or more advanced states of service-learning institutionalization. A stage preceding critical mass building, in other words a Stage 0, would accommodate those institutions that are still conceptualizing the idea of service-learning before they have even begun to build a critical mass. One can also consider adding a Stage 4, which would be the stage in which service-learning is assumed to be part of the institution's daily teaching and learning practice, and would still allow room for further growth, development, and improvement.

CONCLUSIONS

Based on the findings described here, the following conclusions can be drawn:

- **Philosophy and mission.** Sustained institutionalization depends upon an institutional commitment that is well embedded in the fabric of institutional life and can transcend various funding programs and/or changes in academic and administrative leadership. In all cases demonstrated here, institutional mission is a key factor facilitating service-learning participation.
- **Student leadership.** This flows from the philosophical and mission commitment; as programs are put in place that emphasize service-learning, opportunities can be created for student leadership.
- **Faculty support.** Without rewards and recognition, only small numbers of faculty are likely to become very involved in service-learning. Sustained involvement will be reflected in tenure and promotion policies that promote and reward the scholarship of service-learning—both in teaching and in research/outreach.
- **Institutional support.** Through policy, resource commitment, staffing, and commitment to evaluation, service-learning can be sustained. The permanence of any service-learning program is likely to depend on a clear institutional commitment.
- **Community participation and partnerships.** Community members will engage with the institution if there is clear benefit, but to achieve this benefit there must be committed faculty (who need to be rewarded/recognized) and enthusiastic students (who need to see this as a vital part of their learning). All of these derive from institutional support.

The use of the rubric has been shown as a valuable tool for providing a basis for comparisons across institutions with different contexts and missions, yet all with a commitment to service-learning. This initial set of international comparisons suggests the high potential for a more comprehensive comparative study that could track the progress of institutions over time and offer opportunities for mutual learning to further advance our knowledge of how service-learning and civic engagement can be promoted and sustained at institutions of higher education.

NOTE

At the time of writing, the University of Natal–Pietermaritzburg was the affiliation of Trotter and Mitchell, and the university is referred to by that name throughout this manuscript. The institution has since been renamed due to a merger with another campus; however, the work reported here occurred only at the Pietermaritzburg campus.

REFERENCES

Bringle, R. G., Phillips, M. A., & Hudson, M. (2004). *The measure of service-learning: Research scales to assess student experiences.* Washington, DC: American Psychological Association.

Community Higher Education Service Partnerships. Retrieved December 10, 2003, from www.chesp.org.za

du Pre, R. (2003, October). Coping with change in South Africa. *Adults Learning,* 10–11.

Furco, A. (2002). Institutionalizing service-learning in higher education. *Journal of Public Affairs, 6*(Suppl. 1), 39–67.

Furco, A. (2003) *Self-assessment rubric for the institutionalization of service-learning in higher education.* Providence, RI: Campus Compact.

Gelmon, S. B., & Agre-Kippenhan, S. (2002). A developmental framework for supporting evolving faculty roles for community engagement. *Journal of Public Affairs, 6*(Suppl. 1), 161–182.

Gelmon, S. B., Holland, B. A., Driscoll, A., Spring, A., & Kerrigan, S. (2001). *Assessing service-learning and civic engagement: Principles and techniques.* Providence, RI: Campus Compact.

Holland, B. (1997, Fall). Analyzing institutional commitment to service: A model of key organizational factors. *Michigan Journal of Community Service Learning,* 30–41.

Holland, B. (2000). Institutional impacts and organizational issues related to service-learning. *Michigan Journal of Community Service Learning,* 52–60.

Johnson, A. D. (2003, November). Universities 2003: Measuring excellence. An insider's guide. In A. D. Johnson (Ed.), *Macleans guide to Canadian universities 2004* (pp. 140–141). Toronto: Rogers Media.

Kecskes, K., & Muyllaert, J. (1997). *Benchmark worksheet for the Western Region Campus Compact Consortium grants program.* Bellingham, WA: Western Washington University.

Schneider, M. K. (1998, June). Models of good practice for service-learning programs: What can we learn from 1,000 faculty, 25,000 students, and 27 institutions involved in service? *AAHE Bulletin, 50*(10), 9–12.

St. Francis Xavier University. (2000). *Service-learning vision statement.* Unpublished paper, St. Francis Xavier University.

University of Natal. (2000). *Strategic initiatives for the University of Natal.* Retrieved 23 October 2003, from http://www.nu.ac.za/strategic/strat.pdf

PART IV

REFLECTIONS ON TODAY
AND TOMORROW

CHAPTER 11

SERVICE-LEARNING AS CIVICALLY ENGAGED SCHOLARSHIP

Challenges and Strategies in Higher Education and K–12 Settings

Shelley H. Billig and Marshall Welch

ABSTRACT

This chapter identifies the extent of civic disengagement among young people and educational institutions and suggests that service-learning is a pathway for civic engagement. Different conceptions of civic engagement are illuminated and linkage to service-learning for each conception is provided. Authors discuss progress and strategies that are in place in both higher education and K–12 settings, and the challenges associated with each level in using service-learning as civically engaged scholarship.

New Perspectives in Service-Learning: Research to Advance the Field, pages 221–241

INTRODUCTION

During the past three decades, policymakers and scholars within academia began to sense that higher education was not effectively nurturing students' sense of civic responsibility (Sax, 2000). The Carnegie Foundation for the Advancement of Teaching released a report titled *Higher Education and the American Resurgence* (Newman, 1985). It stated:

> If there is a crisis in education in the United States today, it is less that test scores have declined than it is that we have failed to provide the education for citizenship that is still the most important responsibility of the nation's schools and colleges. (p. 31)

The National Commission on Civic Renewal (1998) charged higher education with a sense of "civic *dis*-engagement."

Similarly, building over the past several years on Putnam's (2000) *Bowling Alone* book and data showing the woeful lack of voting and other civic behaviors, a call to renew the civic mission of K–12 schools was sounded in 2003. A report by the Carnegie Corporation of New York and CIRCLE (2003) documented the increasing disengagement of high school students and suggested that the current emphasis in K–12 schools was driving even more students away from learning about democracy and obtaining the skills they need to be engaged, productive citizens.

In response to these concerns and indictments of education, there has been a growing national movement on the part of many colleges, universities, state educational agencies, school districts, and schools to help students become civically engaged and for educators to take an increasing facilitation role to motivate young people. In exploring avenues to increase civic engagement, many have begun to see the potential for service-learning.

This chapter provides analyses of service-learning as an avenue for civic engagement and scholarship, addressing the needs and challenges for higher education and K–12 schools and districts. These analyses reveal commonalities but also stark differences between the two types of educational settings, and suggest strategies that policymakers and educators can consider in helping students to become civically engaged and to support democracy in the United States.

THE NEED TO RE-ENGAGE YOUTH IN CIVIC LIFE

The calls for more engagement are backed by evidence of increasing civic disengagement among youth in the United States. Surveys showed that young people in high school and in higher education settings reported that the majority of students have little interest in civic and political affairs and little knowledge of or trust in the political system (Levine & Lopez, 2002; National Commission on Service-Learning, 2001; Torney-Purta, 2002). In 2002, national poll results showed that many youth did not feel they could influence government or politics nor solve problems in their communities (Lake Snell Perry & Associates and The Tarrance Group, Inc., 2002). Young people did not vote in percentages equal to those in earlier generations (Levine & Lopez, 2002), and they were not connected to political life in the same ways as those in the past (Levine & Lopez, 2002; Westheimer & Kahne, 2002). Kindergarten through Grade 12 schools gave less attention to civic education than they once did, requiring fewer civics courses and ignoring civics outcomes in state assessments (Miller & Piscatelli, 2003).

The 1998 National Assessment of Educational Progress (NAEP) results demonstrated that students were not knowledgeable about many of the social and political institutions that govern American life. Performance measures showed that 65% of 12th-grade students scored at the basic level, 26% at the proficient level, and 4% at the advanced level. Those who scored the lowest were from schools with high poverty (Lutkus, Weiss, Campbell, Mazzeo, & Lazer, 1999, p. 22).

While more traditional engagement in social and political institutions declined, young people started engaging more in volunteerism. Studies estimated that over half of young people participated in voluntary service in the past year (Kielsmeier, Scales, Roehlkepartain, & Neal, 2004; Skinner & Chapman, 1999). In examining this conundrum, Putnam (2000) wrote:

> This development [of increased volunteerism] is the most promising sign of any that I have discovered that America might be on the cusp of a new period of civic renewal, especially if this youthful volunteerism persists into adulthood and begins to expand beyond individual caregiving to broader engagement with social and political issues. (p. 13)

Groups such as Campus Compact (2000) believed that this is part of the "new student politics" and that education may be able to capitalize on the willingness of young people to volunteer as a way to engage in active teaching of those civic concepts necessary for the health and well-being of American democracy. Leaders in states, such as Wisconsin and North Carolina, began establishing policies that explicitly acknowledged the importance of both service/volunteerism and knowledge of government institutions and democratic principles (Education Commission of the States, 2002).

Conceptualizations of Civic Engagement

Civic engagement has been conceptualized in a number of ways, typically including specific knowledge, skills, and dispositions. Some scholars believe that knowledge of governmental and political institutions should be primary (e.g., Galston, 2003) while others promote the acquisition of a set of skills, dispositions, and understandings related to democracy, such as understanding and engaging in democratic decision making, respect for diversity, knowledge of rights and responsibilities, and so forth. Ehrlich (2000) succinctly conceptualized civic engagement as "working to make a difference in the civic life of our communities and developing the combination of knowledge, skills, values, and motivation to make that difference" (p. vi).

Based on a series of panels with scholars and practitioners, the Carnegie Corporation and CIRCLE (2003) report, in a wide-ranging discussion of the topic, specified these four goals for civic education:

1. Helping students to become informed and thoughtful about American democracy through an understanding of history and democratic principles, including awareness and understanding of public and community issues, primarily through the development of skills that help young people obtain and analyze information, develop critical thinking skills, and enter into dialogue with those who hold different perspectives;

2. Increasing students' participation in communities either through membership or through service as a way of addressing cultural, political, social, and/or religious interests and beliefs;

3. Showing students how to "act politically" by facilitating the acquisition of skills and knowledge related to group problem solving, public speaking, petitioning, voting, and serving other public purposes; and

4. Helping students to acquire virtues such as concern for the rights and welfare of others, efficacy, tolerance, respect, and social responsibility (p. 10).

When framed in civic and democratic terms, "engagement" generates new knowledge and a host of skills such as critical thinking, social action, and social ethics that are assimilated through problem solving within community settings (Saltmarsh, 2002). Many believe that engagement is reciprocal in nature through a shared agenda and mutual benefit to all parties (Ramaley, 2002/2003).

Civic engagement has implications for action on an institutional level. For example, Fogelman (2002), Chair of the Task Force on Civic

Engagement at the University of Minnesota, defined civic engagement as "an institutional commitment to public purposes and responsibilities intended to strengthen a democratic way of life in the rapidly changing information society of the 21st century" (p. 104). He continued by stating:

> "Civic" is broadly defined as referring to all the important contributions that colleges and universities make to a flourishing democracy. These civic contributions include the following: access to learning, enhanced diversity, civic learning, public scholarship, trusted voice, public spaces, and community partnership. (p. 105)

The Kettering Foundation convened a series of seminars of presidents, provosts, deans, administrators, faculty, trustees, students, community leaders, and elected officials to promote this dialogue. The nearly 100 participants consistently dismissed the need for reforming, restoring, and restating the mission of higher education. Instead, they recognized and advocated the need for a *new* way of thinking about civic engagement (London, 2001).

THE POTENTIAL FOR SERVICE-LEARNING TO ACT AS A TOOL TO PROMOTE CIVIC ENGAGEMENT

Service-learning is broadly defined as a teaching strategy wherein students learn important academic, social, or civic objectives by providing service that meets authentic community needs. Typically, the service-learning cycle includes students' planning, action, reflection, and celebration. In high-quality service-learning projects, students have considerable voice in determining activities and faculty facilitate knowledge and skill acquisition. By engaging students in community service projects that have an intentional connection to concepts underlying democracy and citizenship, service-learning offers a powerful and widespread strategy for increasing the civic engagement of young people (see, e.g., Astin, 2000; Billig, 2000; Education Commission of the States, 2002; Eyler, Giles, Stenson, & Gray, 2001; Furco, 2002; National Commission on Service-Learning, 2001; and many others).

A gradually accumulating body of evidence suggests that service-learning helps students develop knowledge of community needs, commit to an ethic of service, develop more sophisticated understandings of politics and morality, gain a greater sense of civic responsibility and feelings of efficacy, and increase their desire to become active contributors to society (Billig, 2000; Westheimer & Kahne, 2000; Youniss & Yates, 1997; Youniss, McLellan, & Yates, 1997). Studies have provided evidence for positive effects of service-learning on:

- Civic-related *knowledge*, including awareness of community needs (Berkas, 1997; Melchior, 1999; Morgan & Streb, 1999) and knowledge about government (Berkas, 1997; Hamilton & Zeldin, 1987; Morgan & Streb, 1999);
- Civic-related *skills*, including an understanding of how to design and implement a service project (Melchior, 1999);
- Civic *attitudes*, including aspects of social and personal responsibility, such as:
  - students' concern for social issues (Metz, McLellan, & Youniss, 2000) and concerns for others' welfare (Scales, Blyth, Berkas, & Kielsmeier, 2000);
  - the belief that they can make a difference in their communities (Hamilton & Zeldin, 1987; Melchior, 1999; Morgan & Streb, 1999; Scales et al., 2000); and
  - acceptance of diversity (Melchior, 1999; Morgan & Streb, 1999);
- Service *behavior* (Melchior, 1999) and *intentions* to serve in the future (Berkas, 1997; Metz et al., 2000; Morgan & Streb, 1999); and
- *Social capital*, including increased connections to schools and other organizations and increased social networks (Morgan & Streb, 1999).

At the higher education level, there is additional evidence that service-learning during the college experience can impact multiple dimensions of students' growth including intercultural (Green, 2001), cognitive, personal, professional, and civic development (Moely, McFarland, Miron, Mercer, & Ilustre, 2002). A recent study of three campuses across the United States, for example, showed that service-learning was positively associated with every indicator of civic engagement, from following the news though dialogue about public issues with friends, families, and faculty through intention to vote (Meyer, Billig, & Hofschire, 2004). These studies show that service-learning only has strong civic outcomes when the service-learning activities are more intentionally connected to civic knowledge, skills, and dispositions, primarily through dialogue and assignments that specifically help students see the linkage and understand the meaning of their service (Billig, 2004; Furco, 2004; Meyer et al., 2004).

Systemic Approaches for Implementing Service-Learning to Promote Civic Engagement

Based on a review of the literature on educational change, four systems components appear to be necessary if service-learning is to serve as a vehicle for promoting civic engagement of young people in society. These systems components include:

- Professional development;
- Leadership;
- Mission and vision; and
- Incentives and rewards.

Professional Development

Professional development for teachers and faculty members are a key support for helping service-learning reach its civic engagement potential because, along with parents, educators serve as a primary determining factor in students' ideas and skills related to participatory democracy. Ross and Yeager (1999), for example, conducted studies on young people's conceptions of democracy and concluded: "Teachers' understandings of democracy are a fundamental influence on how children learn democracy in schools" (p. 257).

Teacher education programs are beginning to embrace service-learning, though research by Furco and Ammon (2000) showed that the number of teacher educators who understand this approach is limited. In their 3-year study, these researchers investigated teacher educators' and teacher education deans' use of various pedagogies, methods, philosophies, and service-learning. Teacher educators were less likely to report introducing candidates to the pedagogy of service-learning than any other method listed on the survey. While the researchers found that 65% introduced service-learning as an instructional tool, it is clear that more is needed in teacher education if future teachers are to be exposed to service-learning as a learning method and are to use it as an instructional tool in their careers.

Doctoral programs in higher education can play a critical role in preparing the future professoriate. However, rarely do institutions intentionally address specific knowledge and skills necessary for future faculty to facilitate learning in this realm. In 1996, Robert Atwell, president of the American Council on Education, criticized doctoral education in his last letter to the council as president. He asserted that despite the changing landscape of society and higher education itself to address issues and needs of diversity, generalizable, and cross-disciplinary research, and incorporating new learning paradigms, future faculty are being trained to be "clones" (p. 2) of their mentors trained in the 1950s, 1960s, and 1970s. Applegate (2002) admonished higher education for maintaining the status quo of doctoral education, arguing that doctoral education should not prepare future faculty to "accommodate higher education as it is, but to be agents of change, helping higher education play its proper role in a twenty-first century global society" (p. 2). He continued by noting that many doctoral programs were beginning to heed the call to move away from a focus on the disciplines and their status toward preparing future faculty to improve the lives of citizens. This change was evidenced by the growing number of programmatic efforts such as the Woodrow Wilson Foundation's Responsive Ph.D. program (www.woodrow.org/responsivephd), and the Preparing Future Faculty program (www.preparing-faculty.org).

This trend can be continued if doctoral programs include coursework on topics such as the mission of higher education to examine the very historical role and trends (e.g., as articulated by Harkavy and Mundy in this volume). Coursework could include fundamental principles of pedagogy that examine the theoretical models from which service-learning are based. For example, the Department of Educational Leadership and Policy at the University of Utah now offers a course, albeit an elective, titled "The Leadership and Pedagogy of Service-Learning" that includes these very topical areas as well as skills that would prepare future faculty in higher education to teach as well as prepare service-learning program directors.

It is possible that individual departments have neither the resources, expertise, or curricular "space" within their programs nor the desire to provide this type of coursework. However, many colleges and universities have centers for teaching and learning on their campuses. Traditionally, these centers provide technical assistance to doctoral students who serve as teaching assistants in their respective disciplines. At the very least, these centers could provide seminars or workshops on these topics.

The next step is continued dialogue in the professional literature and at professional gatherings such as the conference that produced the chapters in this book. This dialogue must explore ways to provide professional development opportunities for teachers at the preservice and inservice levels and to the future professoriate in doctoral programs. This will require a *cross-pollination* of sorts by submitting manuscripts to journals of various organizations, associations, and disciplines as well as presentation proposals at conferences. Similarly, the dialogue can be promoted by either establishing or reaching out to established special interest groups (SIGs) and creating "tracts" of paper presentations and/or affinity group discussions with professional organizations such as the American Association of Colleges for Teacher Education (AACTE), the American Educational Research Association (AERA), and Campus Compact.

In K–12 settings, the professional development needed to enhance teachers' capabilities to facilitate the use of service-learning is likely to come head to head with other professional development needs in content areas, and given the limited time allowed for professional development by most school districts, will pose a formidable challenge. However, if schools and districts embrace their civic missions and see the value of service-learning as both an academic and civic engagement strategy, teachers are more likely to be offered opportunities to learn and implement service-learning. Evidence of effectiveness will promote the ability of leaders to embrace service-learning as a normative part of schooling.

Leadership

Research has repeatedly shown that leadership is critical to the success and sustainability of any innovative educational approach. Leadership support can be expressed in multiple ways. Research in K–12 settings (Billig, 2002) showed that support from school and district leaders in the form of policies, resource allocation, and verbal encouragement was related to sustained use of service-learning as an educational reform tool. In higher education, Campus Compact was founded on the notion that university and college presidents have a key role to play in service-learning adoption, implementation, and institutionalization (Ehrlich, 2000). Presidents have continued their commitment by embracing civic engagement in the creation of the *Presidents' Declaration on the Civic Responsibility of Higher Education* (Ehrlich & Hollander, 1999). Campus Compact provides an array of resource materials as well as technical support through a consulting core of faculty fellows that conduct workshops for teams of administrators and faculty to conceptualize, implement, and evaluate service-learning on their campuses.

In partnership with Campus Compact, the Association of American Colleges and Universities has created a number of initiatives and resources to promote service-learning and civic engagement. One example is the establishment of the Center for Liberal Education and Civic Engagement. Similarly, the American Association of Higher Education has devoted attention to service-learning and civic engagement throughout annual conferences and publications such as *Change* and its *AAHE Bulletin*. For example, AAHE convened a Forum on Faculty Roles and Rewards in January 2002 that addressed the challenge of faculty incentives for incorporating service-learning and promoting civic engagement. The dialogue continues at the level of faculty leadership as in the summer of 2000, an entire issue of *Academe*, the bulletin of American Association of University Professors, was titled *Are We Good Citizens? Civic Engagement and Higher Education*. Likewise, a special issue of the *Journal of Public Affairs* was devoted to the topic of civic engagement and higher education in 2002. The American Association of Community Colleges has created an initiative, "CampusCares—Solutions for Stronger Communities," to identify, celebrate, and encourage the involvement of students, faculty, staff, and administration in service-learning and civic engagement.

Mission and Vision

As long ago as 1988, the American Association of Community Colleges encouraged all community colleges to establish service-learning programs (Barnett, 1996). The rationale for this movement was that community colleges serve a unique role in serving as catalysts for community renewal (Parsons & Lisman, 2002). Likewise, community colleges are intrinsically linked to their communities and therefore have a unique mission to use service-learning in mobilizing resources and citizens to address critical issues and needs (Prins, 2002).

In the first chapter of this book, Harkavy provides an extensive historical review of higher education's mission to be good citizens themselves by preparing students to take roles and careers to promote a just and democratic society. He extols higher education to be cognizant of that historical legacy as well as revisit institutional mission statements that typically include promoting service, democracy, and citizenship.

In his essay, *The New American Scholar: Scholarship and the Purposes of the University*, Rice (1991) argued,

> Not only do our institutions have diverse missions—commitments to serving a wide range of scholarly needs within regions, states, and nation—but there is the special commitment to the education of an increasingly diverse population, to the intellectual preparation of the educated citizenry necessary for making a genuinely democratic society possible. (p. 17)

Over the past several years, many institutions of higher education have shifted to include civic engagement as part of their mission and/or vision statements. The presence of such statements paves the way and justifies the use of strategies like service-learning that encourage civic engagement, and further serve to codify and sustain strategies. Campus Compact was established and endorsed by presidents of Institutions of Higher Education to support service-learning and other engagement strategies and to network those who embrace the concept so that ideas can be shared and information can be better disseminated.

At the K–12 level, the National Compact for Learning and Citizenship, housed at the Education Commission of the States, shares a similar function. With a board comprised of state and district superintendents, the group serves as a vehicle for furthering policy, improving practice, and building capacity. Their research shows that scalability is strongly connected to codification of service-learning as an important educational reform strategy.

Incentives and Rewards

This issue has different ramifications for faculty in K–12 and higher education. As the chapter by Mintz and Abramovitz in this book illustrates, there are few incentives for teachers to implement service-learning, and when faculty do adopt service-learning strategies, they tend to be motivated by a combination of cultural variables in a school coupled with more personal, individualistic reasons. Rarely is the use of service-learning a part of tenure and promotion criteria and as such, there are limited extrinsic incentives (Checkoway, 2002).

For K–12 teachers, incentives and disincentives appear to be related to the specific schools and school districts in which they operate. Studies of service-learning adoption in K–12 settings show that often a single champion decides to try service-learning with some support from leadership. Service-learning is sustained when a critical mass of support is engendered and leadership either embraces or at least allows service-learning to endure (Billig, 2002; Billig & Klute, 2002).

Challenges

There are a number of challenges within K–12 and higher education that must be addressed as we attempt to promote service-learning as civically engaged scholarship.

Professional Roles

Faculty in higher education often see their professional roles as being researchers and information purveyors with a prime allegiance to their academic field or discipline rather than to society (Checkoway, 2002). Consequently, to further the practice of service-learning, faculty members' perspectives need to see that their scholarly work can and should continue to contribute to the body of knowledge within their own fields while simultaneously contributing both to community improvement and students' civic engagement. An effective strategy was implemented by the AAHE 18-volume monograph series that integrated and presented theoretical essays, pedagogical models, and bibliographical resources relevant both to specific fields and to service-learning. The disciplinary focus ranged from "hard sciences" (such as biology, medical education, and engineering) to history and philosophy to "professional schools" (such as accounting, nursing, and teacher education). Zlotkowski (2000) noted that a number of discipline-specific associations and journals are publishing monographs or special editions focusing on service-learning.

In K–12, consideration of professional roles typically is not linked with the desire to conduct research but rather the pressure to produce test score results and to cover expected material connected to standards. The larger professional issue for these teachers is whether service-learning will be effective at producing the outcomes that are desired within school and district improvement plans and/or whether service-learning will be embraced by parents, school board members, and others that have decision-making authority.

Engagement Versus Objectivity

Another barrier that is more germane to higher education than to teachers in K–12 education is that academicians are socialized in graduate work, and upon entering academia, to distance themselves from the community as the notion of civic engagement is not part of their role as scholars (Checkoway, 2002). This is based on the cultural expectation and norm of objectivity in scholarship that apparently many educators assume is not possible in civically engaged scholarship.

Objectivity in scholarship is a deeply valued and embedded tenet. In a discussion of historical roots of the emergence of objectivity, Scott (2000) showed that universities functioned for the first 500 years in a medieval society where the pursuit of knowledge was compounded by religion, speculation, and superstition. Frye (1967) acknowledged the scholarly virtue of detachment when its context is intellectual. He also cautioned that detachment becomes indifference when scholars no longer perceive themselves as participants and members of society.

> Going to work on the proverbial hill in the ivory towers does not relieve us of the responsibilities associated with that status.... We exist primarily to meet the needs of the general citizenry and to help society develop, progress, and positively evolve. (Garrison, 1995, p. 6)

Vortuba (1996) pointed out that higher education is not a social service agency whose sole mission is to solve all of society's problems, but rather, to utilize its intellectual resources to address community issues in ways that are consistent with the mission of higher education. This can be accomplished by integrating research, teaching, and service (Bringle, Games, & Malloy, 1999).

Faculty members typically view each component of the academic trilogy as distinct and unrelated scholarly activities. Further exacerbating the challenge is the fact that service has traditionally been viewed with disdain within the culture of higher education. In this traditional context, service often manifests itself as governance on campus committees or serving professional disciplines, such as being a member of an editorial review board, often referred to as the "black hole of meetings," that detracts faculty from the priorities of research and teaching (Marshall, 1999, p. 118).

There are two ways to reframe the academic trilogy. One is to begin to integrate each component. The other is to reconceptualize the trilogy altogether. Ramaley (2002) argued that the historical triad connotes a one-way activity. An alternative approach and terminology consists of discovery, learning, and engagement reflecting shared activities that promote the tenets of civic engagement. Discovery promotes the development of new knowledge through collaboration with community and students that address critical needs in society. Learning utilizes community issues and partners to accomplish educational goals. Engagement creates alliances between educational settings and community to draw upon resources and expertise from both settings.

Rigor of Civically Engaged Scholarship

Another challenge primarily facing higher education faculty is ensuring rigor and quality in this type of scholarship, both in research and service-learning. While many may philosophically embrace the notion of civic engagement scholarship, the legitimate concern regarding adhering to standards of quality and rigor must be addressed. Just prior to his death, Boyer (1990) identified six themes he felt would characterize quality scholarly work. Using these themes as a foundation for further work, Glassick, Huber, and Maeroff (1997) conducted a comprehensive analysis of traditional criteria of scholarly quality. After reviewing what they referred to as "voluminous documents" on hiring, tenure, and promotion from colleges and universities, 51 granting agencies, 31 editors of scholarly journals, and 58 university presses, they essentially validated Boyer's six shared themes. They concluded that praise of scholarly work encompasses these six standards, regardless of discipline or types of methodology. These standards include:

1. Clear goals;
2. Adequate preparation;
3. Appropriate methods;
4. Significant results;
5. Effective presentation; and
6. Reflective critique (p. 36).

These six thematic standards have been modified and adopted as portfolio evaluation criteria by the East/West Clearinghouses and National Review Board for the Scholarship of Engagement, a board created to assess scholarship of engagement by faculty undergoing review for promotion and tenure. The board is comprised of representatives from various types of institutions, disciplines, and roles including administrators and faculty.

Maintaining Integrity and Quality of Service-Learning

Another challenge for higher education and K–12 alike is maintaining definitional and programmatic rigor and quality within the service-learning experience. Many educators apply the label of service-learning to any and all field-based experiential learning or any event that involves community service. Mundy clearly illustrates this confusion within higher education as she describes in her chapter the frustration evident in the curt response from one mathematics faculty member who participated in her survey. This type of misunderstanding was validated in a presentation at the 2003 K–H Service-Learning Research Conference in Nashville, Tennessee, reporting the outcomes of a series of focus groups conducted with administrators (Welch, 2002). One participant was a dean of a college who voiced his consternation that students were "paying tuition to go out and do service projects." This practice of assuming that all service or experiential learning is service-learning compromises the pedagogical and philosophical integrity of service-learning and perpetuates the view that service-learning has no academic purpose.

Some higher education service-learning programs, such as at the Bennion Center at the University of Utah, have a set of criteria based on best practices described in the literature. These must be met in order for a course to receive official designation as service-learning in course catalogues and students' records. A committee of faculty with experience teaching service-learning reviews course proposals and syllabi and gives instructors guidance as they conceptualize their course. In a similar way, some K–12 settings use the Essential Elements of Service-Learning (National Service-Learning Cooperative, 1998), the standards developed by the Alliance for Service-Learning in Educational Reform (1995), or the Service-Learning Quality Review (RMC Research Corporation, 2003) to develop or assess high-quality programs.

Assessing Impact of Service-Learning

Especially in K–12 settings, service-learning is unlikely to be sustained unless there is substantial evidence that desired outcomes are met. Calls for more research abound, along with specific suggestions for the type of research that needs to be conducted. In an earlier volume in this series, Billig and Furco (2002) presented a research agenda for the study of K–12 student impacts. Research agendas have been created in higher education by Eyler and Giles (1999) to help professionals assess the impact of service-learning in multiple contexts, namely, cognitive development, intercultural awareness, citizenry, and community.

As can be seen in this volume, the rigor of the research has increased and replications of others' studies have begun. However, the field still lacks sufficient research to know which aspects of quality are most highly related to outcomes, specific impacts on the community, and information about whether effects are sustained over time.

Reward Structures

Another challenge is to change the existing reward structure within higher education. One strategy is the promotion of civically engaged scholarship. There are a host of issues and misperceptions that must be addressed if civically engaged scholarship is to be deemed as legitimate. Civically engaged scholarship is and should be theoretically grounded. Sound, rigorous methodology must be employed. The results of investigations must be disseminated, especially in traditional venues such as publication in refereed journals. However, dissemination should be viewed in broader terms to include reports to public agencies that can be applied and utilized. When this occurs, faculty should be recognized and awarded for their efforts. Service-learning is an empirically valid and effective form of pedagogy that requires considerable time and effort on the part of faculties who engage in it and therefore should be recognized as effective teaching rather than service.

Limited Resources

Educators grapple with limited resources. While it is important to provide funds to promote civic engagement, the endeavor does not necessarily require new monies but instead creative reallocation and use of existing fiscal resources. Many faculty, departments, and colleges are already engaged in this type of work. Rethinking the way clerical support and adjunct and clinical faculty are utilized is one approach that many entities across campus have begun to implement

At the K–12 level, limited resources often mean that service-learning is conducted within the school or within walking distance of the school. Teachers complain about lack of time (e.g., Billig, 2002) and thus limit the duration of the service-learning activities. Too few schools and districts have coordinators to help identify potential community partners and to ease lesson planning. A regular line item in a school district budget helps ensure that service-learning is sustained (Billig, 2002).

Empowered Networks

Innovations endure longer when they have champions and empowered networks of constituents who support the adoption and diffusion of practice (Billig & Eyler, 2003). While service-learning practitioners and researchers have begun to network, there are still too few opportunities to share information since service-learning is often found in a single campus across disciplines rather than within a single discipline. Intentional networking to advance practice will help to scale up practice and to document evidence of success for students. At both the higher education and K–12 level, disciplinary networks are beginning to form, but will need to build momentum and intentional connection to civic skills and dispositions for knowledge to be generated, accumulated, and shared.

CONCLUSIONS

In 2000, Schneider exhorted, "What is needed now is a far-reaching conversation about education for citizenship as an actively owned commitment of the American academy" (p. 121). Service-learning should be a key part of that conversation. Service-learning can connect educators and students alike to the range of all social spheres, including neighborhood, community, and society at large. Service-learning illuminates the responsibilities and rewards of civic engagement and helps to develop the capacities needed for faculty and students to engage in what Ehrlich (2000) referred to as thoughtful discourse and effective participation in social enterprises. Sustained individual and institutional commitment to meet the challenges is needed, but clearly can be accomplished. With explicit strategies to address the challenges of resource acquisition, policy formation, incentive structures, professional development, assessment of quality, leadership, and culture supports, service-learning can serve to stimulate civically-engaged scholarship for faculty and students alike. Additionally, continuing this dialogue and exploration of these strategies will broaden our traditional view and impact of scholarship. By critically examining service-learning as a form of civically engaged scholarship, the beneficiaries of this type of work goes beyond faculty and student to include community partners and society at large. Thus, our efforts are the first steps to truly integrating and reconceptualizing research, teaching, and service as discovery, learning, and engagement. The dialogue that is initiated here and will continue reflects Boyer's (1997) vision in which he stated:

> Increasingly, I'm convinced that ultimately the scholarship of engagement also means creating a special climate in which the academic and civic cultures communicate more continuously and more creatively with each other, helping to enlarge what anthropologist Clifford Geertz describes as the universe of human discourse and enriching the quality of life for all of us. (p. 92)

REFERENCES

Alliance for Service-Learning in Education Reform. (1995, March). *Standards of quality for school-based and community-based service learning.* Alexandria, VA: Author.

Applegate, J. L. (2002). *Engaged graduate education: Seeing with new eyes.* Washington, DC: Association of American Colleges and Universities, Council of Graduate Schools.

Astin, A. W. (2000). Conceptualizing service-learning research using Ken Wilber's Integral Framework. *Michigan Journal of Community Service Learning* [Special Issue], 98–104.

Atwell, R. (1996, August). *President's letter.* Washington, DC: American Council on Education.

Barnett, L. (1996). Service-learning: Why community colleges? In M. H. Parsons & C. D. Lisman (Eds.), *Promoting community renewal through civic literacy and service-learning* (New Directions for Community Colleges, 93) (pp. 7–15). San Francisco: Jossey Bass.

Berkas, T. (1997, February). *Strategic review of the W. K. Kellogg Foundation's service-learning projects, 1990–1996.* Battle Creek, MI: W. K. Kellogg Foundation.

Billig, S. H. (2000, May). Research on K–12 school-based service-learning: The evidence builds. *Phi Delta Kappan, (81)9,* 658–664.

Billig, S. H. (2002). Adoption, implementation, and sustainability of K–12 service-learning. In A. Furco & S. H. Billig (Eds.), *Advances in service-learning research: Vol. 1. Service-learning: The essence of pedagogy* (pp. 245–267). Greenwich, CT: Information Age.

Billig, S. H. (2004). Heads, hearts, hands: The research on K–12 service-learning. In J. Kielsmeier, M. Neal, & M. McKinnon (Eds.), *Growing to greatness: The state of service-learning project* (pp. 12–25). St. Paul, MN: National Youth Leadership Council.

Billig, S. H., & Eyler, J. (2003). *Advances in service-learning research; Vol. 3. Deconstructing service-learning: Research exploring context, participation, and impacts.* Greenwich, CT: Information Age.

Billig, S. H. & Furco, A. (2002) Research agenda for K–12 service-learning: A proposal to the field. In A. Furco & S. H. Billig (Eds.), *Advances in service-learning research: Vol. 1. Service-learning: The essence of pedagogy* (pp. 271–279). Greenwich, CT: Information Age.

Billig, S. H., & Klute, M. M. *W. K. Kellogg Foundation retrospective of K–12 service-learning projects, 1990–2000.* Denver, CO: RMC Research Corporation.

Boyer, E. L. (1990). *Scholarship reconsidered: Priorities of the professoriate.* San Francisco: Jossey-Bass.

Boyer, E. L. (1997). *Ernest L. Boyer selected speeches: 1979–1995.* Princeton, NJ: Carnegie Foundation.

Bringle, R. G., Games, R., & Malloy, E. A. (1999). Colleges and universities as citizens: Issues and perspectives. In R. G. Bringle, R. Games, & E. A. Malloy (Eds.), *Colleges and universities as citizens* (pp. 1–16). Boston: Allyn & Bacon.

Campus Compact. (2000). *The new student politics: The Wingspread Statement on student civic engagement.* Providence, RI: Author.

Carnegie Corporation of New York and the Center for Information and Research on Civic Learning and Engagement. (2003). *The civic mission of schools.* New York: Carnegie Corporation of New York and CIRCLE.

Checkoway, B. (2002). Renewing the civic mission of the American research university. *Journal of Public Affairs, 6,* 265–294.

Education Commission of the States. (2002). *Learning that lasts: How service-learning can become an integral part of schools, states, and communities.* Denver, CO: Author.

Ehrlich, T. (2000). *Civic responsibility and higher education.* Phoenix, AZ: Oryx Press.

Ehrlich, T., & Hollander, E. (1999). *Presidents' declaration on the civic responsibility of higher education.* Providence, RI: Campus Compact.

Eyler, J. S., & Giles, D. E., Jr. (1999). *Where's the learning in service-learning?* San Francisco: Jossey-Bass.

Eyler, J. S., Giles, D. E., Jr., Stenson, C. M., & Gray, C. J. (2001). *At a glance: The effects of service-learning on college students, faculty, institutions, and communities, 1993–2000* (3rd ed.). Washington, DC: Corporation for National Service, Learn and Serve America; Scotts Valley, CA: National Service-Learning Clearinghouse.

Fogelman, E. (2002). Civic engagement at the University of Minnesota. *Journal of Public Affairs, 6,* 103–118.

Frye, N. (1967). The knowledge of good and evil. In N. Frye, S. Hampshire, & C. C. O'Brien (Eds.), *The morality of scholarship* (pp. 1–28). Ithaca, NY: Cornell University Press.

Furco, A. (2000, Fall). Establishing a national center for research to synthesize the study of service-learning. *Michigan Journal of Community Service Learning,* 129–134.

Furco, A. (2002). Is service-learning really better than community service? A study of high school service program outcomes. In A. Furco & S. H. Billig (Eds.), *Advances in service-learning research: Vol. 1. Service-learning: The essence of the pedagogy* (pp. 23–50). Greenwich, CT: Information Age.

Furco, A. (2004, April). *Service-learning and civic engagement.* Presentation at the annual meeting of the American Educational Research Association, San Diego, CA.

Furco, A., & Ammon, M. S (2000, February). *Service-learning in California's teacher education programs.* Berkeley: University of California.

Galston, W. W. (2003). *Civic knowledge, civic education, and civic engagement: A summary of recent research.* Syracuse, NY: Campbell Public Affairs Institute, Maxwell School of Citizenship and Public Affairs. Retrieved June 3, 2003, from http://www.maxwell.syr.edu/campbell/Civic_Virtue/CivicVirtue.htm

Garrison, G. R. (1995). *The social responsibility of the academy and its academician.* New York: American Council of Learned Societies.

Glassick, C. E., Huber, M. T., & Maeroff, G. I. (1997). *Scholarship assessed: Evaluation of the professoriate.* San Francisco: Jossey-Bass.

Green, A. E. (2001). But you aren't white: Racial perceptions and service-learning. *Michigan Journal of Community Service Learning, 8*(1), 18–26.

Hamilton, S. F., & Zeldin, R. S. (1987, Winter). Learning civics in the community. *Curriculum Inquiry, 17*(4), 407–420.

Kielsmeier, J.C., Scales, P.C., Roehlkepartain, E.C., & Neal, M. (2004). Preliminary findings: Community service and service-learning in public schools. In J. Kielsmeier, M. Neal, & M. McKinnon (Eds.), *Growing to greatness: The state of service-learning project* (pp. 6–11). St. Paul, MN: National Youth Leadership Council.

Lake Snell Perry & Associates and The Tarrance Group, Inc. (2002, March). *Short term impacts, long term opportunities: The political and civic engagement of young adults in America.* College Park, MD: Center for Information and Research on Civic Learning and Engagement.

Levine, P., & Lopez, M. H. (2002, September). *Youth voter turnout has declined, by any measure.* Report from Center for Information and Research on Civic Learning and Engagement (CIRCLE), College Park, MD.

London, S. (2001). Higher education and public life: Restoring the bond. *Connections, 11*(2), 15–17.

Lutkus, A. D., Weiss, A. R., Campbell, J. R., Mazzeo, J., & Lazer, S. (1999). *NAEP 1998 Civics report card for the nation* (NCES 2000–457). Washington, DC: U.S. Department of Education, Office of Educational Research and Improvement.

Marshall, W. J. A. (1999). University service. In V. E. Bianco-Mathis & N. Chalofsky (Eds.), *The full-time faculty handbook* (pp. 113–128). Thousand Oaks, CA: Sage.

Melchior, A. (1999). *Summary report: National evaluation of Learn and Serve America.* Waltham, MA: Brandeis University, Center for Human Resources.

Metz, E., McLellan, J., & Youniss, J. (2000). *Types of voluntary service and the civic development of adolescents.* Unpublished manuscript, Catholic University, Washington, DC.

Meyer, S., Billig, S. H., & Hofschire, L. (2004). *Wai'anae High School Hawaiian studies program.* Denver, CO: RMC Research Corporation.

Miller, J., & Piscatelli, J. (2003). *State citizenship education policies.* Denver, CO: Education Commission of the States.

Moely, B. E., McFarland, M., Miron, D., Mercer, S., & Ilustre, V. (2002). Changes in college students' attitudes and intentions for civic involvement as a function of service-learning experiences. *Michigan Journal of Community Service Learning, 9*(1), 18–26.

Morgan, W., & Streb, M. (1999). How quality service-learning develops civic values. Bloomington: Indiana University.

National Commission on Civic Renewal. (1998). *A nation of spectators: How civic disengagement weakens America and what we can do about it.* College Park: MD: University of Maryland.

National Commission on Service-Learning. (2001). *Learning In Deed: The power of service-learning for American schools.* A report from the National Commission on Service-Learning. Retrieved November 21, 2001, from http://www.learningindeed.org/slcommission/report.html

National Service-Learning Cooperative. (1998, April). *Essential elements of service-learning.* St. Paul, MN: National Youth Leadership Council.

Newman, F. (1985). *Higher education and the American resurgence.* Princeton, NJ: Carnegie Foundation for the Advancement of Teaching.

Parsons, M. H., & Lisman, C. D. (2002). Promoting community renewal through civic literacy and service-learning. *New Directions for Community Colleges.* San Francisco: Jossey-Bass.

Prins, E. S. (2002). The relationship between institutional mission, service, and service-learning at community colleges in New York state. *Michigan Journal of Community Service Learning, 8*(2), 35–49.

Putnam, R. D. (2000). *Bowling alone: The collapse and revival of American community.* New York: Simon & Schuster.

Ramaley, J. A. (2002). Creating a focus for the engaged institution: K–12 science and math reform. *Journal of Public Affairs, 6,* 139–160.

Ramaley, J. (2002/2003). The engaged institution, the twenty-first century, and the new university extension. *Journal of Higher Education Outreach and Engagement, 8*(1), 13–28.

Rice, R. E. (1991, Spring). The new American scholar: Scholarship and the purposes of the university. *Metropolitan Universities,* 1–11.

RMC Research Corporation. (2003). *Service-learning quality tool.* Denver, CO: Author. Retrieved June 21, 2004, from www.servicelearningtool.com

Ross, D. D., & Yeager, E. (1999). What does democracy mean to prospective elementary school teachers? *Journal of Teacher Education, 50(4),* 255–266.

Saltmarsh, J. (2002). Introduction from the guest editor. *Journal of Public Affairs, 6,* iv–ix.

Sax, L. J. (2000). Citizenship development and the American college student. In T. Ehrlich (Ed.), *Civic responsibility and higher education* (pp. 3–18). Phoenix, AZ: Oryx Press.

Scales, P. C., Blyth, D. A., Berkas, T. H., & Kielsmeier, J. C. (2000). The effects of service-learning on middle school students' social responsibility and academic success. *Journal of Early Adolescence, 20,* 332–358.

Schneider, C. G. (2000). Educational missions and civic responsibility: Toward the engaged academy. In T. Ehrlich (Ed.), *Civic responsibility and higher education* (pp. 98–123). Phoenix, AZ: Oryx Press.

Scott, D. K. (2000). Spirituality in an integrative age. In V.H. Kazanjian & P.L. Laurence (Eds.), *Education as transformation: Religious pluralism, spirituality, and a new vision for higher education in American* (pp. 23–36). New York: Peter Lang.

Skinner, R., & Chapman, C. (1999, September). *Service-learning and community service in K–12 public schools.* Washington, DC: National Center for Education Statistics, U. S. Department of Education.

Torney-Purta, J. (2002). The schools' role in developing civic engagement: A study of adolescents in twenty-eight countries. *Applied Developmental Science, 6*(4), 202–211.

Vortuba, J. C. (1996). Strengthening the university's alignment with society: Challenges and strategies. *Journal of Public Service and Outreach, 1*(1), 29–36.

Welch, M. (2002, October). *Results of a quantitative and qualitative trends analysis of service-learning courses at a research university: A 10-year retrospection.* Presentation at the 2nd Annual International Conference on Advances in Service-Learning Research, Nashville, TN.

Westheimer, J., & Kahne, J. (2000, April). *Assessment and the democratic purposes of schooling.* Paper presented at the annual meeting of the American Educational Research Association, New Orleans, LA.

Westheimer, J., & Kahne, J. (2002, August). *Educating the "good" citizen: The politics of school-based civic education programs.* Paper presented at the annual meeting of the American Political Science Association, Boston.

Youniss, J., McLellan, J. A., & Yates, M. (1997). What we know about engendering civic identity. *American Behavioral Scientist, 40*(5), 620–631.

Youniss, J., & Yates, M. (1997). *Community service and social responsibility in youth.* Chicago: University of Chicago Press.

Zlotkowski, E. (2000, Fall). Service-learning research in the disciplines. *Michigan Journal of Community Service Learning,* 61–67.

ABOUT THE CONTRIBUTORS

Albert J. Abramovitz earned his Ph.D. from Case Western Reserve University (CASE) in Curriculum and Instruction. He currently consults for a range of organizations in strategic thinking and planning, organizational development, curriculum design for professional development, and grant writing since his retirement from CASE. He was on the faculty of the Mandel School of Applied Social Sciences (MSASS) and the Mandel Center for Nonprofit Organizations at CASE as Professor of Community Service.

Shelley H. Billig, Ph.D., is Vice President of RMC Research Corporation. She directs the Carnegie Corporation of New York national study of the impact on service-learning on civic engagement as well as several other research studies involving service-learning, citizenship, and educational reform. She is series editor of *Advances in Service-Learning Research* and coedited the first three volumes in the series. She also has authored multiple journal articles.

Debra David, Ph.D., is founding Director of the Center for Service-Learning at San José State University and Professor of Health Science. Her research interests include intergenerational service-learning, interdisciplinary programs, and faculty development.

Peggy Fitch, Ph.D., is a Professor of Psychology at Central College in Pella, Iowa, whose research interests include service-learning, student intellectual development, and the development of intercultural competence. She has

New Perspectives in Service-Learning: Research to Advance the Field, pages 243–246
Copyright © 2004 by Information Age Publishing
All rights of reproduction in any form reserved.

been using service-learning in her developmental psychology courses for several years.

Ira Harkavy, Ph.D., a long-time leader in the field of service-learning, received the Thomas Ehrlich Award for Service-Learning in 2002. He has been Associate Vice President and Director of the Center for Community Partnerships at the University of Pennsylvania since the center was founded. His current teaching "seeks to combine academically based community service, collaborative, democratic learning, and real-world problem solving on campus and in the community."

Linda Hofschire, Ph.D., is a Research Associate at RMC Research Corporation. She serves as a member of the service-learning team and manages multiple research and evaluation projects.

Marla Gaudet, M.Ad.Ed., is Program Officer with the Service-Learning Program at Saint Francis Xavier University in Antigonish, Nova Scotia, Canada. She has interests in experiential learning and community-based services.

Sherril B. Gelmon, Dr.P.H., is Professor of Public Health in the Mark O. Hatfield School of Government at Portland State University, in Portland, Oregon. One of her primary areas of interest is the development, institutionalization, and assessment of civic engagement in higher education institutions.

Brenda Marsteller Kowalewski, Ph.D., is Professor of Sociology at Weber State University. Her teaching and research areas include the sociology of family, gender, and work and social psychology. Much of her research focuses on gender equity and stereotypes, as well as the use of service-learning as a teaching tool.

KimMarie McGoldrick, Ph.D., is an Associate Professor of Economics in the Robins School of Business at the University of Richmond in Virginia. She is author of several publications describing the use of service-learning in economics that have appeared in leading economic journals, such as the *Journal of Economic Education,* and has co-edited (with Andrea Ziegert), the volume, *Putting the Invisible Hand to Work: Concepts and Models for Service-Learning in Economics.*

Stephen J. Meyer, Ph.D., is a Senior Research Associate at RMC Research Corporation. His interests include service-learning, civic engagement, and program evaluation. He currently conducts evaluations of K–12 service-learning programs in Colorado, Michigan, and Texas.

Patricia J. Mintz currently serves as a Dean of Academic Affairs at Cuyahoga Community College in Cleveland, Ohio. Her research in service-learning was completed through a collaboration with Youth Philanthropy and Service at the Mandel Center for Nonprofit Organizations. She completed the Executive Doctor of Management Program at Case Western Reserve University in May 2003.

Carol Mitchell, M.Soc.Sci., is a counselling psychologist and lecturer in psychology at the University of KwaZulu-Natal in Pietermaritzburg, South Africa. She has been responsible for the development of service-learning in the School of Psychology and assisted with service-learning development across the university.

Meaghan Mundy recently completed her doctoral dissertation on faculty and service-learning at Vanderbilt University. For the past two years, she has worked with Vanderbilt's Assistant Provost for Service-Learning to institutionalize service-learning within the curriculum. She is currently conducting an assessment of student learning and development through a service-learning exchange project between students at Vanderbilt University and the University of New Mexico–Gallup.

Malu Roldan is a member of the faculty of the Management Information Systems Department at San José State University. Her research focuses on electronic commerce, mobile computing, and engaged learning. Her publications have appeared in *Communications of the ACM, EDI Forum, Journal of Informatics Education and Research*, and *Internet Marketing Research*. She is currently the director of a Hewlett-Packard-supported project to conduct technology-based, cross-disciplinary service-learning activities at community-based organizations.

Ana Ruiz, Ph.D., is Associate Professor of Psychology at Alvernia College in Reading, Pennsylvania.

Ann Sherman, Ph.D., is the Coordinator of the Service-Learning Program, as well as the Acting Director of the School of Education, at Saint Francis Xavier University in Antigonish, Nova Scotia, Canada. One of her areas of interest is alternative teaching and learning methodologies.

Amy Strage is Professor of Child and Adolescent Development in the College of Education at San José State University. She is presently involved in three large-scale investigations of the effectiveness of service-learning as a pedagogical tool for college-age learners. She served as codirector of the *It Takes a Valley* program, a nationally recognized, federally funded service-learning-based program to prepare future teachers to serve in high needs schools.

Kirsten Trotter, M.Comm. (CHESP), is a lecturer in Policy and Development Studies with the Centre for Government and Policy Studies at the University of KwaZulu-Natal, Pietermaritzburg, South Africa. Her primary research area is historical policy analysis, and she has significant interests in the institutionalization of service-learning.

Judith Warchal, Ph.D., is Associate Professor of Psychology at Alvernia College in Reading, Pennsylvania. She is also a licensed psychologist engaged in clinical practice at the Center for Mental Health at the Reading Hospital and Medical Center.

Marshall Welch came to the University of Utah in 1987 as a faculty member in the Department of Special Education and began teaching service-learning courses in his field. He became the Director of the Lowell Bennion Community Service Center in 2001. He now teaches an undergraduate honors course using service-learning to promote service-politics and civic engagement as well as a graduate-level course on the pedagogy of service-learning.

Andrea L. Ziegert is Associate Professor of Economics and Director of the John W. Alford Center for Service-Learning at Denison University in Granville, Ohio. She has a long-standing interest in student learning and pedagogy in economics, which has resulted in the use of service-learning in a variety of policy-related economics courses. Her interest in service-learning in economics resulted in a coedited volume (with KimMarie McGoldrick), *Putting the Invisible Hand to Work: Concepts and Models for Service-Learning in Economics*.

INDEX

New Perspectives in Service-Learning: Research to Advance the Field, pages 247–253
Copyright © 2004 by Information Age Publishing
All rights of reproduction in any form reserved.